THE
FORECLOSURE
OF AMERICA

Life Inside Countrywide
Home Loans, and the Selling
of the American Dream

Adam Michaelson

BERKLEY BOOKS, NEW YORK

For my sons, Alex and Spencer, and for Nancy.

THE BERKLEY PUBLISHING GROUP
Published by the Penguin Group
Penguin Group (USA) Inc.
375 Hudson Street, New York, New York 10014, USA
Penguin Group (Canada), 90 Eglinton Avenue East, Suite 700, Toronto, Ontario M4P 2Y3, Canada
(a division of Pearson Penguin Canada Inc.)
Penguin Books Ltd., 80 Strand, London WC2R 0RL, England
Penguin Group Ireland, 25 St. Stephen's Green, Dublin 2, Ireland (a division of Penguin Books Ltd.)
Penguin Group (Australia), 250 Camberwell Road, Camberwell, Victoria 3124, Australia
(a division of Pearson Australia Group Pty. Ltd.)
Penguin Books India Pvt. Ltd., 11 Community Centre, Panchsheel Park, New Delhi—110 017, India
Penguin Group (NZ), 67 Apollo Drive, Rosedale, North Shore, 0632, New Zealand
(a division of Pearson New Zealand Ltd.)
Penguin Books (South Africa) (Pty.) Ltd., 24 Sturdee Avenue, Rosebank, Johannesburg 2196,
South Africa

Penguin Books Ltd., Registered Offices: 80 Strand, London WC2R 0RL, England

The publisher does not have any control over and does not assume any responsibility for author or
third-party websites or their content.

THE FORECLOSURE OF AMERICA

PRINTING HISTORY
First Berkley hardcover edition / January 2009
First Berkley trade paperback edition / April 2010

Berkley trade paperback ISBN: 978-0-425-23376-4

PRINTED IN THE UNITED STATES OF AMERICA

10   9   8   7   6   5   4   3   2   1

Contents

Foreword to the Paperback Edition

Well, all I know is what I read in the papers.
—Will Rogers, American Humorist

MARCH 2009

Prime Rate: 3.75%

Cumulative Foreclosure Rate: Approximately 3%

Bank of America Stock Price (bought Countrywide): $3.20 (from a high of $55)

Since the initial release of *The Foreclosure of America* in January 2009, America—especially the media—has debated the causes, lessons, faults, and fallout from the Countrywide story. Clearly this book has struck a nerve. As the story would occasionally and intermittently take center stage of ongoing twenty-four-hour news cycles, I would get requests for my viewpoint, having been at ground zero of the company as the crisis was born. March 3, 2009, was one of those days.

I started my day like any other: I made a pot of coffee and looked forward to another long day of meetings, conference calls, and other assorted advice sessions that I provided to my marketing clients each day to help them build their businesses. Since leaving Countywide, heading my own consulting firm had been gratifying, fruitful, and entrepreneurially exciting. As I was pouring my first cup of dark French roast before I jumped in the shower, I caught a glimpse of my cell phone message light, blinking in my peripheral vision. I flipped it open and began listening to my messages.

"You have . . . twelve . . . messages . . ." stated the creepily human voicemail lady.

What the hell? Who died? Another Countrywide flare-up? I wondered as I began pressing the buttons to get to the litany of apparently urgent messages.

As I began listening to the voicemails one by one, a story—or a nonstory, depending on one's point of view—emerged. Reporters, bloggers, television and radio news producers all wanted to get my thoughts on an item that had appeared in that morning's *New York Times*. A few just wanted a quick quote, but some wanted me to come into the television or radio studio to provide on-air commentary regarding the story that Stan Kurland, the former Chief Operating Officer of the collapsed, once-great titan of home loans, Countrywide Financial, had created a new company called PennyMac, which was, according to the *New York Times* article, ". . . buying up delinquent home mortgages that the government took over from other failed banks, sometimes for pennies on the dollar. They get a piece of what they can collect."

Like almost every aspect of the Countrywide story, this new development, as well as many others to follow, immediately and viscerally polarized the media. Most media outlets were clearly biased, leaning either far left or right, trying to lead the witness [me] in every interview. Within seconds I could tell whether the host or anchor of any particular program had even read this book, or had received notes from some poor producer who'd had to read it in one night, or read only the cover copy. In my experience, it was very rare to engage with a truly fair and balanced media venue.

As I always did, I first called back the media outlet with the largest audience (from my marketing background I knew the relative audience sizes—"reach"—of the different shows), which was in this case a producer from a nationally known, syndicated radio news show. The conversation with this producer was typical.

"Thanks for calling me back, Mr. Michaelson. We wanted to see if you could come into the studio today to talk to [host] about the item that appeared in the *New York Times* today about Mr. Kurland's *profiteering from the crisis*," she said.

"Well, some people may not think he is *profiteering*, but, rather, *profiting*, while also solving the acute problem of getting toxic mortgage assets off the books of these struggling banks, right?" I responded, probing as I went to determine if I was entering hostile or fair, unbiased territory.

"Well surely you'd agree that he helped create the crisis, and now he is profiting from that same crisis he helped create?" she continued.

"Perhaps; I can easily see how some people would take on that point of view. But I'd be happy to come in as long as [network] wants to really have a thoughtful discussion about it, versus a slamming session."

She listened silently, and hesitated to respond. I continued speaking to fill the awkward void on the phone.

"I'd rather have the marketplace solving the toxic assets problem instead of the government trying to do it all themselves, and who better to help than someone who clearly knows how to repackage and sell mortgages?" I said.

After another awkward moment of silence on the telephone, she replied, "Yes, maybe . . . let me check with [host] and call you back in ten minutes."

As the call ended I allowed myself an eye roll and gave it a 10 percent chance at best that they still wanted me on the air that day. Sure enough, twelve minutes later they called back and thanked me for offering to rearrange my schedule to go to the studio that day, but they instead were going with "another guest," probably the head of some organization called the *Coalition for Arbitrarily Slamming and Vilifying All Former Executives of Corporations Because It Was Now Populist to Do So and Somewhere Along the Way It Became a Crime to Seek Legal Profits* (known as the CASVAFECBIWNPTDS-SATWIBACTSLP, for short).

Of course, this kind of thing never bothered me. I was busy with my consultancy, and of course I could see how folks could get upset from such a story. In fact, as it was a "business-to-business model" that Kurland was setting up (as opposed to a consumer-facing "Toxic Assets 'R' Us" store), partially funded by institutional investors, I questioned the public relations wisdom of whoever invited the *New York Times* to come visit their offices at all. Surely they must've known, no matter how fair the story may have been written, that some people in the media, especially left-leaning media, could paint the effort as gross profiteering from a crisis they themselves may have had a hand in creating, however inadvertently or not.

That was just one new chapter that showed how the continuing Countrywide drama has solicited strong opinions from both sides, spoke to the acidic polarization in America about the financial crisis in general, and sadly confirmed the old adage that you can't please everybody. As such, I figure you might as well tell the story straight and let people think what they want to think, which is what I endeavored to do in the pages that follow. I hope you feel that I succeeded.

At about the same time that the Kurland story broke, and the press scrambled to define it in their own editorial opinions for a polarized audience, academia also began seeing the compelling Countrywide case as a powerful teaching tool.

Since the book's release, I have lectured on the Countrywide saga and my role in it at several prominent business schools at the graduate level, including the Anderson School at UCLA, and the Tuck School at Dartmouth, where I also facilitated a discussion with their MBA students. I believe strongly in telling this cautionary tale to as many classes of business students as possible as a strong warning to future generations, especially those future leaders of capitalism. Also, I like to think of it as my way of trying to cleanse my mixed feelings about how I participated in helping to sell the dream of homeownership, and how it may have contributed to the "irrational exuberism" of the boom, that only now has become frighteningly clear in hindsight.

The discussion occurred at that venerable campus in remote Hanover, New Hampshire, next to a roaring fireplace in a building that looked as old as America itself. At least a hundred students, faculty, and administrators filed into the large room for this "fireside chat" about my book, the crisis, the ethics of profit-based capitalism, the definition of greed, and other academic thought experiments.

(In my hotel room that morning I flipped through the Dartmouth alumni magazine to see timely yet mildly ironic references to now-high-profile graduates such as current Treasury Secretary Timothy Geithner and his predecessor, Henry Paulson. As arguably one of America's smartest schools, producing some of our most brilliant minds and successful leaders in business and government for more than two centuries, I couldn't help but wonder if this association with their fame—or notoriety, depending on one's point of view—was pleasing or horrifying to Dartmouth's powerful alumni network.)

One seminal moment during my evening with the Dartmouth crowd reminded me of my one constant struggle with the isolated perspective of some aspects of academia: textbooks, business cases, and the framework of the classroom may not always teach everything about life in the real world, or surviving the daily politics, pressures, and personalities of America's corporate hallways. It is important to have teachers who have lived in the real world, too, and can pass on that experience.

While most of the questions were deeply intelligent, thoughtful, and insightful (unlike many forums in which I had spoken, it was clear that almost every audience member had actually read this book in preparation), the safety of the academic cocoon became apparent when one bright-eyed grad student asked a legitimate question.

"Is it wrong, unethical even, for a public company to be so intensely focused on sales?" he asked from the front row.

I paused for a moment as I pondered his perspective on this issue, and decided to then pose a question back.

"How many of you have real-world experience working in a sales-driven company?" I asked, knowing that some of these grad students may have indeed spent time at Fortune 500s before they went back to grad school.

One hand went up in the back of the room, and I pointed to him and followed up with "Was it a high-intensity or low-intensity sales culture?"

"High intensity," he responded meekly. (Maybe he was shell-shocked from his high-pressure corporate sales experience.)

"So then you've seen firsthand that in for-profit companies that are high-pressure sales cultures, ethereal academic ideas may not apply day to day. You also probably know that in a sales culture there is one reality: you simply make your sales numbers (legally and ethically as best you can), or they take you out back and (figuratively) shoot you, right?" I asked the brave audience participant.

He nodded timidly.

I decided to lay it out to them plainly.

"Countrywide, for all of its white-picket-fence brand imagery surrounding the American dream, was, in the end, just like all the other intense sales cultures in the U.S.—just like cars, technology, and all across financial services. Within the halls of Countrywide, at that time within the frenzy of the bubble, making the goal sales numbers 'this week, this month, and this quarter' was the primary focus." I paused, letting the thought echo over the crowd.

I concluded, "And maybe that was the greatest mistake of all."

An introspective silence hovered above the room as this army of future CEOs considered the potential ethical quandaries they may face in the future.

A FEW WEEKS LATER, in April 2009, the name "Countrywide" quietly vanished into the history books of business, marketing and, some would say, the annals of greedy villainy, after forty years of helping people get into homes.

Bank of America had finally decided, after much internal debate, that the Countrywide name, as strong and as alluring as it once was, was now too tarnished, too toxic to remain viable under the Bank of America banner. And while the internal buzz within the small remnants of the original Countrywide marketing staff wistfully hoped that the old name might somehow live on within BofA as some sort of sub-brand, it can be reasonably assumed that the retiring of the Countrywide brand was always the plan from day one of the buyout. In my then-boss's office almost five years ago while working for Countrywide, I predicted that only the mighty Bank of America would have the brand power, and sheer size of its balance sheet, to absorb the massive $2 trillion Countrywide mortgage portfolio, with all the assets and frightening current and potential future liabilities within as delinquencies continued to rise (and still do).

Possibly due to the increasing public exhaustion regarding the crisis, few national news outlets even mentioned it. But marketers like myself, who at one time blindly idolized the awesome power of this all-American brand, which used to stand among Chevy, Wal-Mart, Disney, and other icons of American dreams, must have felt yet another disappointing loss, or, at the very least, a tinge of regret for what could have been if the market and all its players—corporations, consumers, government, and the media—hadn't collectively gone nuts and created the financial tsunami.

One media outlet, the venerable yet occasionally left-leaning *Los*

Angeles Times, decided to run a story about it, as Countrywide was headquartered in the Los Angeles area where tens of thousands of people had lost their jobs. I had sent the writer of the piece, Scott Reckard, a copy of my book a few weeks earlier, and I felt he was one of the few fair and balanced journalists in the entire industry. We met and shared a lunch, which included a thoughtful and challenging background discussion and debate about the causes, culprits, and casualties of the debacle. He asked tough, smart, thorough questions (some of which indeed made me squirm), but he was (and still is) always informed, earnest, and focused on the facts.

Scott's piece in the *LA Times* was arguably one of the few articles that was not focused solely on pending Countrywide investigations, lawsuits, or the ever-upward spiraling trajectory of continuing foreclosures and the toxic assets that continue to grow like a frightening and unstoppable cancer on the few financial institutions that still remain (although he writes about that as well). The article hinted at the sometimes-cruel evolution of brands that had passed into the "untouchable" zone of consumer disgust, and he wrote with a strong combination of eloquence and pragmatism, which is his style. Reckard cited this book and quoted portions of it related to my prediction that Bank of America was arguably the only similar "white-picket-fence" brand that was in alignment with what used to be the Countrywide "feeling." I want to thank him for referencing this book in his article.

Some media outlets felt I didn't go far enough, as I tried to offer a fair and balanced view from within Countrywide, through my own personal journey, then let readers decide for themselves and ask what they may have done differently in my shoes. Media from the left were annoyed that this book was not about a "smoking gun"—no factual support for the total vilification of corporations, or the CEOs themselves. But of course they missed the point; there *was no single smoking gun*, and like oil or dot-coms or gold or real estate, *sometimes bubbles occur when every element of the system is doing exactly what it was designed to do, and every player is pursuing his own self-interests*, whether it be a public corporation that was enhancing its profits to dutifully return value to shareholders, consumers getting more and more loans because they wanted them, a government who was not stopping it because (at the time) a rich electorate was a happy electorate, or the media who was churning out "house flipping" shows by the ton because people were watching them.

Some in the right-leaning media, while clearly more understanding of the realities of that time, the marketing of the craze, and the role that corporations play in our lives to provide goods and services, questioned why I included some real stories of people who had actually gone through the nightmare of foreclosure, and the dramatic details of how their lives were ruined. I felt this was, and still is, a critical reality to discuss even as pundits argue about setting blame. Many families who deserve help because the financial cataclysms in their lives were not due to their *own poor choices*, have still not received help, even as banks receive massive bailouts and the nation never-endingly bickers, blames, bungles, and bombasts.

Yet both far left and far right shared a disturbing objective; they both seemed solely focused on obsessively finding, blaming, and scorching a single villain in their rhetoric. The right wanted to blame uneducated or overconsumptive people for the entire crisis. The left wanted to vilify all CEOs, all profit-seeking corporations, and the "greedy evildoers" who took little old ladies' life savings as they twirled their waxed mustaches and snickered over cigars in smoke-filled backrooms. Both extremes are, of course, ridiculous and dangerous oversimplifications.

The collapse would never have happened without all sides interacting together in a perfectly poised waltz of self-delusion, denial, and dumbness. To cite an overused metaphor, it really was the "perfect storm." But pity the poor media, with their new focus on "infotainment," vitriol, and the unenviable task of having to fill up twenty-four hours of airtime every single day—not to mention being accountable for primarily generating *profit,* yet not necessarily facts, which may have, ironically, fallen into the same corporate "give the public what it wants" model that eventually slammed the financial services industry that the same media loves to blame. Blame creates conflict, conflict creates drama, drama creates viewers (just like a car wreck does), and viewers achieve the new news machine's primary objective: ad revenue.

It has been said that the media is the fourth "check and balance" in our government, societal power, and influence structure (vs. executive, legislative and judiciary). Yet the hypocrisy of the media machine, some would say, is almost too much to contemplate, and ironically, it may have become the only "check and balance" that has run amok and has not been held accountable for truth and a check on its power. Walter Cronkite would have never allowed screen graphics of uncharged CEOs with iron jail bars overlaid onto them just for histrionic effect. We'll miss you, Walter.

But the continuing saga did not end with that once-venerable brand name Countrywide vaporizing into nothingness.

In June 2009 the Securities and Exchange Commission made good on its threat to formally charge Angelo Mozilo with fraud. The charismatic, tanned, and now-besieged former CEO of Countrywide was being charged with alleged insider trading, and "deliberately misleading investors about the significant credit risks being taken in efforts to build and maintain the company's market share."

The announcement was made by the SEC in a theatrical, high-profile press conference. With flashbulbs flashing and cameras clicking, the SEC laid out charges of senior executives misleading investors, citing internal emails about what they were saying about the nature of the risks the firm was taking, among other things.

That day my phone began ringing off the hook again, from many of the same radio and television producers asking me to comment, weigh in, and/or show up at their studios that night and the next day.

Overloaded with consulting work that week, I chose to call into only one regional radio talk show, for a host who had been thoughtful and insightful and fair during my first appearance a few months earlier.

His first question blew my previous experience to pieces.

"So, do you think he is guilty of perpetrating this fraud?" the host asked me.

I paused for a moment, cautiously realizing that whatever I said would be public commentary on a pending federal legal case of the highest visibility, and a lightning rod of public outrage. I was instantly angered that once again the media was drawing premature conclusions just for ratings.

"The last time I checked, [host name], that is for a *jury* to decide." I responded plainly.

"Oh c'mon you must feel one way or another," he pressed.

"In my book I describe my personal feeling about Angelo as a one-time idol for us 'young turks,' as well as my eventual disillusionment because of what happened. But I do feel that anyone charged is innocent until proven guilty in a fair trial."

The interview went on for a while, but the reality of modern-day media had been hammered home yet again. Each time the radio show host and his callers continually and loosely used words like *perpetrated*, and *knew the risks*, they oversimplified a complex issue and swayed public opinion toward exactly what they themselves wanted to hear.

Every CEO by role, definition, and responsibilities has some level of "insider knowledge" about how the firm is running at that time. But how far into the future can they predict outcomes, and with what certainty, especially in fluid and unpredictable markets? [It is important to note that during the boom, every Countrywide Annual Report noted the possibility that the boom may not last forever.] And for a CEO nearing retirement, which Angelo was, it is not abnormal for him to begin accelerating his stock sales as he nears that retirement, which he allegedly did. But were his actions due to any clear and sure knowledge of exactly what would happen, and when, in the markets? Indeed, the timing of all of these events may appear suspicious to an already emotionally raw public seeking a villain, and a government watchdog eager to "do something," but proving sinister intent by accurately predicting the future is another thing altogether.

And what exactly is the definition of "knew the risks?" Every time the space shuttle goes up, every single scientist, engineer, and astronaut knows that there is a risk that the thing will blow up. But how much risk is too much risk? And what officially constitutes a "toxic risk," when the future is unknowable? These are subjective concepts, and tough issues for a jury to consider, as all "toxicity" and all "risk" are purely relative. The same two aspirin that might cure your headache can also kill a baby; the same is true of subprime mortgages on your balance sheet.

I once had a great professor who answered the question, "What should the price be?" with his own immediate response, "Whatever the market will pay." Similarly, for years the marketplace—lenders, borrowers, the securities markets, the government—all gleefully accepted the risks involved in the lending and housing industries, because so many people and consumers were getting rich quickly; the marketplace carried the weight of those risks—until they couldn't. Is it fair to claim that one individual knew exactly where, when, and how badly the bubble would burst?

If the Mozilo case actually goes to trial, these will be some of the tough questions a jury would need to decide in determining not only "what did they know, and when did they know it," but, more important, "what could anyone have possibly done to stop that runaway freight train?" Could the CEO of the largest mortgage firm in the country really have stopped lending and let the other banks lend instead while his firm died? How could we have gotten consumers to stop overborrowing? It's like saying that fast food companies should refuse to serve their food to obese people. Where does corporate responsibility end and personal responsibility begin? These issues are complex, and will no doubt continue to be debated, with no resolution, until the end of the republic.

But perhaps the most important question is, how will we see the danger sooner next time, and knowingly stop it before catastrophe strikes? If *The Foreclosure of America* helps just one current or future CEO, business student, government regulator, consumer, or media outlet to question the sanity of the next bubble sooner, be more cautious in their spending, or better check their own hubris, then it will have achieved its mission.

The themes I discussed in business schools and on the air in various media were the same themes and debates that have ensued all throughout America. So by that standard, this book has certainly achieved one of its objectives by getting America to discuss issues critical to our future as a nation: the essence of capitalism and its natural conflict with ethical frameworks; the role of private enterprise and free markets versus government oversight and control; the definition of greed and the scope of its effects; the role of personal choice and responsibility in a free society; how and when to speak truth to power (or the futility of doing so); the essence of homeownership as basic right or earned privilege; the long-simmering issue of out-of-control consumerism and personal debt; intergenerational differences in values and morals; and, generally, whether or not the American empire is about to collapse in on itself as a result of our own doing.

Also, I wrote the book for the people on Main Street, not for the isolated elitists on Wall Street. I wrote it for the 90 percent of Americans who do *not* work in corporations, and were asking one-still-unanswered question: What on earth were these mortgage companies *thinking* inside those meeting rooms?

Well, it appears that I answered Main Street's question, because they responded in droves. I received many emails from readers, as the book seems to have triggered emotional reactions from three key audiences that feel clearly underserved by the story, and wanted to be heard, loudly.

First: seniors. Some from the so-called "Greatest Generation," others a bit younger, many of whom wrote that they appreciated that the book finally raises an issue that few media outlets are discussing, but should. That is, the apparent collapse of personal responsibility in America, the rewarding of poor choices, and the approval of gluttony. Their emails talk about generations past, when folks bought only what they could pay for, when their word was their bond, and "good credit" meant having a good standing in the local community versus filling out one of the billions of credit card applications to buy more shoes. Some had lived through the Depression, and knew this cycle would someday repeat; many proudly paid off their mortgages and prioritized their mortgage payment first each month; some remember the second great war, the rationing of food, planting Victory Gardens, pulling together, and not being able to buy a new car for years because the car companies dedicated their plants to making tanks and planes. Seniors wonder why many people who are in trouble are blaming others for their woes. Yet notably, every profiled foreclosure story in this book includes that ex-homeowner's answer to my question about "who do you blame?" Most of them freely said that they blame themselves for some of their poor choices, and they know they don't deserve a "bailout" per se; they just want a chance to recover. Even now, immersed in our great national healthcare debate, the role of taking personal responsibility for our own health, by eating right and exercising, for example, continues to be the elephant in the room that no politician dares mention.

Second, I received many emails from angry homeowners who have *not* defaulted on their loans, and are asking, "Where is *our* bailout?" There is a vast, seething rage in America from what Nixon used to call "the Silent Majority." As the foreclosure numbers quietly and steadily keep rising (even though the "crisis" story is waning), many are still, arguably, sad stories. But for every foreclosure in this country there are still at least eight or nine other households who are current on their mortgage, even though many of their loans were also initially "adjustable" and the loans have reset to higher levels of monthly payments. Maybe they planned for their three-year adjustable rate loan to reset in the thirty-seventh month and budgeted accordingly; maybe they are scrimping and saving and putting off purchases and vacations and luxuries because their mortgage payment comes first, and because they signed a document—they gave their word—to pay the debt as noted in the paperwork that they actually read. They are outraged when they hear defaulting homeowners claim that they "didn't understand the paperwork" or they were "forced to take the loan." The last time I checked, this is a free society, and it is the sole decision of the thoughtful buyer whether or not to make a good choice for himself and his family, to know that he can "afford it," to sign the documents and put his own word on the promissory notes. Many homeowners are quietly boiling under the surface of the debate, as somehow in the media it has become taboo to question why so many people made so many poor choices, and question whether or not all of them really deserve help. In the end, though, it is simply easier to blame faceless corporations instead of looking at our own poor choices in the mirror. I would argue that the same poor, rash, fast, and easy rush to judgment that led the market to approve millions of bad loans, is the same poor, rash, fast, and easy process by which we are assigning blame and labeling people as villains.

Third, I get many emails from within the audience of millions of dedicated, educated, and well-meaning financial services professionals who feel unfairly demonized in the media. Clearly, as in any overheated business, there were some unscrupulous individuals who may have engaged in illegal or unethical behavior or solicitation, but the other 99.9 percent of people in insurance, banking, lending, and other related careers are now embarrassed to put that career, and in many cases, those formerly impressive company names (Countrywide, AIG, Lehman, Wachovia, etc), on their resumes. Stories of AIG employees being personally threatened with violence even though they may have had no part in the collapse harken back to the days of the Communist menace and the drumbeat of McCarthyism. Having personally known many professionals in these industries during my own career, I know that many of them took great pride in the good they were doing for customers; helping them save, buy a home, protect their families and their assets, diversify, invest, and generally secure the American dream. They resent being pooled together in headlines that talk about "Fat Cats," "Corporate Greed," and "Excessive Pay." Some financial services professionals did return profit to their companies through their hard work, provided valuable and trusted services to happy customers, and perhaps do deserve a bonus.

SO NOW, WELCOME to 2010, and the future. America will continue to reel from the mortgage crisis in many ways. Encompassing fits and starts, our national backbone will continue to endure false senses of easing—so-called market "suckers rallies" and "dead cat bounces"—combined with intermittent days of market and banking terror as yet another shocking financial announcement spooks the world. The current wave of profit announcements include many "false positives," in that "profits" reported, in many cases, include one-time bumps in revenue due to asset sales, borrowed revenue, and some tweaks in various accounting rules; but the underlying cancerous and toxic assets continue to default at increasingly higher levels, ominously growing under the rosier surface. Yes, 2010 will be interesting.

James Madison once wrote, "If all men were angels, no government would be necessary." And yet our new and old cadre of leaders, love them or hate them, continue to waver in their solutions, convulsively responding to the marketplace and public sentiment with a seemingly never-ending series of intensely chaotic, knee-jerk, and reactionary plans, solutions, programs, laws, commissions, czars, panels, task forces, hearings, acronyms, counterproductive posturing, and, generally, running around acting like their hair is on fire, or not running around enough.

Some view our government's actions—or inactions, depending on your point of view—as opportunistic politicking. Others say, well at least the government is trying *something*, doing *something*, attempting to *help* ease the situation. The layman view of history says that FDR's New Deal, implemented relatively quickly, ended the Great Depression, although many economists and historians now believe it really didn't; the war did. But history records that, like throwing a bucket of water on an inferno, at least he *tried*, and, arguably, it didn't hurt as it created the perception of motion, of a solution, that rallied others to try as well. That is what good leaders do; they set the example. They *try*.

And this is what we expect from government; to *do something*. Yet, this enormous pressure to act can sometimes cause flailing, which in turn may overwhelm and confuse an already jittery public. The initiation of so many programs so quickly in so many different directions, while probably well intentioned, can make things worse. Confidence and trust come from a consistent experience that we can depend on, that stays focused on the mission. The more complex the problem, the simpler the solution needs to be, and then marketed with a consistent, dependable message.

For example, the array of urgent government and lender efforts has been dizzying. To name just a few, there have been the *Helping Families Save Their Homes Act*, the *American Recovery and Reinvestment Act*, the *Making Home Affordable* program, the *Hope Now Alliance*, the *Hope for Homeowners* program, the *Homeowner Affordability and Stability Plan*, the *Home Affordable Modifications Program*, the *Foreclosure Alternatives Program*, and many others.

Still, the media continues to report that even though the number of households originally projected to be potentially eligible for assistance within one or many of these programs numbered in the millions, the number of households actually helped have numbered only in the thousands. There has been public confusion about these programs, service challenges as the banks scrambled to properly staff help centers to handle demand, and, of course, the ubiquitous catch-22's that cynics cite, that sometimes a household may not be eligible for help until they default, and yet they are seeking help to prevent their default before it happens. And it may only get worse. Stock market gains notwithstanding, foreclosures continue to rise nationally, and many banks are beginning to lift the recent, temporary moratoriums on foreclosure proceedings, so the backlog may suddenly grow even larger.

Moreover, some of the language used in our national dialogue has been misleading. Arguably our economic situation is truly a "crisis," as the scope and depth of the pain felt by so many Americans is so frighteningly real. But historically speaking, the collapse of the real estate, mortgage, and housing bubble was also a long-overdue, natural, albeit severe market "correction," back into normal levels. Clearly the bubble was unsustainable, and like the laws of physics, what goes up, must come down. And for context, although unemployment, now in excess of 10 percent nationwide, is awful, it does not even come close to the 25 percent or higher unemployment of the Great Depression. Not yet, anyway.

Most of the government's focus on creating solutions has been institutional, not personal: Bailouts on a scale never before seen for automakers, banks, insurance companies, and, some are predicting, credit card companies, airlines, and similarly gargantuan "too big to fail" businesses that are critical parts of our economic quilt. It is true that many of these bailouts save jobs, albeit artificially, bordering on socialism because we have no choice.

And although it can be argued that the government could and should have stopped the overexpansion for our own good before it tipped over (a consistent chorus from economic Monday-morning quarterbacks), the government cannot be expected to "solve" or "stop" the crisis; the lattice structure of the house of cards that was our bloated market has already given way. All the government can do now, and be expected to do, is to ease the severity and length of the corrective event as much as possible. Enabling a soft landing, versus a crash, should be considered a win.

IN MY VIEW it's become immensely clear while watching the crisis unfold that the United States desperately needs a Chief Marketing Officer—a single person to guide, manage, and market the ideas, programs, vision, and consistent message for the administration (although some would argue that this is part of the president's job, selling ideas, programs, and policies to the American people via consistent messages and tone just like a car company does).

Consider even the basic tactic of properly naming something, which in our case has demonstrated an amateur-hour approach to marketing considerations at the highest levels: What genius decided to label the most critical element of the plan to save financial markets from collapse—based upon the ideal of total transparency—the *TARP* Plan? Did anyone in the administration realize that they chose to call the most important program to reestablish *trust* in our system, a word that literally means "a cover-up"? That's like Crest launching a new toothpaste version that has a new ingredient, ROT [Removing Oral Tartar]. *New Crest, now with ROT!* Names matter, whether you are marketing toothpaste, or the financial plan to save the world.

So the story continues. And since *The Foreclosure of America* first hit bookshelves in January 2009, the twists and turns of my wild ride through the smiling gauntlets of media punditry and polarized public opinion has been matched only by the original story of my wild ride within Countrywide itself. The saga that has continued after the book was released evolved into the same structure of the book itself: parallel paths of both my own personal experience, combined with the external evolution of Countrywide's final, very public implosion, which, like a dying star not quite large enough to supernova, first ballooned into a white-hot controversy, then cascaded through a series of smaller controversies, only to finally end as a wispy afterthought, quietly absorbed by a much larger entity (Bank of America). Now, only the charred ruins and faint echoes of a once great financial empire remain; one that was, at one time, considered invincible. I can't help but wonder, now that anything is conceivable, what other previously thought-to-be-invincible empires will be the next to fall?

Adam Michaelson
Santa Monica, California
August 2009

Preface

MANY PEOPLE ADVISED me not to write this book. They cautioned against writing an "insider's" tale of what was the largest mortgage lender in the United States, and arguably one of the most critically powerful pistons in the engine that drove the U.S. economy. But I had to write it. Someone needed to put onto paper the events of what actually happened inside Countrywide before it was the first giant to fall. With this book I wanted to accomplish a number of objectives.

First, I wanted to provide for future generations of business leaders a cautionary tale of hubris, a lesson on the infectious groupthink of bubbles, and scribe the actual thoughts of those who were deep inside them as the bubbling began its own momentum. When business school classes study this collapse in hindsight many years from now (and I hope the course is not titled "The Great Depression of 2010"), they will certainly pore through reams of rich data, charts, and graphs, and seek out various flaws in the present-day business models, looking for what went wrong and what was the tipping point. But no data, no textbook, no chart can ever illustrate the *human* aspects of what causes bubbles, and provide the firsthand account of the thinking—the flavor of those moments—from within those conference rooms at that point in history. The excitement, the groupthink, the momentum and fear that squelch resistance, the systemic power of the mighty current pushing the fish along, this is the inside story of the feelings within the walls of Countrywide during that time, which textbooks will never be able to re-create.

Perhaps this will prevent it from happening again in the future, although this is unlikely. From gold to oil, from dot coms to real estate, the nutty, frothy momentum of unchecked greed, and then our penitent penchant for cleaning up the messes at terrible costs, seems to course through our veins as capitalists and as Americans.

Second, I wanted to dispel myths that have grown out of the story; that Countrywide and many other lenders were sinister in their intent; that foreclosed homeowners were all either irresponsible losers, or were rampant spenders or speculators, or that we indeed should save everyone. All of these myths, and many others, are unfair generalizations that I have tried to fairly dispel, or confirm if necessary, in these pages.

Perhaps most profoundly, I wanted to try to answer, from a personal perspective, the question that all America seems to have been asking since the credit markets began their collapse in the summer of 2007: "What were they *thinking*?" As I was one of the "they" that helped create the boom, after you read this, you will know.

I also wrote this for several key audiences.

I wrote it for the more than one million families (at least at the time of this writing; who knows? the total could be several million by the time this book is released) who are facing, or who have already endured default on their mortgage or foreclosure on their home. My interviews with some of those hardest hit really brought the crisis to life for me. Their tears were real and compelling. Trucks being repossessed; crying children not understanding why they had to move out of their big house and into a small apartment, saying good-bye to friends; attempted and successful suicides; and the terrible stigma and embarrassment these people have faced. These are not numbers in a newspaper headline; these are all Americans; all suffering. So for all of you in the midst of this crisis in your own homes, know that you are not alone.

And I wrote this book for the other 45 million or so mortgage holders who have *not* defaulted—those who read the fine print, took their promissory note seriously and responsibly, and planned for the time when their loans were due to reset. Perhaps they too are suffering, under the weight of new, higher monthly payments, but are making them and are holding on. They are canceling vacations, cutting back on luxuries, working longer hours, and doing without to fulfill the promise they made to whatever financial institution *gave them hundreds of thousands of dollars,* all based on the trust that came with their signature.

I also wrote this book for all the policy influencers who may be reading it—legislators at the state and federal levels, the press, the pundits, the economists, the army of dedicated business school professors in America, some of whom I had the honor to study under myself, and future first-time homebuyers who may be smarter about the promises they make. Perhaps within the first, critical hundred days of the new administration, the new president will be tucked under the presidential quilt in his big new bed upstairs in his big new White House some evening, and will read this. (*Hello, Mr. President, I'm Adam. Thanks for reading my book.*)

Perhaps the details surrounding how and why this happened to homeowners, as told by them, and what exactly the executives in the lush conference rooms at the largest mortgage company in America were thinking as they helped fuel the boom, will help create thoughtful reform and smarter mortgage policy for future generations in the twenty-first century.

Or, perhaps, vast thousands of unsold copies will be used for oil drum fires to keep hungry people warm as they wait on soup lines within two years. Who knows; I simply had to try to get the story out and inform the future.

Finally, I wrote this for all of the people, who, like me, once believed in Countrywide long before its sudden vilification, thought they were "doing good," and are now wondering if they should even list Countrywide on their résumés. Hopefully this book will allow you to do that without reservation.

I will provide an accurate record, to the best of my recollection, of what happened there during my tenure in the fast rise of the boom, as well as early signs of the beginning of the end that started to appear just as I departed from the firm, and from information gathered about the final collapse itself from interviews and research. While I did not keep a formal journal during my time at Countrywide, I have tried to recall the events that transpired within the heyday of the storm as accurately as possible. Some scenes have been enhanced slightly for dramatic effect, but all are true accounts as I remember them.

This will not be a salacious "tell-all," and will not divulge any proprietary "insider" information about Countrywide's financials or processes. I did not wish to do any harm to the entity that was Countrywide before Bank of America bought it, so no confidential information or trade secrets will be shared. In fact, I don't even need any confidential information to tell this true, dramatic story about the behavior of corporate people, and the moral conflicts they faced from within a bubble. Corporations, it can be argued, may indeed be mindless beasts of profit, but they are still run by people, and such people, including those within Countrywide, were driven by human motives, self-interests, desires, incentives, and value structures that I hope to illustrate thoughtfully within these pages.

Nor is it to be an act of "whistle-blowing," as I believe there is no whistle to blow, and that is part of the point. Political finger-pointing and blame-seeking notwithstanding, during my time working all throughout Countrywide Financial, including the Home Loans and Banking divisions, I never witnessed any malfeasance or wrongdoing. In my eyes, Countrywide was driven by a creed of always doing what's right and adhered to the stated mission of Angelo Mozilo, the founder and CEO of Countrywide: "Help All Americans Achieve the Dream of Home-ownership." The staff was dedicated and committed to this and to their duty as a public company to maximize the return of shareholders' equity.

In the end, they may have been guilty only of giving Main Street what it wanted, and Wall Street what it needed; just like, as some would argue, "fast-food companies are killing people by forcing them to be obese" for a hungry, demanding market. This is a key theme in this story as well.

While certainly there were personalities and styles that may not have completely fit my comfort zone, I in no way seek to hurt any of these professionals who did their jobs as best they could in the circumstances they were handed. As these people did not ask to be written about, and out of respect for their privacy, I have changed the names, identifying traits and in some cases, even the genders of those I worked with who were not in the public eye, and some characters are amalgams of several real individuals. I used only the real names of the most senior executives who already made the choice to be officers of this public firm and were profiled on Countrywide's website for all the world to see.

At the beginning of each chapter, I present a snapshot of the foreclosure rate, as well as the Prime Rate and average Countrywide stock price at the time, for historical context. Although the term *foreclosure rate* can be defined in many ways, such as the number of loans entering the process, concluding the process, or just in default (not yet foreclosed), for consistency I have based this on the definition, as publicly reported by the firm RealtyTrac, as "the percentage of loans in some stage of the foreclosure process." But any way you slice it, it has soared.

This is a complex story with many characters; some are people, some are not. Some are static institutions, some are chaotic, fluid systems, and some are even entrenched states of mind in our culture. But Angelo Mozilo, the charismatic and paternal CEO of Countrywide, is a central character to be sure. Whether you like him or not, his is truly one of the last only-in-America success stories of the twentieth century, and is, arguably, the father of what was the modern mortgage business. For almost 40 years, he "did good"—he helped Americans get into their own homes. Although I don't expect to see any bronze statues of him with hand extended upward to the financial future to be unveiled anytime soon, he was a powerful force within the firm, especially for those of us, like myself, who aspired to also one day become a corporate rock star. He motivated and inspired everyone from the most senior executives right down to the guys in the mailroom. When he visited your office, it was a special day.

Countrywide itself as an entity, and as a powerful brand in its own right, is a character as well. But what I hope this book will illuminate, and what I hope will become clear when the dust settles on this sandstorm of negative media and finger-pointing, is that neither Angelo, nor Countrywide, nor homeowners, nor I are truly the most important antagonists in this modern financial tragedy.

In truth, the forces of the marketplace, in its natural state of unrelenting self-destruction, its tendency to bubble, then to overcorrect, is really the villain here. Everyone was just naturally pursuing their own self-interest; perhaps guilty, but not responsible in their actions. All of this, the mortgage crisis, the housing crisis, the foreclosure crisis, the crisis of confidence in free markets, our leaders, and our economy— all of this was *our own doing*.

Thomas Jefferson might have seen this coming. He warned us of this financial mess in his brilliant homespun wisdom of early America, his famous "Ten Rules." In fact, he dedicated three of those ten rules to concepts relevant to this debate:

Never spend your money before you have earned it.
Never buy what you don't want because it is cheap.
Pride costs more than hunger, thirst, and cold.

Ironically, Jefferson broke almost every one of his own rules, and died *owing* more than $2 million in today's dollars. *Sounds like a typical American to me.*

Adam Michaelson
Santa Monica, California
September 2008

1

The Vault, and the Meeting That Changed America

I can get no remedy against this consumption
of the purse: borrowing only lingers and lingers
it out, but the disease is incurable.
—William Shakespeare, *Henry IV*

JULY 2004

Prime rate: 4.25%

Foreclosure rate: 1.14%

CFC stock price: ~$36.00

ONCE UPON A time, I attended a meeting that may have contributed to the Second Great Depression in the United States. And it occurred in a nuclear-proof underground bunker.

By the summer of 2004, the housing and mortgage boom had accelerated to unheard-of levels, and it seemed that the sky was not even the limit.

I oversaw new customer acquisition marketing—the creation of new customers across most media—for Countrywide Financial during the biggest refinancing boom in U.S. history. Then, as housing values soared stratospherically, the Refi boom mutated into the home equity boom, and as the new customer acquisition marketing guy, I drove the growth. The president of the firm said that Home Equity Loans (known as "HELOCs" in the industry vernacular) were the "next frontier" in financial services, and we were selling them. Hard.

Americans were using their homes' increased value as ATM machines. HELOC "draws" (cash people took out from the inflated values of their homes for even more spending) in excess of $50,000, $100,000, even $150,000 and beyond saw corresponding and mind-boggling growth in the amounts the homeowners owed. But "don't worry," everyone said. Home values would continue to rise, and one could always refinance. Again. And again.

America has had a love affair with debt in recent decades. Credit card balances in the United States average more than $8,000 per household, and they're still on the rise.

Let's go to Florida! Billy needed braces. Suzie's off to college. That bathroom just *had* to be redone. Oh, did you see that new Lexus? Yes, things were good. It was the late 1920s all over again.

Then, as Refi levels waned and as HELOC applications started to crest, a new, insidious trend began to emerge, driven by the winds of the marketplace—consumers' needs for ever-increasingly exotic forms of credit, and Countrywide's natural market motivation to fuel that need.

Like many corporate cultures, Countrywide prided itself, at least outwardly, on being a meritocracy, rewarding those who demonstrated a commitment to the cultural mores and who were able to add value to the firm each and every quarter. While it seemed that everyone was *only* as good as their latest weekly numbers, especially in this sales-driven organization, the reality was that many "stars" earned this reputation by sleight-of-hand. You know the ones I mean; every company has them. Some create the illusion of overload by waiting until the last minute to accomplish everything. Others are constantly putting out "fires," desperate to be perceived as martyrs who, in fact, would have no fires to put out if they had planned things properly. (There's a great *Seinfeld* episode based on this company dynamic, where George acts frustrated every time he wants to appear busy to his bosses; a classic.)

Most corporate cultures in the United States are a lot like high school, and Countrywide was no exception. I can remember vividly the caste-based pecking order of high school, delineated by the unwritten "separate but equal" law of the teenage jungle, via the different cliques. The jocks; the band geeks; the hot ones; the smart ones; the foreign ones; the overachievers; the potheads; the nerds (do they even still use that word?); and, most importantly, the popular ones. All blended in a mix of what I call "woo culture," also known by other euphemisms such as "school spirit," and in Fortune 500s, simply known as "corporate culture." Countrywide had its "finance jocks," its "tech geeks," its popular cliques, its "woo!" cheerleaders, and its politicians, of course.

Having worked with hundreds of corporate entities throughout my previous ad agency career, the only thing that was consistent in corporate cultures was how different they all were. One day I might be with the dot com start-up, which was like a dorm. Employees would be doing tai chi in the lobby, playing billiards on the table in the conference room, "brainstorming" in their wool caps and flip-flops, and generally making as much noise as possible. (There is an old Microsoft legend that employees could spot a visiting vendor a mile away because he would be the only one in the office wearing a tie.)

Then on another day I might be presenting an ad campaign to a bank, where employees were at their desks at 8:00 A.M. sharp, decked out in the standard issue uniform of pinstripes, shined shoes, neatly pinched ties and crisp white shirts, all toiling away at their spreadsheets silently in a librarylike environment.

Cultures are powerful entities, with a momentum all their own, and are designed to engender conformity. Working with, and acclimating to, an existing culture is usually rewarded. Working against an entrenched culture can cause you to be alienated and eventually purged. A frequent error that I have especially seen many young people make is not to realize that once you agree to join a firm, every e-mail, every call, every voice mail, every meeting, even the car you drive and the clothes you wear—everything about you—either works with a culture or against it. And it starts on the first minute of the first day. So if they love to golf, you better not decline the invitation for the foursome. If they like to go out to bars after work, you better like drinking. Whatever ingredients mix together to make their "Kool-Aid," you better embrace it, for the thought police of the "woo!" culture will usually demand that when great sales numbers are announced, you yell the loudest "Woo!" you can muster, and high-five everyone, hard. Or you're out.

One key element of the Countrywide "Kool-Aid" that fueled some of the mayhem of the mortgage boom was a mix of two cultural concepts: one of "velocity" and the other of "fire in the belly," an odd mix of "don't put off 'til tomorrow what you can do today" and "if you ain't runnin', then you don't have enough to do." In retrospect, I wonder if the Human Resources cheerleaders who created these phrases truly knew that someday the money, and the opportunity, and the reign of Countrywide would end. *Better get it while the gettin' is good.* But during this new gold rush, these mantras, created on some whiteboard at some off-site to thunderous applause at some resort, did accomplish some of their desired objectives. Every week, across every department, within every meeting room, the culture was driven forward via a "velocity" that had to be driven by everyone's "fire in the belly." Or else. And each race had a common start: the *Meeting Invitation,* (known colloquially in corporate culture simply as an "Invite").

I truly believe that one of the greatest inventions of the twentieth century was not e-mail but rather the singular function of being able to send out an Invite to many people instantly. For within the *Lord of the Flies*–driven, lead-or-be-led laws of the corporate jungle, few creations have given so much power to so many so fast as this magic wand of virtual leadership. With one touch of the send button, anyone can exert leadership (or try to) over any topic or group. Simply tell them to be at some predetermined place and time, with either orders to come prepared to discuss a topic authoritatively, to present their ideas (ergo, prove their value—or lack of it—in front of others), or to listen passively to another authority figure, and, *whammo*, instant conch shell. In short, when you need to quickly exert or demonstrate leadership, never underestimate the power of simply being the one to call the meeting via these Invites, these wonderful little virtual butterflies of power.

But beware. Like any exertion of leadership, you better be sure that your call to arms will be heard, heeded, and respected. There is nothing worse in corporate culture than to act like a leader but then be ignored. *Ouch.* Every Invite sent out in Countrywide became a microcosmic joust with any and all peers, subordinates, and senior directors above you, so you had to make sure you won. If they cancel, or deny the Invite, that's bad enough. But the worst case is if, God forbid, you send an Invite, and no one responds, not even with declines. Many managers slit their own throats by going to the Invite well too often. Like the boy who cried wolf, you had better be sure of affirmations before you hit Send.

One day at the office, a meeting Invite popped up in my Inbox. This unto itself was not extraordinary, for as Senior Vice President of Marketing for New Customer Acquisition, I received at least 50 such invitations each day across many business lines, departments, and topics. Fortunately, I had learned over the years how to separate the wheat from the chaff with only a quick glance. The quarterly review meeting for sales was a definite, quick *yes*. The meeting to present the customer research about one of our escrow services, *no*.

But this one was different; it caught my eye. *Where* it was set to occur is what made me notice it right away. It was set to occur inside the *Vault*.

The headquarters of Countrywide Financial in Calabasas, California, was outwardly an unassuming, nondescript place, with a legendary history that not many people knew about. The three-story, 350,000-square-foot, Mediterranean-style villa complex across 20 acres was originally built as the headquarters of Lockheed Corporation decades ago, during the Cold War. There, projects both public and secret were developed to help America win the space race, the arms race, and probably many other races we may never know about. Most notably, as owner of the world-famous Skunk Works, that headquarters building for Lockheed probably also oversaw the technological marvels that were developed secretly for the United States at that time, such as the U-2, the early concepts for stealth technology, and others. Hell, maybe alien technology, too.

With an almost Frank Lloyd Wright–like style, it had an eerie similarity to the exterior of his masterwork, *Falling Water*. And, like that architectural wonder in the deep woods of Pennsylvania, part of it was built into the surrounding earth, underground. I suspect that the reason was twofold: some rooms needed to survive an attack by the Soviet Union, and some conversations must never be heard by the enemy. This underground section, shielded below layers of earth, was where they decided to put the Vault.

The Vault was just that. According to legend, this massive conference room was specifically designed to be part bomb shelter, part panic room, and part silent haven, safe from eavesdropping. There were no clocks, no windows (obviously), and the ceiling felt unnervingly low—definitely not for claustrophobics. The underground room had a strange deadness to it. The air was cooler inside, with a damp muskiness. Like a cave with nice carpeting.

I had heard the stories about the Vault, but entering it myself for the first time was a surreal experience. The only way in or out was via one door. The door was actually a massive steel wall, a giant safe door, like banks have in heist movies, or the airtight bulkhead door on a battleship, and had to weigh at least several tons. When the door was open, and I walked in, I could clearly see that the gray, cold steel was at least six inches thick, with hinges enormous enough to support that massive weight. Like entering a fantastic place conceived by both Lewis Carroll and Tom Clancy, I felt a childish yet real trepidation as I went inside. I crossed over a small bump in the floor, housing God knows what kind of sensitive equipment. Were they going to seal this door for the meeting? Would I hear the stereotypical vacuum seal sound effect as the door was bolted shut from the inside? I wondered if the door had not been sealed since some tense day during the Cold War. It was like the submarine in the film *Das Boot*, but for mortgages.

The room was stark, dark, dank, and musty. I wondered what the original Lockheed architects and interior designers were thinking. How, exactly, does one design a room that may one day be the scene of postnuclear holocaust decision-making and administration? It seemed set up to inspire conformity and quell independent thought. Perhaps it was to establish calm. It had solid black carpeting, and dark brown walls covered with some kind of sound-absorbent material (there's your alien technology, probably). Oddly, it also had a plain dark brown table, which seemed too cheap for a room with such importance. It was dimly lit, with buzzing fluorescent lights overhead. But the size was enormous. At least 30 senior executives might fit around that table, like knights in the round, or rather rectangular, perhaps at one time deciding the fate of a nation or, in this case, the American economy.

Being an amateur scientist all my life, and having heard about the Vault being designed as a real nuclear-proof shelter, I immediately wondered if it was also a Faraday cage. Named after the famed nineteenth-century physicist who invented it, Michael Faraday, it is essentially a room with an outer box, with metallic mesh within the walls, such as copper. It can be used to shield electronic equipment from the electromagnetic pulse of a nuclear blast, or prevent electronic signals from entering or leaving an enclosure—perfect for making sure your enemies cannot hear you. Under the table, I discreetly pulled my cell phone out of my pocket and flipped it open. *Yup*, no signal. *Cool*. Maybe this was simply due to the fact that the Vault was underground, but it was more fun to imagine its intentional stealthy design.

Some key players were there, from "the five families," which is what we snidely called the groups from marketing, product, and the sales organizations, as well as some other areas. I immediately noticed Allison Pringle there, a midlevel executive whom I simply called "Harvard," because she had the annoying habit of obliquely reminding everyone in every meeting that she had gotten her MBA from Harvard Business School. *Yawn*.

The meeting was called by Bibi Karimi, an attractive woman and a well-regarded thinker within the organization, who worked within the Product Development group at Countrywide Home Loans. In the number-one home loans company in the United States, the euphemism "product development" referred to a group of so-called "finance jocks" who were expert calculators of strange and new financial products. They were passionate about what they did.

People milled about, waiting for Bibi to arrive with her team. As I was getting Countrywide's standard-issue, horrible, watered-down coffee that had been set up for us, I wondered once again how a firm that made billions of dollars a year could serve its employees this swill they called coffee. As a native New Yorker, I liked my *cawfee*—it had to be like motor oil. I imagined that ExxonMobil served their minions Starbucks, and wondered silently if *they* were hiring.

Then I saw Tim Shay, a colleague who worked on marketing for the Full Spectrum Lending Group, Countrywide's Subprime division. We weren't often in the same meetings, as typically Prime and Subprime didn't overlap in messaging, offers, or loan products. I decided to be the one to start the small talk.

"Hey, Tim," I said, searching for Splenda.

"Hey, Adam. So what's this big product announcement?" he asked.

"Who knows? Maybe now we're giving away a free house with every home loan," I half joked.

Tim half laughed back, "Maybe you're right."

At that point, a few other midlevel people entered the room, from sales, public relations, finance, and operations, which handled application processing, the call centers, and other loan-based administrative functions. Large meetings were unusual for Countrywide. Even for "committee" meetings, culturally, Countrywide felt as I did that the use of smaller "SWAT teams" was a more efficient approach to getting things done. And if someone had no role or speaking part in the meeting, then that person would add no value and should be working on something else.

But this meeting felt different the moment it began.

Bibi finally entered with her financial entourage. They left the safe door open during the meeting. Perhaps some folks in previous meetings experienced claustrophobic panic attacks, jumping up during a particularly disturbing review of loan portfolio servicing revenue, pounding on the inside of the door madly, sweating, screaming to be let out. They could not have known that some three years later, they might all be screaming to get out of Countrywide.

A laptop had already been set up on the conference table for Bibi's presentation, and in usual style, she jumped right into the meeting, finishing the pleasantries right away with a simple "Good morning, everyone. Can we dim the lights please?"

As she fired up the laptop that had been in sleep mode, I took in the sight surrounding me. The anticipation for whatever she had to say was palpable in the room, partly because it was so secretive. The moment or two of silent preparation created a hush across the table, which seemed even more pronounced as the walls absorbed all forms of sound.

Bibi began.

"Several months ago, this product development team was directed to create our own version of a new form of loan product that is changing our industry. With the Refi boom waning, and home equity sales booming and potentially cresting soon, Countrywide decided to invest in this new product development focused on extending our leadership as the path to American homeownership."

Good opening, I thought. Bold, compelling, enticing, and grounded in our mission. The room was captivated. Maybe we really *were* going to give away a house with every loan. She continued.

"Ladies and gentlemen, we would like to introduce the Countrywide suite of *PayOption* loans," she announced. I half-expected music to begin to swell, but instead, an awkward silence filled the room. *What* loans? It felt like five minutes, but it was more like five seconds before her eyes darted around the room, paused, and she continued:

"The PayOption is an adjustable-rate loan where the borrower has the *option to pay less* than a standard mortgage payment every month. Let me show you what I mean," she continued.

Bibi went on to explain that a PayOption Adjustable Rate Mortgage is not a fixed loan. A traditional fixed loan amortizes down over time because the borrower must pay a set amount each month (comprised of both the interest and principal) over the term of the loan. That payment discipline forces the borrower to pay down the loan each month, little by little. With each passing month of the term, the borrower owns a little more equity in the property and a little less on the debt. That's a good thing. And that's how it worked well for many generations in the United States. With this method, my parents paid off their home in 1999, after 30 years of disciplined, steady monthly payments. They own it, free and clear.

But the PayOption is a monthly Adjustable Rate Mortgage that allows the borrower the *choice of payment*, even giving them the ability to pay *less* than they owe on the loan every month. This is called *negative amortization*, which in plain English meant actually increasing the size of the amount owed on your loan each month. Here's an overly simplified explanation of how it worked: if you owe $300,000 on a home loan, and your loan payment normally would be $3,000 a month, but you decide to pay less than that, your total loan could actually increase each month. First month, you now owe $301,000, second month, $302,000, and so on. *Yikes!*

The PayOption product offered four choices of payment. The first two choices could actually make your total loan larger every month; the last two were traditional payment styles.

Choice number one would be a "Minimum Payment," which, depending on whether or not you got an "Introductory Rate," may actually be *lower* than the principal and interest payment you would normally owe for that month. Choice two was "Interest Only," where you would pay only the interest due that month, not paying anything into the principal you owe. These first two choices could put you into negative amortization.

Choice three was the standard principal plus interest payment, like the old days, and choice four was for the courageous who wanted to pay a much higher payment as if the loan was only a 15-year term.

Think of it like a credit card (because that's how the customers did). Those of you who carry a credit card balance every month know that your card statement will typically provide you with the "Minimum Payment Due." That's not the minimum payment required to pay down your revolving credit card debt or even keep you at the same level. It is the minimum that the card company is willing to accept to even keep you as a customer. Now, imagine getting a card that set the minimum amount due but allowed you to pay *less* than that number. Your balance would grow larger, your payment discipline would crumble, and, basically, you'd be going backward, fast. Not good.

A spreadsheet hit the projection screen as Bibi continued her presentation. I swear I could hear the faint sounds of "oohs" and "aahs" like I heard while watching summer fireworks at Shea Stadium as a kid. I could see the numbers in the reflection of people's glasses across the table as they studied the visual. Countrywide always, immediately, properly focused first on the numbers. I did, too.

The fundamental reasons for the creation of this product were threefold. First, home values were rising at trajectories and speeds never before seen. Borrowers needed ever-increasingly exotic products that would allow them to get into ever-increasingly expensive homes, and yet still be able to pay only tiny payments. Consequences be damned, the future was bright.

Second, Countrywide could make great amounts of money from these loans. As they were Adjustable Rate products, borrowers would eventually need to refinance, presumably through Countrywide, and, voilà—more loan fees, more income, more happy shareholders.

Third, and perhaps most ominously, Countrywide moved forward with these risky loan products *because we could*. There were no laws, no regulations restricting these loans that could conceivably put half the country underwater.

Countrywide did not invent the optional-payment concept. Many players in the industry—Wachovia called theirs "Pick-A-Payment" loans, for example—were starting to build similar products for the same reasons we were, because borrowers loved their lower monthly payment option. But as the largest home loan company in the country, with arguably the strongest marketing engine anywhere, we would do it larger, better, and faster like the blazing market share conquistadors that we were. I liked that part, frankly. I was "in it to win it" just like everyone else in a profit-driven, sales-focused organization like Countrywide. And, more directly, my bonus was tied to achieving sales goals. *Bring it on.*

As Bibi walked the room through the numbers before us, something jumped out at me and I began to become alarmed. They showed that, yes, they were going to allow some borrowers to pay less than their monthly principal plus interest payments called for. They were going to allow borrowers' loans to increase every month. But that was not what made me queasy.

I read the numbers more closely and saw the major flaw immediately. They made the fundamental assumption, wrongly in my view, that housing values were going to go up for the foreseeable future, perhaps forever—"in perpetuity," as finance jocks called it. It was assumed that PayOption borrowers who continued to pay less than their minimum or interest only, whose balances would grow higher and higher, could always refinance their loans, again and again, because their $300,000 home would continue to be worth $350,000, then $400,000, then higher and higher. Don't worry, they said, things were good, and they were only going to get better.

But I assumed at that moment that everyone else was seeing what I was seeing. Of course everyone can see that these numbers are pure fantasy at best, and cataclysmic folly at worst.

"Any questions so far?" asked Bibi, about midway through her presentation.

Several hands went up, including my own. She called on some other folks first. *Oh good*, I thought, *someone is going to raise this concern before I need to.*

Jeff Stone, a buddy of mine and one of the leaders of the inbound call centers, asked about how it would be sold, what language would be used in messaging, etc. I jumped in.

"Jeff, we'll work closely with Bibi and her team to build the optimal messaging that maximizes conversions to applications within your scripts. My team will be sure to keep you in the loop, Jeff—you know your call agents best, and we'll make sure we test those scripts with real callers first," I said.

Jeff nodded appreciatively. Part of my responsibilities running the New Customer Acquisition marketing group at that time was not only to do the big and visible marketing like television commercials. Yes, we developed national television, sent out tons of direct mail per month, ran many online banners, and managed vast numbers of online search keywords at optimal profitability every week. But we were also responsible for the more mundane elements of the "loan lead generation and conversion-to-application process," including assisting with call center scripts, postage management, inbound television calls data, and more.

Then there were some questions about various administrative functions: operations people asked about how these loans might be processed differently; technology people were inquiring into the timing of this product launch, as software systems needed to be updated, tested, and ready in time. My team was asking about marketing materials needed and the like. The number of moving parts necessary to launch a new product or service in a company and a product process of this size is mind-boggling. Most consumers don't realize that in today's infinitely complex corporate operations, even launching a new line of breath mints is a major undertaking, requiring the perfectly synchronized efforts of thousands of people in research, testing, operations, sales, marketing, distribution, production, finance, and many other teams.

Still, no one around that table questioned the assumptions they were making.

I suddenly felt like an astronomer, looking at the same sky as my colleagues, seeing the same dot of light, and somehow being the only one to realize that that dot was an asteroid that could hit the Earth. But who was I to question it? Although I was a senior vice president, I was just the "marketing guy," not one among the fraternal order of finance jocks—a clique that was tightly bound and powerful in that metrics-based company.

I was also struck by how *proud* they seemed. Like parents, glowing as they unveiled pictures of their newborn. Or, more aptly, like scientists, weapons designers, proudly displaying their new models of financial nuclear weapons.

The "core" was Countrywide's financial capital seemingly great enough to risk these loans, and their predesigned motivation to do so. The "trigger" could be the combination of an implosion in housing values, the epidemic of consumerism, and the marketplace's greater and greater demand for exotic loan products. The "yield" was going to allow people to get into homes they could never have possibly been able to afford otherwise, which, given a worst-case scenario, could wreak havoc on the broader economy via the ripple effects of any potential fallout. Each piece of the presentation showed how these financial devices would be more efficient, easier to launch, and faster to produce. God help us, were we now about to actually deploy these tools of potential financial destruction? It seemed so. Then again, I thought about what Harry Truman supposedly once said about the atomic bomb: "*Why'd we build the damn thing if we never planned to drop it?*"

My heart pounded. My pulse quickened. My ego and conscience both came to the forefront as I processed the internal dialogue of whether to speak up. Do I risk being the only dissenter in a room full of enthralled drones? It could mean political suicide, not "wooing" with the others. Or it could mean creating a reputation as an aggressive, independent thinker. Was I senior enough to carry any weight? Maybe it was time to roll the dice and bet on the equity of my experience and seniority. I knew I would not change the world, but perhaps I might be able to at least live with myself after the fact.

I suddenly felt a rush of remembrances: of every lesson, every negotiation, every confrontation, every bit of interpersonal, ethical, academic, and moral teaching from which I had ever learned, and every time I had to summon the courage to speak truth to power, no matter how trivial it may have seemed at the time. In an instant, I was back on a windy street in Boston with my father almost 20 years earlier.

RAISED IN WORKING-CLASS suburbs on Long Island, I had a typical, relatively uneventful upbringing. Never for want of anything, but not rich, I was the oldest of three overachieving boys, and a product of my creative father and my doting mother.

Throughout high school, I demonstrated proficiency for math, science, school politics, and music. As college applications approached and as my love of science and math bloomed (or so I thought), my parents quietly began gathering information about the military academies—mostly the Naval Academy at Annapolis and the Air Force Academy in Colorado. The allure of prestige and a top-notch education were strong motivators. Although I got carsick, the thought of flying was exciting.

But like most teenagers, I found it hard to decipher where my parents' wishes ended and mine began. The thought of a military life, devoid of many of the freedoms I might be defending, frightened me. Also, the physical fitness requirements would be challenging. I had never been part of any of the sports teams in high school, and I would need to compete for slots with some of the best jocks in the country.

Through a series of twists and turns that I won't bore you with, I wound up accepting an offer to attend Boston University in the fall of 1984. I had been offered a full scholarship by the United States Air Force Reserve Officers' Training Corps (ROTC), and I was to become an aerospace engineer. Boston University was then and is now a relatively expensive school, and this scholarship represented approximately $50,000 worth of education (in 1984 dollars, which equals approximately $110,000 today).

It turned out that I loved the military: the discipline, the uniform, the "club," the "best-of-the-best" culture. To this day much of my corporate professionalism and any leadership skills I possess I owe to the teachings of the Flying Tigers of the 355th Training Detachment of the Air Force Reserves in Boston. Be punctual. Neat. Know your job. Be prepared and confident. Tie straight. Shoes polished. Never leave your wingman, never leave a comrade behind. It also got me into shape, got me up at 6:00 A.M. on many a frigid morning to do physical fitness drilling in a giant army armory in Boston, and forevermore taught me how to intertwine physical fitness into all aspects of my adult life. There was only one problem: my genius powers of math and science quickly gave way to what would become known in my history as the "Great Grades Train Wreck of the 1980s."

I discovered I wasn't as good at physics, fluid dynamics, and advanced calculus as I had once thought. In fact, I sucked at them. Maybe my high school taught Romper Room math and science or something, maybe I just realized that I didn't have the maturity or the dedication required for such a vocation, maybe maybe maybe...

When I literally scored a 12 out of 100 on my physics final freshman year, I knew I was in big trouble. I assumed they awarded 10 points for getting my own name right.

Sophomore year would be the year I would get my act together, hunker down, and bring those grades up. If not, I could lose my scholarship, and that was bad. I had no Plan B. My parents, who had always seen me excel at whatever I attempted, were mortified by my apparent sudden lack of ability to get straight A's. They also could be facing the scarier problem of paying for the rest of my education.

But that second year was worse than the first. Moreover, I came to realize that I did not want to be an engineer. And the conversation that ensued with my parents at that point made for one of the most difficult years of our relationship. It was an odd mix of fear, sadness, disappointment, and optimism on both sides.

I will never forget the day I grew up, the day I finally changed course and courageously spoke my mind and followed my own path. It was the first time I truly developed the guts and the maturity to speak a difficult truth to entrenched, overpowering authority, both institutional and personal.

My father drove to Boston to meet me and the Major at the Air Force office on campus that warm May day. Today would be the day when my new life path would be determined in a meeting that lasted no more than 10 minutes.

My Major was all spit and polish. His shoes gleamed with a mirror shine that I could never replicate exactly. His tie was straight and neat. His clothes fit him like the quartermaster himself had tailored them perfectly to his muscular girth. If he had been a fictional creation I am sure the author would have named him *Dirk Concrete, USAF.* He was tall, imposing, and intimidating, and got right to the point after the introductory pleasantries.

"Son, do you want to stay in the Air Force?" he asked sternly, his tightly cropped, silver hair matching his silver-rimmed glasses framing his chiseled, stoic face.

"I love the service, but I do not want to be an engineer," I responded resolutely.

"Then what *do* you want to do?" the Major asked.

There was an awkward pause in the room as I searched for the sentence that might define my life. My dad made a face that mimed his eagerness for me to answer. Truth was, although I knew what I *didn't* want to do, my chosen alternatives were less clear.

"I want to switch to some marketing or communications field, I guess. I'm not sure yet."

The Major gave me an incredulous blank stare and then informed me and my father that "the only applicable job slot for that vocation in the service was in the Public Affairs office, but there was no scholarship for such a slot."

My father looked ashen, and I could see that the Major saw that, too.

The Major continued, "Son, your military scores are very high, you are one of the best cadets in the detachment, and we would hate to lose you. But if you stay in while pursuing a marketing or communications degree, we can no longer pay for your education. Perhaps you should discuss it with your family and let me know by Friday."

The meeting ended and we exited. My father and I walked out of the building onto windy Bay State Road in Boston, the home to many historic moments.

"Do you really want to ruin your life this way?" my father asked me straight.

I loved passive aggressive questions.

I was petrified. For my entire life this man had been a towering presence, filled with complete power over my life, bordering on inadvertent intimidation at times. Although equipped with great patience, he had it within him to display anger, which I had witnessed occasionally when growing up. But this time the calm, resigned disappointment that dripped from his sentence and hung from his face overwhelmed me. His brief silence and nauseous look of sadness cut me to the bone.

Slowly, I managed to stand up straight and say, "Dad, I am ready to go my own way now, and find a path for *me*, not you."

"Okay," he said, as we walked together back to his car silently. He got in, and drove off on the six-hour trip back to New York. I watched his car disappear into the city streets as a light drizzle began to fall. I stood there, determined to purposely remember that moment.

I had spoken truth to power—to an intimidating Air Force officer, and the ultimate power thus far in my life, my father. And the world didn't end. Nobody died. I had identified that something was not right in my life, I set the wheels in motion to alter my course, and I changed my world for the better, as fate would have it. And, of course, back then, as things often do, everything worked out fine.

BUT BACK IN the Vault at Countrywide, I suddenly wasn't so sure things would be fine—for me, for Countrywide, for borrowers, for

America. I wasn't a confused kid on a Boston sidewalk anymore, and this wasn't about just picking a career, which would affect only me. This issue could be real, could be serious, and could directly affect the well-being of millions of Americans. I decided to try to do *something*.

As the questions began to subside, one of Bibi's sycophantic subordinates openly said, "We are really proud of this new suite of products—thanks to Bibi for leading this charge for us." Applause filled the room, with smiles and nods all around.

Bibi was preparing to close out the meeting. "Any further questions?"

"Um, yes, I have a couple of questions," I said.

"Yes, Adam," Bibi said as she began putting her papers into a nice neat pile, clearly assuming that any questions now would be anecdotal.

"How did you reach the conclusion that home values, and therefore their ability to be refinanced, might go up forever?" I asked.

She paused, and thought for a moment.

"Well, forecasting has run the numbers and, based on recent history, and thinking through the risks, we believe that housing values will continue to rise for the foreseeable future, especially in major metros such as Los Angeles, New York, and others."

"Hmm," I continued the debate. "But what if we're *wrong*? What if housing values come down? How will these riskiest loans—these people—be able to Refi?"

She took a moment and absorbed it. I could feel all the heads in the room turning to her, then back to me, then back to her, like at a tennis match. As we were both Senior Vice Presidents, the underlings might have been enjoying watching us engage in this hypothetical debate.

I had no way of knowing at that time that I would turn out to be exactly right. Beginning in 2007, and increasing in 2008 and 2009 (and as I'm writing this it looks like it will continue into 2010), housing values have crumbled, the confidence in financial markets has been shaken, banks have stopped lending and millions of homeowners are trapped in huge mortgages they cannot afford, nor refinance because many people are "underwater" (owing more than their homes are now worth). Many of them are being foreclosed upon, and the fallout is causing blight in millions of communities across the United States. And these PayOption loans turned out to be part of the reason.

Bibi began to speak. "We feel strongly that we have vetted the scenarios, and the risk is offset by the opportunity for market share and revenue gain, let alone helping more people get into more expensive homes that they want, which, as you know, means bigger loans we can fund. And these products are consistent with our overall mission." She spoke calmly and resolutely but not angrily. She, like many at Countrywide, truly believed in what she was doing, and this was a good thing for the company. I partly agreed with her. She finished with a stern conviction. "We believe...it is *worth*...the risk."

Apparently senior management believed it as well, as they directed her to flush out these products and their numbers already. I was keenly aware of that political fact as I spoke. This was simply an informational session, not a request for approval.

"Okay, I have one more question," I continued. Outwardly I was calm, but as had happened to me many times before, I could feel my blood pressure increase.

"Are you...*nuts?*"

The room was an odd mix of hushed silence, murmurs, and giggles, but I wasn't laughing.

Bibi just looked at me, a little stunned at my statement.

I just kept going, trying to make her realize that I meant that organizationally, not personally.

"What if housing values *do* come down? Isn't it possible that *half the country* could be upside down on these loans?" I looked pleadingly at Allison across the table, blurting out an obnoxiously dry, "C'mon, help me out here, Harvard." She shrugged, giving me that "don't look at *me*, *you're* on your own" look.

"Yes, of course. Anything is possible. But we feel the chances are slim," Bibi conceded reluctantly.

I felt like rambling on, but I did not need to. My point had been made, albeit rhetorically, for I knew that this train had already left the station.

She seemed to appreciate my words, and with a knowing smile, concluded the meeting, saying simply, like a good soldier obeying orders, "Well, you're welcome to take up your concerns with senior management, of course. Otherwise, let us know about the schedule of those marketing materials, as I believe these products will be approved next week for launch."

As the meeting broke up and people exited, few looked me in the eye. My buddy Tim Shay smiled and gently patted me on the back. I could not tell whether that gesture meant "good job," "nice knowing ya, ya just ruined your career here," or "thanks for saying what we were all thinking but were afraid to say."

As the others filed out, I remained for a moment, making believe I was jotting some notes on my pad. And then for a few eerie moments I was alone, in the Vault.

I thought about the Cold Warriors who may have been in this very room, and argued about sensitive subjects that would affect the welfare of the United States long ago. I thought about the ones who stayed quiet when they should have spoken up. I thought about the ones who spoke up, at the risk to their own careers, to say what they believed. I thought about that Air Force officer. I thought about my father. I sat there, stared at the soundproof lining on the wall, and wondered if anyone had heard me at all.

I knew what would happen: we would launch these products with much fanfare and success. We knew that many of our competitors were going in this direction, so market forces would push us there as well. I was powerless to stop it. I knew that.

This was not like other times in my life when I had spoken truth to power because I had to, because I *could*, and because it was my own personal truth; this was different. This would require the strength, position, and power to change our entire company mission, culture, and reason for being; to change the capitalist system within which we resided; and to stop consumers' rabid need to buy more and more *stuff*.

I didn't have such power. No one did.

I left the room, and as I made my way through the gilded, vast atrium and lobby of the headquarters building, I thought about the devastating effects these types of products could reap. On Countrywide. On the loan business. On the economy as a whole. I drove the five miles back to my main office in Westlake Village, California, lost in thought. Was I overreacting? Perhaps.

There are two types of people in this world: those people who always see the bright side of things (you know who you are), and those who are annoyed by those people. I am the latter. You know, the "glass is half empty" type. So I had to slap myself as I predicted doom for the whole world. Perhaps it was just a case of too much caffeine, perhaps I was burned out, or perhaps I was right. I felt lost. I needed some wise counsel. And as I had learned in the Air Force, when in doubt, properly send it up the chain of command first.

At that time I reported to two different senior people within the Marketing group, who for purposes of this story, I shall call "Bob Griffin" and "Emily Simmons." Like many corporate lackeys with multiple bosses, I often felt like the child of divorced parents, both of whom I admired.

Bob Griffin was a warm and nurturing leader, a veteran of Countrywide, who headed the Brand group. Although he was a skilled thinker in many ways, with an impressive talent for reaching out to people, his joy seemed not to be the hard-core metrics of the business, but rather the equally critical *emotional* bond to all of Countrywide's audiences—customers, prospective customers, sales groups, investors, employees. He was the ballast within the organization, the brand yin to the ever-present, and sometimes overpowering, hard-core financial yang. He had a wonderful, keen sense of what Countrywide should and did mean to people, as well as being arguably the finest corporate diplomat I had ever met. No one knew how to bring people together like Bob did. He had brought me on board Countrywide, and I was forever grateful. But for feedback on my recent Vault experience, he was not the mentor I needed this day.

My other boss, and Bob's equal counterpart in the group was Emily Simmons, arguably one of the internal leaders of the finance jocks. Emily was a brilliant analyst, strategist, and loan production metrics overseer. I reported to her when I began the New Customer Acquisition group, which was primarily a response-driven, focus-on-the-metrics endeavor to drive thousands of new loans per month. She had no patience or expertise for the branded emotional elements of our marketing role, but was solely focused on profits, revenue, and margins—the perfect counterweight to Bob's "touchy-feely" marketing role. In time I would come to realize that both sides of this internal Countrywide marketing brain trust—emotional branding *and* rational metrics—were truly symbiotic; both were critical to the holistic success of the business, and each would have failed if they did not have the other's support.

After years in the ad agency business, and having just earned my MBA at UCLA's Anderson School, Emily had become the analytical and financial mentor I needed to round out my growth and corporate maturity. With her steady, confident walk and perfectly tailored power suits, her presence was palpable, and could be maternal, if you were making money for the firm. If not, she had no tolerance for you, and could cut you in half quickly. But you'd probably deserve it. Like me, she had no patience for slackers, losers, or drains on the firm. We shared this view, and this was part of the reason why I felt we bonded quickly in the initial weeks we worked together.

When I got back to my cluttered office, she was making the rounds as she often did, quietly observing who was at their desks toiling away and being productive. Seeing Emily walking the halls could strike fear in the heart of any slacking worker. She especially seemed to love to sadistically walk through the cubicles around 6:00 P.M., quietly noting who had left "early" that day.

Empty coffee cup in hand, she breezed past my office door, stopping in her tracks and taking a step back when I gave her a rare look of dread.

"Whatcha got, kiddo?" she said, in her best mentor voice. I could tell that she immediately knew something was up, and it was real.

"I think I may have just witnessed the beginning of the end of Countrywide and maybe the entire U.S. economy," I replied seriously.

She entered my office, closed the door behind her, and sat in my guest chair, slowly, calmly interlocking her fingers on her lap. Slowly crossing her legs to get comfortable, she briefly looked down at her new Italian shoes, then looked directly at me, and spoke.

"I'm listening," she said, with a slight smile.

DEBBIE, A MARRIED mother of three boys, was one of the first fore-closure interviews I did for this book, and one of the most heartbreaking.

For years, she and her husband, Mark, had rented an apartment in Queens. It had three bedrooms, one bath, and was located on the main floor of the building. They lived in the tough part of town. Gunshots could always be heard at night, there was drug dealing in the street, and used condoms and needles could easily be found in front of their building. Debbie's children could not ride their bikes, as sometimes roving gangs of "punks" would canvass the neighborhood and steal the bikes at knifepoint.

Debbie and Mark were honest, good, working, middle-class folks who loved their kids, and loved each other for many years. Together they had built a close-knit family, including Sam, an intelligent teenager who was proudly part of the Air Force Junior Reserve Officers Training Corps at his local high school; Steven, the sensitive middle child; and the youngest, Parker.

In 2004, as their oldest son was heading toward high school, they thought about moving out to Long Island and buying their first home. They had had enough of the crime in their rental neighborhood. They had heard the buzz about the housing boom, and how prices would go up and up and up. It sounded like it was time to jump in, to make the leap into investing in, finally, a home to call their own for themselves and their boys. For the pride of ownership, and being able to provide a backyard for their sons to play in, they were connected to a friend of a friend who also happened to be a mortgage broker.

Their main objective, besides getting into the house itself, was to keep the monthly payments to a minimum and not have to put money down on their new purchase. From Debbie's job as a lab technician and Mark's salary as a bus driver for the Metropolitan Transportation Authority of New York, they had a combined take-home income of approximately $6,000 per month. This equates to about $110,000 in total gross yearly income for the family. Now, this might seem like a huge amount to some people, and paltry to others, but as with most things in life, income, too, is relative. While the average home price in America was about $175,000 when Debbie and Mark started looking for a home to buy, prices on Long Island were much more expensive comparatively. The modest house they eventually bought cost $321,000. So relative to the cost of living in suburban Long Island, taking home about $6,000 per month is not rich by any means, but doing all right.

(This concept of income *relative to local cost of living* is a crucial perspective throughout this book, and part of the reason why trying to create a single, national definition of "wealthy" [as politicians often do] can be misleading; a household income of $100,000 in New York may mean something very different from having the same income in Montana.)

They had good credit, as Debbie, the money handler and bill payer in the family, always made sure to pay off their credit cards every month. They enjoyed the freedom and comfort that having no revolving debt gave them. They were responsible with their money and always paid on time. They did not make tons of money, but because they always paid their bills, they were considered "Prime" borrowers, with lower risks, not Subprime. And they were good, law-abiding citizens.

They found the perfect house. It was a two-story, three-bedroom, two-bath colonial about 40 miles from New York City, in a working-class suburb of Long Island called Patchogue. Like many towns scattered across one of the nation's large islands, it had the name of the local Native American tribe who had resided in that area centuries ago.

It was far from the city, and Mark would have to commute each way every day to get to his bus driver job, but, for their family, it was worth it. It was surrounded by lush pine trees, just like the forests upstate where Debbie had grown up. The school district was great and the neighbors were even better. This was the one.

Their good credit score allowed them to be approved for an 80/20 loan, which was essentially two loans rolled into one monthly payment. With no money down—paying nothing to get into their new home—they opted for a fixed-rate loan for the 20 percent of the purchase, and for the other 80 percent they went with the most popular, most flexible option at the time, an Adjustable Rate Mortgage.

This loan would be set at a low monthly payment for the first two years; then, on the first day of the twenty-fifth month, would "reset" to the new potentially higher rate based on the interest rates when the resetting would occur.

I asked Debbie if, at the time, she felt pressured or intimidated into signing onto such a loan. She responded honestly, with a typical refrain from 2004.

"No," she said. "The mortgage broker told us that in two years, we would be able to refinance." She could not recall the name of the mortgage firm, although she did say she believed it had since gone out of business.

In 2004 they, and the rest of America, including many within Countrywide, also saw home prices going up steadily, mightily, for years. Yes, of course Debbie would be able to refinance. Again and again. Huge fees would be reaped by the mortgage brokers, the lenders, appraisers, and title companies every time she did. And those fees, sometimes in the thousands of dollars, would be neatly blended, or "rolled up" into the new refinancing, so she would not have to pay those fees out of her family's pocket. They simply might add another $10 or more to the monthly payment on the new loan. Everyone would win, every time.

So they took the plunge, signing the papers, buying the house for $321,000 with nothing down. They knew completely and openly that their monthly payment of $2,100 inclusive of taxes and insurance would change in the twenty-fifth month. But they wouldn't worry about it for now. They also knew that they got into a new home, far from the smells and swelter of the city, and out near better schools, and cleaner air wafting with the scents of freshly cut lawns, for them and their kids.

Things were good. For a while.

In 2006 the loan reset. The first letter said that the new payment would go up to $2,500. No problem; time to refinance, and they did, with yet another broker. The $321,000 house was now reappraised at $375,000—a value growth of almost 17 percent—in only two years. And why not? For like "pennies from heaven," homes on the island and all over America were going up at an astonishing rate no one had ever seen before. Umbrellas would indeed all be turned upside down for the foreseeable future.

With this amazing new equity, they decided to invest in some fun fix-ups. They thought about redoing the inside of the house, but instead they opted to invest in a new underground pool for the backyard. This seemed a fun way to spend the money, and at least be assured of recouping their investment if they ever sold the place.

So they bundled their new Refi with a Home Equity Loan, pulling out $32,000 in cash from the equity on the house for the pool. Now they owed a total of $353,000 (a $321,000 mortgage with a $32,000 Home Equity Loan piled on), for a home that was just reappraised at $375,000.

Their monthly payment was now $2,500, an easily manageable increase. Work some extra overtime hours here, scrimp a little there, no problem. But the new Refi loan was a completely Adjustable Rate Mortgage, with no fixed period, so the payment continued to rise. Every few months Debbie would open a new letter from the lender at her kitchen table and read the bad news. The payment would increase steadily thereafter, as interest rates continued to rise from their 2003 lows, eventually rising to $2,900, then $3,400, then all the way to almost $4,000 per month, almost double what they were originally paying.

Then Mark got hurt. A back injury while on the job caused him severe back and neck pain, making him unable to work. This pushed him onto disability, and into receiving workers' compensation benefits. This provided only about $1,000 per month, causing their total monthly cash flow to plummet to only $2,800 per month, from their previous level of more than $6,000. With three kids to feed, and now a whopping mortgage of more than $4,000, they were now officially in trouble.

A $12,000 disability check to cover Mark's doctor bills was instead put toward food, car payments, and the ever-increasing cost of gas. It had become a struggle to survive. Eventually they dipped into their once pristine and unused credit cards to quickly rack up more than $50,000 in revolving debt at double digit percentages over six different cards. Eventually they fell behind on their minimum payments, and Mark's leased truck was towed away as he watched with tears in his eyes.

Their American dream quickly dissolved into an American nightmare, one which was quickly becoming all too ubiquitous in small towns and large cities across the country. By 2007, America's borrowed wealth had begun to burn, with the speed and fury of the largest of wildfires, eating up decades of dried, overgrown false equity, true debt, and conspicuous consumption.

Debbie knew that they wouldn't be able to make the house payments anymore. To escape the creditors across their mortgages, their cards, and their leased cars, they declared bankruptcy. They would need to somehow tell the children they could not live in their home anymore.

The dutiful parents did what they had to do. They had a somber family meeting in the living room, and told the three boys that the family had to move out. Sam, the oldest and most mature, seemed to take it in stride. Steven, the middle child, wept at the thought of leaving his home, his school, his friends behind. When you're a child, your home is supposed to be your universe, your base, your comfort zone, where all is well, and familiar details and a loving family make it worth coming home to. How shocking it must be to be told, suddenly, that all that was changing and you were powerless to do anything about it. Understandably, their youngest son did not fully grasp the impact of what was happening, of what was going to happen.

As she was telling me this story, I was moved by the stoic strength Debbie showed while describing her children's heartbreak. Her steadfast determination to get by, to survive, reminded me that America will be all right. We are still made of the steel and grit and guts that made us pioneers in so many areas. And this woman represented the best of that strength as she spoke to me.

They tried to fix it; they begged the banks for more time, for help. But with the new appraisal coming in at only $375,000, and, with credit cards and medical bills and the many Refis now adding up to a total debt load in excess of $400,000, they were underwater, and no bank would provide another Refi. Why would they? Their debts outweighed their collateral.

They tried to reach out to one of the many noble organizations whose sole mission is to help people save their homes, much like the national Hope Now effort by the federal government. They approached the Long Island Housing Partnership for assistance but were told that their case was too far gone. With so many complaints being sounded by so many in need, these organizations' criteria to be able to render assistance are very narrow and may not help all those who need it.

In a last desperate attempt at saving their lifestyle, they approached credit counseling services, who told them plainly that declaring bankruptcy was their only option. This modern-day "get out of jail free" card is indeed available for those who cannot pay their creditors and who can deal with the embarrassment and stigma of that label. Debbie was referred to a lawyer, who charged a competitively reasonable $800 for filing the paperwork. Yes, as if adding insult to injury, our system charges families for processing their own bankruptcies. The label will stay on their credit report for the next few years while they pay cash for everything from now on.

And so they left the first owned home they had ever known, moving into a rental, about 15 miles away. They wanted to leave before the foreclosure was completed. Debbie did not want her sons to have to experience the humiliation of seeing an armed sheriff escort them off the property. So to try to minimize the trauma of leaving their school in midyear, Debbie drives their youngest back and forth to school each and every day between work shifts, even though they can barely pay for the higher gas prices.

Their new rental is only $2,000 per month, but the backyard is a dangerous mess of concrete blocks and old wires from previous construction, so the kids can't play there. It is also on a main thoroughfare, so they can't ride their bikes on their street either. The tracks of the Long Island Railroad are visible from their front windows. When the train goes by, as it often does, the house shakes. But for now, it is a roof over their heads.

I asked Debbie who she blamed for all this.

"I blame myself a bit," she responded after a silent pause.

I could feel her disappointment, in the loss, in her and her husband's own errors in judgment, planning, and fiscal responsibility to themselves. But who knew that housing values would not go up forever?

I asked her if she felt that the government should bail her out. She responded, "Sure, it would be nice, but I don't believe the government should bail out everyone. I don't think that's the answer. I just think there needs to be more education."

I asked her if she could imagine this book someday next year being read by the next president of the United States. What would she say to him? What could he do to make sure this does not happen again? She responded thoughtfully, "If a person is looking into buying a house, I think a mandatory counseling session...for the consumer, to educate them, so they know all the pros and cons before they get into it. If I had had something like that...I would have held off."

Did you hear that, Mr. President?

She knew the risks she was taking, but said that if counseled closely in the very real possibility of having a $4,000 mortgage within four years, she would not have signed. But then the swirl of brokers, lenders, and all the peripheral players would not have received their fees.

I mentioned to her that it seemed like she had a very strong family. Debbie paused and then responded:

"Well, in the end, that's all you have."

2

Agency Man

Half the money I spend on advertising is wasted,
and the problem is, I do not know which half.
—Lord Leverhulme, 1851–1925, British founder of Unilever

MAY 1987
Prime rate: 8.25%
Foreclosure rate: 0.90%
CFC stock price: ~$ 1.30

A ND SO THERE I was, with my boss—one of Countrywide's top finance minds—sitting in my office, ready to hear my "Chicken Little" case for why I felt that I had just witnessed the beginning of the end of the most powerful mortgage company in America. My head spun as I considered my words carefully, fully prepared for her to leave my office laughing as I wondered, *How the hell did I get HERE?*

The path that eventually brought me to this scene, at what was to be the Big Bang of the mortgage mess, was 15 years long and circuitous, and if you had stopped me on the street in college and told me that one day I would be at the center of one of the greatest economic stories of the last hundred years, I would've looked at you funny and kept walking. Then I probably would have turned back and asked, "What's a mortgage?"

After I received my honorable discharge from the U.S. Air Force Reserve in June 1986, I set to work on figuring out what I really wanted to do.

I immediately gravitated to Boston University's College of Communication, and narrowed my search for a major. Although I had dabbled in journalism, broadcast, and film, advertising is what really intrigued me. Headlines. Art direction. Glitz. Glamour. At once both understanding the mood of hip culture and partly creating it, advertising had it all, including convincing people to buy this product or service, and making it sexy, intriguing, delicious, or otherwise tempting. Advertising would encapsulate for me all of the elements of the other careers I did enjoy: the cadenced approach of journalistic writing (ad copy frequently being a derivative yet colloquial, pithy version of the same structure); and the minimovie, ministory creative approach of production of broadcast television commercials.

And ad execs dressed up. Pinstriped suits, white shirts, cool ties, shiny shoes. I believe that our career choices are influenced by the other cultural and social aspects of the field. It may sound silly and be an unfair stereotyping, but maybe I did not want to be an engineer because I didn't want to spend my life keeping a satellite assembly room microscopically clean while wearing white overalls, goggles, a shirt-pocket combination mechanical pencil and brand-new pocket-sized Hewlett-Packard Aerospace calculator.

I loved both the creative advertising and the analytical marketing courses. The entire curriculum seemed the perfect mix of creativity, just enough math so as not to be engineering; a great social life, as many cute girls went into advertising; and, most importantly, the concept of controlling the behavior of millions of people, however subtly, was an aphrodisiac.

Like many vocations, securing an apprenticeship or internship was critical in learning the trade. As summer approached, all of the communications students who were focused on advertising were scrambling for slots in the major agencies in Boston, New York, Los Angeles, and even Europe. My grades were now all A's and high B's, to the delight of my parents, but I had few connections in the advertising world, so I was starting from scratch, or so I thought. Then two serendipitous connections developed that would change the course of my life forever.

American Express at that time was nearing the end of their 20-year masterwork campaign "Don't Leave Home Without It," and preparing to embark on their blockbuster sequel campaign "Membership Has Its Privileges." To generate interest on campus for the student Green Card, Amex hosted a national student contest to find the best student-produced American Express commercial within the last run of the "Don't Leave Home Without It" campaign, using the famous line *Do You Know Me?*

I wrote and filmed my own spot, and it won the American Express contest at Boston University. In retrospect the spot was god-awful, wrought with clichés and sexist stereotypes, but hey, I was 20 years old.

From there it went on to compete with the other film schools' entries from across the country. It did not win, but it was a runner-up, enough to provide me an interesting connection to Amex's agency who judged the entries: Ogilvy & Mather, a worldwide advertising, public relations, and communications powerhouse in New York.

The second lucky connection came through one of the top textile and houseware firms in New York, where my dad was creative director. He was in charge of all the designs for their products, from soap dispensers, to shower curtains, to the colors and patterns of the assorted woven dinner table mats that take up an entire aisle at Bed Bath & Beyond. My dad's boss, the chairman of the firm, also happened to be golfing buddies with the Chairman and CEO of the same Ogilvy & Mather. *Bingo.* With no earthly connection of my own to speak of as I attempted to begin a career, this connection and this timing were too powerful not to seize upon.

I begged my dad for this "six degrees" favor. Using my immature 20-year-old logic, I figured that all my dad's boss had to do was carry a bulky VCR and a small television onto the golf course, find an outlet, plug it in, play the Ogilvy CEO my brilliantly witty, funny, and smart student Amex commercial, and immediately I would be overnighted a five-year contract to be the newest senior officer of their worldwide agency. I could already taste the cigar as I placed my feet onto my glass desk overlooking Central Park from my corner office on the forty-eighth floor of their headquarters.

In May 1987 I got a call from the office of the president of one of Ogilvy's divisions, Ogilvy Direct, which focused on Direct Mail and Direct Response Television for Ogilvy's clients. Shelly Lazarus was one of their top executives (eventually becoming the Chairman and CEO of *all* of Ogilvy Worldwide, a position she still holds as of this writing). I was nervous as I had Shelly's assistant on the phone, asking me if I would be available that Thursday at 10:00 A.M. *Would I? Um, yes, I would cancel my own wedding for this meeting*, I thought.

"Yes, I would love to come over then," I quipped. *Dumb*, I thought. *Too enthusiastic, bad grammar, dumb. Dammit, I hope they don't cancel the meeting because I sounded so stupid on the phone.*

This was it. The chance of a lifetime. I vacillated between terror and glee as I borrowed $150 from my mom and dragged her to the men's fine clothing store at the mall. Everything had to be perfect. New shoes; crisp white shirt; a bright yellow spring power tie I would borrow from my dad's impressive wardrobe. The new suit would be tailored perfectly, picked up on Wednesday. I typed and retyped (no computers yet in my house) my résumé what seemed like a hundred times, making sure the final five copies (always have extras) were perfect, no typos, no smears. I carefully slipped them into a manila envelope as if they were delicate, priceless Fabergé eggs. And they were. It was my whole life on one piece of paper.

Thursday. D-Day. I awoke at 4:30 A.M. that humid morning, and was dressed perfectly and out of the house by 5:30 A.M. My train arrived at Pennsylvania Station just after 8:00 A.M., and I proceeded to walk the mile or so to the offices of Ogilvy & Mather Direct at 350 Park Avenue South, arriving just after 8:30 A.M. The humidity was already unbearable as I struggled not to perspire on my nice new crisp white shirt. I found a small coffee shop near the office, and ducked in for the coldest drink I could find.

There, at a corner table, I read agency founder David Ogilvy's bible *Ogilvy on Advertising* for the hundredth time, making notes on my pad so I could quote his gospel at my meeting. Years later I would be never-endingly dismayed at how many of the candidates I interviewed for jobs, whether at agencies or even top candidates for Countrywide, knew nothing about the firms for which they interviewed. *Always be fluent in all aspects of the company before the interview; always do your homework. Knowledge cannot be faked. Ever.*

My stomach churned slightly as I made my way up the elevator at precisely 9:45 A.M. I was alone in the elevator. I straightened my tie. I cleared my throat. I saw myself in the reflective metal doors and moved one tiny hair that was out of place. I felt the elevator slow to its destination as I thought, *This could be a pivotal day in my life.*

The doors opened onto the upper floor, and the stuffy air of the elevator was replaced by the welcome blast of cold, air-conditioned nirvana. I made my way to the reception desk, which looked like something out of a movie *about* an ad agency. My heels tapped against the crisp white marble of the floor as I saw the hustle and bustle of agency life before me. It was as if someone had yelled "ACTION!" just before the elevator doors opened.

Creative people in jeans (in jeans?!) carrying storyboards; beautiful women walking briskly with collegiate glasses on their small noses, steno books in their long fingers, and pencils behind their petite ears; executives in three-piece pinstriped suits running to important meetings; mailroom boys pushing carts full of critical packages from Paris.

The white marble floor was delightfully juxtaposed with a sea of bright, deep red everywhere. The Ogilvy color, blood red, adorned what looked like new carpets, new wall paint, and accents everywhere. On the walls were marquee samples of their iconic work: ads for Maxwell House, Pepperidge Farm, Rolls-Royce, AT&T, of course, American Express, and many others. *Wow*.

"Hi, I'm Adam Michaelson... I'm here to see Ms. Lazarus at 10 A.M.?" I could barely get the words out. The stunning, dark-haired receptionist told me to take a seat. I was surprised when she asked me if there was anything she could get for me. I had never had anyone in an office ask me that before, so I wasn't sure if it was a trick question or part of the interview "test." I paused awkwardly as she clearly saw that I was confused, and continued, "Coffee? Water?" I politely declined. I knew that if I drank anything, I was so nervous that I would be sure to be wearing it on my tie within five seconds.

At exactly 10:00 A.M. on the dot, another older but very attractive woman came to greet me. "Shelly will see you now. Please follow me." She led me into a huge office with windows that displayed what seemed like the whole city. Behind the desk was Shelly Lazarus, one of the giants of the advertising business. She immediately rose and greeted me with a warmth that was unexpected.

"Come on in, Adam. Can we get you anything?"

"No, thank you, Ms. Lazarus. I am just glad to be here."

"Call me Shelly, please." She smiled. She could tell I was nervous.

She offered me a seat in front of her desk, a neat yet overwhelmed area of ideas, proposals, and paperwork of an overworked leader, and dozens of mementos of a long and distinguished career. I awkwardly handed a copy of my résumé to her. The seconds she took reviewing it felt like hours of silence.

When she finally lifted her head, she put the résumé aside and began speaking.

"Do you know much about our firm?" she asked.

Bingo. "Why, yes," I said, dorkily holding up my copy of the Ogilvy book. I began spouting random facts about the agency, about David, about the philosophy, as she nodded politely. Then I began telling her about my student commercial, which I could tell she found amusing, perhaps for its silliness, or for the pure, as-yet-unjaded passion I demonstrated as only a young person can.

I had never before met a person so successful, so powerful in their field, let alone a woman. Ten years before the magazine cover stories about women the likes of Meg Whitman of eBay or Carly Fiorina at Hewlett-Packard, and long before the Oprahs and Marthas of the world would rise, Shelly Lazarus was a maverick leader in her field, a respected four-star general in command of a huge army of advertising soldiers.

Shelly began telling me about the intern programs they had at Ogilvy, and the long and important traditions and teachings at the venerable shop. David Ogilvy himself believed strongly that agencies were like hospitals. Their job was not only to treat patients (clients), but, also and more importantly, to make great new doctors in the form of bright, energetic account executives who would become the brand builders of tomorrow.

As she spoke, my mind wandered a bit, and I used my peripheral vision to take in the eclectic and interesting items around her office. So this is how the bigwigs live, huh? Huge sofa, lots of books, awards and plaques on the wall. *Cool.* On her desk I saw many pieces of advertising, some half finished. Some were color marker drawings, some were lines of typed copy, and one was what looked like a print mechanical of a brochure. Upon closer staring I could see it was a brochure—a "Take One," as they called it—for the American Express Green Card. (Years before the Internet existed, a ubiquitous presence on millions of restaurant and store countertops, the "Get the American Express Card" application brochures were still powerful sources of new card growth.) I could see the final art on the matte board on her desk, although it was upside down from my point of view, and about three feet away from me.

In the minute or two that she continued to speak about the history and ethos of the Ogilvy "family," I was fascinated by the Amex brochure. This was real advertising, not some school project. I strained to read the upside-down copy as she spoke, finally finding a use for my eyesight that the Air Force at one time had considered worthy of pilot training.

"With the American Express Card, there're no preset spending limits..."

"...you get 24-hour award-winning customer service..."

"...and with millions of dining and retail establishments worldwife..."

World*wife*?

I looked at it again.

Yup. It said "worldwife."

I snapped out of my proofreading exercise as I heard her say "...but unfortunately all of our internship slots are filled for this summer, but next year we could continue our chat about it...."

What did she just say? I was crushed. I was too late. Clearly, her allowing me to visit was simply a courtesy call, as part of the standard manners within the professional network of New York's advertising and CEO community. For whatever reason, the summer internship slots for 1987 were already filled by other students who were nephews of friends of pals of golf buddies or employees. My head quickly moved to trying to secure one of those precious slots for next year, and keeping a smile on my face, while inwardly I was devastated.

"I would love to keep in touch with you and try for next year," I said, feigning a happy energy.

"Yes, please keep in touch over the next few months," she said, as she began to get up and walk me to her doorway. The whole meeting had lasted maybe 10 minutes, and I was grateful that she had given me all the time she did.

I turned to shake her hand as the hallway approached, saying, "Thank you, Shelly, for this meeting, I really enjoyed it."

"Me, too," she said, gripping my hand in a firm but gentle manner. She let go and began to turn back into her office, and I began walking out. Courtesy meeting, pity interview—whatever it was—I was angry. Knowing there was no intern position open, they had dragged my ass all the way from the suburban boonies to spend money I didn't have to come into a sweltering city to be shown the career I could not yet have. I could feel my best-behavior veneer of professional maturity crumbling as my immature temper began to emerge. *Keep it in check, Adam. Don't embarrass Dad. What the hell, I didn't get the job anyway. SAY something.*

Halfway down the hall, I turned around and walked back to her doorway, where I saw she had sat back in her chair behind her enormous desk, already scanning some other important new campaign idea. I knocked at the open door firmly and loudly, then brashly walked right into her office again. Freaked out myself at what I was doing, I quickly pointed a slightly quivering finger at her cluttered desk.

"By the way," I said with a panicked stutter as she looked up, surprised. I paused, then went for it.

"There [gulp]…there is a *typo* on that Amex brochure. Third panel, fourth line down. 'Worldwife' should read 'worldwide.'" The words hung in the air for several agonizing seconds.

I was shaking inside. I was 20 years old, speaking to the CEO of one of the largest agencies in the world. I saw her slowly look down at the brochure art.

Convinced I had just ruined my whole life, I simply added, "Have a great day," then silently turned and again made my way down the hallway to get the hell out of there as fast as I could before security guys could grab me.

Within three seconds, from her office doorway where she was now standing, I heard her shout, "Adam! Wait..."

I turned back and approached her, with a polite "Yes, Ma'am?"

"You saw that typo upside down from across the room?"

I nodded.

She paused, obviously thinking to herself.

"Impressive..." she said. Then, a small smile emerged and she said, "Be here, Monday, 9:00 A.M. We'll find something for you to do."

I smiled back at her as she disappeared from view, back into her office. I walked toward the reception area, projecting a beaming smile to the receptionist as I entered the empty elevator. As the doors closed, I burst into a frenzied, deep laughter, the kind that almost caused me to cry. Good thing I was alone.

I did it. I would become an ad agency man.

DURING THAT HOT summer of 1987, and for the next 15 years, I would discover that agency life was not at all like *Bewitched*. In fact, never *once* did I have to run back and forth from my living room to my kitchen entertaining two clients at once (a scenario that represented about 99 percent of all *Bewitched* episode plots, and, come to think of it, *Three's Company, I Dream of Jeannie,* and many other sitcoms as well).

However, long before I had ever heard of Countrywide, and years before it would become an ever-present name on the front page of most newspapers in the United States as the mortgage crisis grew, I would use this career in advertising to amass all of the business, marketing, sales, and organizational skills and experience necessary to qualify me to eventually become their Senior Vice President of Marketing, and help drive one of the most powerful sales machines this country has ever seen.

Dedicating my career to encouraging people to buy what they didn't truly need—or worse, couldn't afford—had inherent moral dilemmas that were profound and integral parts of my daily work life. But it is what I wanted to do, and within weeks of that seminal moment in the doorway of Shelly Lazarus's office, I was neck deep in it.

But when I saw the first Amex *Membership* television commercials that I assisted with, on television at my parents' house one night, I felt, simply, *cool*. I was having the time of my life. At this point I just *knew* that making ads was *way* more exciting than flying airplanes would have ever been.

I always tried to work on as many varied and different accounts as I could. From healthcare to cars to technology, from kids to travel to entertainment, and from financial services to consumer goods and packaged services, I did them all. I had seen people, like actors, be pigeonholed into only certain ad categories, and it was not always where they wanted to end up. The car guy. The toy lady. The technology creative. There was danger in spending too much time in one category, and one day waking up finding they would never qualify to do any other.

Some of this ping-ponging was not intentional, however. Agency life can be a harsh, nomadic, transient existence, and not for the timid. If the concept of "job security" has waned in corporate America over the past few years, then, lemme tell ya, it left the agency business at its inception. Over the course of 15 years I worked at several different agencies, including some giants such as Ogilvy, the global Japanese firm Dentsu, and Grey. I also worked at some smaller agencies, such as Hill, Holliday (headquartered in Boston), the remnants of Della Femina (an icon of creative talent), and many others.

Account service, or Client Service, as it is called, is what I did. Typically seen as the "suits" who wine and dine the clients, schmooze on the golf course, and are the lackey errand boys of the creative group, I and all account people were, in all fairness, more than that. Like a great conductor of a vast orchestra, the best account people would align, choreograph, and otherwise help ensure the perfect, compelling execution of whatever the agency was selling. And we were *always* hunting for new business.

But, of course, there were other critical agency roles as well.

The stereotypical ad man is typically the creative person in a wacky, creative department. And, truthfully, if an ad agency was a factory, the creative is the product around which all other roles revolve. I always got along with those talented art directors and writers; I felt that I understood their unique temperments, as my dad had been a "creative" for years. Analysts can talk for hours with their charts and graphs, but at the end of the day it's all about throwing a bitchin' cool ad on the table.

Media was another key part of any agency service. Typically seen as the department that helps pay the bills, because of the commissions it generates, the Media Department is in charge of the assessment and allocation of the critical media dollars across thousands of potential outlets. With so many venues to choose from, including TV, magazines, newspapers, outdoor billboards, radio, and the web, each with its own tiny slices of channels, sites, times, sizes, etc., Media is a daunting responsibility and underappreciated department. And the financial responsibility can be substantial, where some of the top companies in the United States, such as General Motors, Pepsi, and other giants, can spend upward of $1 billion a year. Some agencies do nothing but media planning and buying for clients.

Depending on the size of a full-service agency, there can be other departments that comprise the machinery, such as competitive, customer, or trend strategizing and research (also known as Account Planning); there is typically an in-house art studio and, at the bigger shops, in-house commercial filming and production units; sales and data analysis teams; and the usual support and administrative resources.

Half of my advertising career was spent doing pure Branding, and the other half doing pure Direct Marketing. Most people not familiar with advertising believe that branding people did the fun stuff—huge, emotional commercials, giant budgets, big stars, prestige placements such as the Super Bowl. Direct-Marketing people supposedly did junk mail, hacky, cheesy, loud, and obnoxious television commercials at 3:00 A.M. telling people to CALL NOW for some widget or combination salad dressing and foot ointment in new lemon scent. Both stereotypes are unfair generalizations.

Branding, and being a brand marketer, is very, very difficult. Like in any emotionally driven, relationship-oriented philosophy, many great thinkers have tried to unravel its mysteries and truly understand what gives us goose bumps at Disneyland, what thrills us when we step into a Mercedes, or what makes us cry when we see that light blue Tiffany box. Like gravity, branding cannot be measured directly, but rather we can only measure the effects of it on other things; attitudes, perceptions, etc. We can see how customers may alter how they feel about the brand; we may see sales rise when an animated polar bear drinks a Coke—or we may not. The toughest thing that any Brand marketer will ever need to do is justify his own value. Yes, the cute polar bears may have helped sell Coke, but frankly, price and distribution mainly sell Coke. And I once saw a study that showed that at least 50 percent of consumers thought that the Energizer Bunny was selling Duracell.

Direct marketers also get a bum rap, having been unfairly labeled the "junk mailers" who do that "schlocky work." Many brand people look down on such work, in part because they don't understand it, because it's complicated, and because it's been steadily eating away at more and more of the "branding" budgets, but mainly because the creative is results-driven, not emotionally driven, at least on the surface. Unlike Brand people, who may need to *infer* that their new $2 million commercial directly created those rising sales, Direct Mail or Online marketers know exactly how much money a client makes back for every $1 spent. Through unique web banners, landing pages, search keywords, or unique 800 numbers on single commercials, the Direct marketer is able to tell the client that directly from their efforts they sold 1,264,342 widgets at $10 each. And they do it through an established method of testing, calibrating, retesting, and investing in only that creative/offer/message/ timing that the marketplace shows is the most profitable.

But the success or failure of every single TV commercial, mailing, offer, call script—everything—in the end, can be distilled into three simple words: does it *engage, inform,* and *motivate* sales?

No message will get through, no matter how relevant it is to the consumer, unless the creative message immediately, compellingly, and powerfully *engages* the person. This is the essence of most great Brand work. Whether it's the use of striking white screens (Apple commercials) or the unheralded but incredibly successful, blue, over-sized "20% off" Bed Bath & Beyond coupon postcard mailing, it is critical to engage the customer with something interesting. If only this succeeds, you are still adding to a brand's *awareness*. Well done.

Second, it is critical to *inform*. Nobody will gain anything from your dazzling computer effects if no one knows—quickly—what the hell you are selling. Inform them of what is for sale, and how it solves their problems or enriches their lives or saves them money, or you can kiss that graphics budget good-bye the next time around, I assure you. This migrates the consumer from the initial stages of *awareness* to levels of *knowledge* and potential *consideration* of your product.

Finally—and this is where some brand campaigns stop short of success—it is critical to close the sale with a "call to action," to *motivate*: encourage the prospect to act—to do something—today, right now, immediately. Buy that movie ticket, take that test drive, call now for that salad mixer, go online and apply for a Debt Consolidation No-Fee Home Equity Loan, *now*. This continues to take the consumer along the cycle from where they were—awareness, knowledge, and consideration—to now action, trial, purchase, and eventually, hopefully, repurchase.

Doing both well—that is, creating an emotionally compelling branding experience as well as a response-driven direct marketing campaign—is exceedingly difficult. Direct marketing alone without good branding wastes the opportunity to build an emotional relationship with the audience; pure Brand marketing without any call to action could be accused of being a glitzy waste of money. The web is where these originally competing disciplines have finally come together, a holy grail mix of emotional engagement, information, and motivated action.

It is a rare thing to see a marketing effort that balances all of these disciplines in one message with stunning power and clear, motivating clarity or purpose. I would argue that great examples of "branded direct" marketers include Dell, and many financial services firms—American Express, Bank of America, Schwab, and yes, at its height, Countrywide, but not many others.

My advertising career, made up of Branding experiences as well as Direct Marketing training, prepared me to be part of the enormous marketing engine of Countrywide. There we orchestrated a hybrid of both approaches, driven by the proliferation of technology and data, the growth of the web in our daily lives, and the ever-smaller pockets of customers with particular preferences.

But there was one piece missing.

A few years into my career I discovered another skill set that I enjoyed and was eager to develop: *new business*. Some call it sales, or business development, but it's the lifeblood of any firm, including advertising, to generate new sources of revenue, because, as I learned early on, *all new accounts begin to be lost on the day you win them* (so you should always be seeking new ones).

I soon discovered that while doing cute ads was fun, the real money and power came to those rainmakers who could seek out and nurture new client relationships, build trust, get the meetings, present great ideas, and close the deals.

Creatives loved doing the new work. Media folks loved the new commissions for the agency. A new piece of exciting business could completely reenergize a team and increase retention and recruiting successes. And whoever helped win it was a hero for a day (until the next day, when the boss would ask, "Okay, what other leads have ya got?").

And damn, was it fun. Just like in the movies, I have spent countless nights watching the sun rise from ad agency conference rooms, covered in doodled tissues of creative ideas and storyboards, fixing the broken color printer at 5:00 A.M., drinking cold coffee and eating hardened bagels from yesterday, hoping to find one hour for a shower and new clothes and be back here for the big client presentation at 9:00 A.M. that same day for the giant account. Every pitch meeting was advertising war, and there was glory in the trenches. Nothing brought out the camaraderie and best work of the greatest people more than a deadline for a life-changing piece of business that we had a slim chance of winning.

I began to gravitate toward agency roles that focused more on sales and less and less on marketing. I had experienced the bliss of the "win" and was hooked. This migration would culminate in what would eventually turn out to be my last agency job, as Director of New Business and Client Service at the Direct Marketing Division of Grey Advertising, one of the last giant firms in the ad world.

I have heard countless hallway chats in sales-driven companies where the typical refrain is "Marketing guys don't know sales," and in marketing-driven companies where the marketing geniuses are smugly saying, "Those sales guys wouldn't know a marketing strategy if it hit them in the face." Truth is, they are one and the same, two sides of the same coin, and cannot function without the other. Sales is part of life. And even in a marketing department in a giant Fortune 500, every single conversation, meeting, e-mail, and bathroom chat is always a part of the sale of your ideas, agenda, and goals.

Like marketing, sales has fundamental components to the process, each of which requires skill, experience, and tenacity. Sales requires the ability to hunt, to seek out prey, to know when and how to pounce to close the deal. With cunning, drive, and fearlessness, it demands the best of patience, diplomacy, resilience, and, when appropriate, subtle aggression.

But a life in sales had its downside as well. I traveled constantly, flying all over the country at least 20 days a month, rarely seeing my kids. Bad food, bad service, bad beds, jet lag, ugh. I will always have enormous respect for that silent army of sales road warriors who hump it out every day to feed their families, servicing clients who don't care, and prospects who care even less.

A year into my job at Grey, I decided I did not want to be an agency new business sales guy forever. Maybe I should become a client, I thought, and dedicate my life to one brand I could be passionate about. It would have to be something profound, something important, something meaningful, and something I could be proud of. But what?

Then 9/11 happened. For a time the economy stopped. Clients pulled back on spending. Those with existing agency relationships were entrenching deeper into them. All my sales methods, all the leads, seemed to dry up for a time. My frustration grew, as did my boss's. Armageddon be damned, he wanted new revenue, no matter what, and I wasn't delivering it anymore. Another key lesson I learned in sales, and that I would be ever mindful of at Countrywide later, is that *any salesperson is only as good as his or her most recent results*.

But my heart wasn't in it anymore; I was burned out. By the fall of 2002, I attended what would turn out to be my last client pitch of the hundreds I had done in my agency career. After two hours of dazzling them with our knowledge of their business, their competition, and our creative, the clients sat there, all in a row, agape at the creative boards we laid out on the table. "Well, whaddya think?" I asked.

Seconds of silence turned into minutes as I sat there, waiting for them to at least thank us for all our work. I knew I wanted to be sitting on the other side of that table, being that one client who was smart, driven, charismatic, and exerting leadership. I wanted to lead, to make the decisions, not to present a creative idea and pray that the client "got it." I had outgrown the agency business.

Finally my thoughts snapped back to the room, where I saw everyone staring at me incredulously. Apparently I had been tapping my pencil so loudly on the table that it stopped the meeting. We didn't win it.

Within weeks, I was out at Grey, out of work, and, although I did not know it at the time, out of my agency career.

3

Punching the
Corporate Ticket

We at Chrysler borrow money the old-fashioned way.
We pay it back.
—Lee Iacocca, July 1983

FEBRUARY 2003

Prime rate: 4.25%

Foreclosure rate: 1.20%

CFC stock price: ~$13.00

LOOKING FOR A job is, as anyone who has been there can tell you, the hardest job in the world. It is the ultimate in tense, emotionally draining selling, with extreme highs and lows, and you yourself are the product. Yet, that November of 2002, I got to work seeking work.

I kept getting calls for senior agency positions I didn't want. November and December are also the worst months to generate job search momentum, as holidays approach and decision makers go on vacation, typically stopping the hiring process. As 2002 moved into January 2003, I got a suggestion from an old agency buddy: "Give Bob Griffin a call; I think Countrywide might be looking for someone."

I knew it was a mortgage company, but I didn't know much else about Countrywide except that their headquarters was all the way out in Calabasas, a desertlike enclave of hilly terrain and wealthy gated communities of golf courses, horse ranches, and corporate parks, so a job at Countrywide would mean a daily commute of at least an hour each way. I can remember mentioning this complaint to my dad, who was quick to snap me out of my cushy complacency. "Stop your whining," he said. "The whole country gets their asses up every morning and commutes. I've been doing it for 30 years so you and your brothers were able to have a nice backyard to play in." He was right. I had a family to feed, I needed a job, and this was the corporate track I sought.

Also, the options for corporate marketing gigs in Los Angeles were limited, and each had its own unique downside. Working at the movie studios or other abundant entertainment firms was glitzy and glamorous, but because the studios knew this, they generally paid lower salaries. The other major players in town were some car companies (Toyota, Nissan, Hyundai, Suzuki, etc.), as well as Nestlé and Mattel. I loved working on the Infiniti team in the early 1990s, but car companies were notoriously difficult to break into because the executives there tended to stay in their positions forever. Nestlé was primarily a packaged foods firm, of which I had limited experience, and I couldn't see myself dedicating my life to marketing Libby's canned pumpkin. And pushing children to "just gotta have" that latest Mattel product was a morally ambiguous area of marketing that wasn't my cup of tea.

So I called Bob at Countrywide.

There are few things more wonderful in this life than reconnecting with a supportive old friend or colleague just when the entire world seems against you. And this was the experience I enjoyed when Bob and I reconnected on the phone. Still nurturing, paternal, and approachable even after a decade had passed since I had worked with him in the agency world, Bob Griffin was a class act, a warm person in what could many times be an icy business world, and was responsible for the Countrywide brand.

Deciding not to impose at all on him at this point regarding any opportunities at Countrywide, I suggested we get together for a casual lunch just to catch up. A date was set for a few weeks later.

It was drizzly, cold and unusually raw in Southern California on that February day when I would meet Bob for lunch in "Countrywide country"—Calabasas, California. I held no expectations of the meeting. My goal was simply to reconnect with an old friend and perhaps secure some new leads via Bob's network to other firms. Although Countrywide was huge—even before the soon-to-explode Refi boom that was to emerge that summer—working for what I perceived to be a stodgy mortgage company was not my idea of a successful new career path at that point. I still had my hopes on achieving a corporate gig in a sexier enterprise. Still, perhaps out of habit, I brought some of my work samples and my laptop to show my web work just in case. Maybe I could impress him enough with my recent marketing experience so he would recommend me to someone in his network at a much cooler company.

I arrived at the restaurant early for our 12:30 P.M. lunch. It was at the Marmalade Café in Calabasas, just down the street from Countrywide's sprawling headquarters. A frequent haunt for many executives, it was also, I would find out later, sometimes referred to as the "Countrywide lunchroom."

As he arrived at the restaurant, I could see that his hair was still a fiery red as he eagerly reached out his hand to shake mine, as he exclaimed with a big smile, "Aaaaaadam! How are ya man?!" Immediately I was put at ease by his paternal presence and at that moment I was glad I made the trip. What I could not have known at the time is that this lunch would lead to a critical turning point in my career.

It would also literally be the longest lunch of my life. Beginning at about one o'clock, we would continue talking well past five o'clock. The first hour or so was the standard catching up: where he had been, how he wound up at Countrywide, his family, his kids, where my life had taken me as well. At the very least this meeting would be a fun and warm reconnection. We laughed about those long, lost agency clients, about the all-nighter presentation preps we endured, about the pros and cons of agency life, as it was.

But then he started talking more about Countrywide. All I had to ask was, "Do you like it?"—and off he went. His eyes grew wide when he talked about how wonderful it was to be part of a mission that was a part of the American tapestry. The feelings that they brought to people when they were handed the key to their very first home, and the transcendent joy it created. He leaned in to the table as he talked about Angelo Mozilo, their CEO; how amazing he was as a founder, a leader, a motivator of others to help this dream. I sipped my second iced tea, finding myself being drawn into his enthusiasm, like I was watching the most exciting adventure movie I had seen in years, eager to find out what happens to the hero.

He threw his arms wide when he bragged about the huge array of products and services Countrywide offered—not just home loans, but also banking and insurance, to customers, to partners, to builders. He said it was a marketer's dream company because one would never, ever get bored with so many challenges and so many diverse projects, channels, and media to choose from. From the web to TV to mail, the Countrywide story was, in the next five years, he said, going to be *everywhere*. I commented to Bob that I was impressed with his passion for this company, and I understood it. I, too, did not want to do marketing for some other firm that sold relatively insignificant products or services. For me, no silly gadgets, doohickeys, or the like; no paper cups or breath mints. I wanted something really meaningful in people's lives, something I would be eager to dedicate a part of my life to, and frankly, something for which I would be willing to commute more than an hour each way every day.

Knowing me, and hearing my words, he looked me straight in the eye with an earnestness I had not witnessed in all my years of advertising meetings with hundreds of clients and said, "I have never believed more in what I'm doing, Adam. What could be more wonderful than helping someone get a home, really?"

Just then he pulled out his keys, holding up his own house key.

"This...*this* is what Countrywide does," he said.

At that moment, I deeply understood the magic of Countrywide.

"THIS...*THIS* IS for *you*," said my father, beaming with pride as he handed my mom the key to their very first home.

I was only three years old in the summer of 1969. Yet seeing her hug him in their new modest Long Island home for what seemed like forever would become one of my earliest, warmest memories.

Both from semifractured Jewish homes, they had found each other on the stickball streets and steamy summertime stoops of Jerome Avenue in the Bronx, in the then-unprecedented boom of postwar 1950s America. Longtime friends and kindergarten classmates from "the neighborhood," they would eventually blossom into a couple. They married in 1964, at what was then the normal marrying age (they both were only 20 years old). From there, they set out on their lifelong adventure together, with barely two sticks to rub together between them. He was a struggling yet talented artist and graphic designer, she a dental hygienist, still finishing her associate's degree at the local college. They nestled into their small one-bedroom, sixth-floor walk-up apartment in Far Rockaway, Queens, with their rare brown and white Dalmatian, Gigot, and began their quest for the American Dream, along with millions of other young couples of the Kennedy generation.

When my mother was growing up, her family was not rich. In fact, they were barely not poor. When they were living in their sparse two-bedroom apartment in the Bronx, my grandfather's steady job as a salesman at a men's fine clothing store would afford them the ability to scrape enough money together to support his family. My mother's father, stepmother, and eventually her half sister all shared that two-bedroom apartment until my mother moved out to start her new life with my dad. Her family never bought their own home.

My father grew up in markedly different yet similarly fractured circumstances. He shared a two-bedroom walk-up apartment with his mother and older brother, while his father spent most of my dad's childhood abroad in Japan, developing his clothing businesses. My grandmother worked, supporting her two sons, and struggled to keep the family together as best she could. She, too, would not buy her own home until much later in her life, when my grandfather would finally return to the United States for good, and they retired to Temecula, California, together in the 1970s.

But in July 1969, as Neil Armstrong was taking "one small step for (a) man," (legend has it that a short burst of static during the transmission of his moon-based signal obscured the word "a" from his now-famous recorded quote), my parents were taking their own giant leap into the American Dream of homeownership.

Earlier, in March 1969, while sitting at the kitchen table in their apartment, my father was skimming the *New York Daily News*, alternately puffing on his first cigarette of the day and sipping his morning coffee just how he always liked it: black as motor oil. He came across an interesting ad depicting the charming image of a perfectly welcoming, peaceful, safe new home in the suburbs, built by the famous Levitt and Sons Homebuilders. (I can imagine the other-worldly refrain from the "Hallelujah" chorus ringing in my dad's ears when he saw this ad for the Promised Land of suburbia.) That day, my parents loaded me and my one-year-old brother into my dad's little Renault and took a 60-mile trek out of the city to the Levitt model homes, out on the northern end of Long Island that would change our lives forever. (Interestingly, during that same March, only a few miles away, another young man in New York City named Angelo Mozilo was also pursuing a dream, starting a new mortgage company called Countrywide.)

I can still remember that day, touring construction homesites with fun piles of dirt atop concrete slabs, and grassy sod squares forming manicured lawns where forests once stood. American Dreams were ready to be made, new lives to be started, on each site. This was the New World to a generation of city kids starting new families, and that day my parents decided to do something their parents had not achieved. They were going to buy their own home.

They opted for a three-bedroom, two-story colonial model, a popular one. With a large front lawn and even larger backyard, the property covered approximately half a square acre. Faux shutters adorned the window frames; a small front porch would be perfect for sitting outside on mild summer evenings. The house was white, the shutters black, and the roof was covered in dark brown tar shingles, with the brick of the fireplace chimney crawling up one sidewall, and a giant metal TV antenna on the roof. At more than 30 feet high, it was, to this child, a huge, impenetrable castle of regal proportions.

They secured a 35-year Fixed-Rate Mortgage at a set rate of 7.25% for a sale price of only $65,000. For context, loan rates would soar to 15 to 18% during the inflation of the late 1970s (sparking the proliferation of a new line of loan products—"Adjustable-Rate Mortgages"—to provide for continued affordability), then fall back to the 5% range in 2003. Also, that same $65,000 home would, adjusted for inflation, be the equivalent of buying a three-bedroom colonial for almost $400,000 today.

My parents were arguably the last "30-year fixed" loan generation; back then, *everyone* used to get a fixed-rate, long-term loan, typically a 30- or 35-year mortgage. Home equity loans, or "second mortgages" (as they were called back then), were usually reserved only for the neighborhood's "troubled" homes, which were the target of gossip by ladies who lunched during Tupperware parties. Maybe there was a bad divorce. Maybe he was a drinker, or had endangered his family by racking up irresponsible debts. A second mortgage was like a signal flare for a troubled home in the idyllic utopia of suburbia.

One thing hasn't changed across generations, however. It has always taken, and always will take, guts for young couples to buy their first home. It took real courage for my parents to make this colossal financial commitment. He had just started his own design business; they had two babies, and no money. Also important to note, unlike many of today's starting families, they had no preexisting debt.

My parents scraped together the starter money, saving up a few hundred dollars that spring. They paid the $500 down payment, with some minimum closing costs. Levitt had just started offering an option of adding a basement to the home, at an additional cost. My parents could not afford that. Not many tornadoes on Long Island, so no biggie, I guess. They wanted a double garage, but could not afford that upgrade either. They only "luxury" they added, for the whopping add-on of $8 per month, was a wood-burning fireplace in the living room. Sounds odd, but to lifelong tenants of New York City apartments, to have the sweet scent of wafting embers float through the rooms of your very own home was heaven. They "made it"—they had achieved the American Dream.

And then on that steamy day in July 1969 when we finally moved in, I saw my dad give my mom the key to their very first home. I had never seen them so happy. Using all their savings to buy our new home, they had $58 left in their bank account.

While they were still hugging, I ran upstairs and leaped into my new bed, then rolled on the new carpet, laughing uncontrollably at the profound fun of it all. In that moment, I was inside pure magic.

That night, in our new living room, we watched a man walk on the moon.

It was quiet. It was safe. It was far from the smells and noises of the city. Crickets chirped as fireflies danced in the air in the backyard at night. For the first time, I saw stars in night skies that had not yet been inundated with city light pollution.

Everything was new, clean, and magical. This was our new frontier. It was now not just a house, it was *home*.

(Exactly 30 years later, my parents made their last mortgage payment, paying it off five years early. They settled the debt that they had promised to pay back when they signed the loan papers. They had made that monthly mortgage bill their number one priority, through good years and bad, never missing a payment. Their home was finally theirs.)

As I LOOKED across the restaurant table in Calabasas, staring at the magic key Bob Griffin held in his hands, I saw the genuine gleam in his eyes. It was a potent mixture of pride, purpose, and commitment. At that moment, Bob *was* Countrywide. To me, he was the essence of a brand that suddenly I found myself excited about, a mission I would become energized to support. With almost the power of gospel, Bob had converted me into being a believer in *helping Americans achieve the dream of homeownership.*

Too bad I didn't have an offer from him. But I still had some concerns.

For years I had heard buzz among agency people that Countrywide could be a challenging place to work, and was conservative in its dress, its culture, and its no-nonsense beliefs and commitment to professionalism, hard work, and dedication to the firm.

I had even heard an urban legend (who knows if it was true) that in the early days of Countrywide, when Angelo would be leading a meeting, he would lock the door at the exact time the meeting was to start. Anyone who was late would spend the duration of the meeting waiting out in the hallway.

Bob laughed out loud when I shared that little nugget of a story with him, answering, "That's ridiculous!" as he waved his hands and took another bite of salad.

He dispelled the agency myths that the company was Orwellian in its monitoring of employees and steadfast determination to push every worker to the grindstone all day, every day, although he did stress the culture of hard work, whatever *that* meant.

About midway through the lunch he mentioned, almost in passing, that he was looking for a senior-level person to run the online web marketing. *There's my opening*, I thought. But almost as a throwaway, he quickly followed up with "but that's probably something you wouldn't be interested in."

Hmm, interesting indeed.

I kept listening, nodding as if he were right. Then, as the waiter poured my third iced tea, I asked Bob to tell me more about the role "so I could send him a few great candidates from my own Rolodex." He was talking so compellingly and so fast that I tried to ignore the fact that my bladder was about to explode from all that iced tea.

This role would include responsibility over the immensely prolific and critical Countrywide.com website. This was a massive "portal," as they called it. Part storefront window, part outer mailing envelope, part salesperson, part personality, the Countrywide website was the focal point—the perfect hybrid of tool and sale, of brand and response, the front door through which most people came—prospects, customers, partners, employees—to engage with the firm. Across Home Loans, Banking, Insurance, Securities, it fielded literally millions of visits a month and required a herculean oversight. With my relevant web and financial services marketing experience, I quietly thought that this could be a good fit.

On a napkin Bob doodled the proposed organizational structure, the staff it would need, and the scale and scope of this position, which was looking more and more perfect to me with every glass of iced tea. I finally had to excuse myself to take care of business. As I rose to head off to the restroom, I said to him, "When I get back, let's talk some more about this."

Once my task was completed in the men's room, I washed my face, and looked into the mirror. *Wow, this could be the start of an exciting adventure*, I thought. I fixed my tie, and looked at my watch: 3:12. Time to shift this meeting from a friendly catch-up into a soft sales pitch for my abilities for this job. For the next hour or more, I would *engage, inform,* and *motivate* Bob to buy the most important product I have ever marketed: me.

I returned to the table and shifted the dialogue quickly.

"Bob, you know, the way you describe it, I might be able to add some value there for you," I said.

He seemed pleasantly surprised, responding, "Oh, I know you could do the job, and well, but I just thought it might be too limiting for you. It won't include any other media besides online, for now. Unless that is where you want to be?"

As I had often done, I not only looked at this job opportunity as an immediate, tactical series of positives—new job, good money, prestigious Fortune 100 firm—but also saw two very strong, long-term strategic possibilities. First, even though I would start handling their online efforts, the scale of the company was truly huge, and if I did a good job, it would probably lead to more diverse and grander responsibilities. Second, entering Countrywide, even with a lateral salary move, would help me achieve the critical next step in my career if I ever wanted to be a CEO. I would need to "Punch the Corporate Ticket," as we used to say in the agency world.

Every defined, professional group in our business culture has an unspoken "secret handshake." While not a literal greeting, every working collective has a tight network of insiders, from agencies, to corporations, to government, to academia, even religions and the mob. They know if you're "one of them" or not. And you must get your ticket punched, somehow, somewhere.

I would forever be "an agency guy" unless I could figure out a way to break through into another clique. I can't tell you how many corporate people I had met in my travels, and during interviews I had had, where the HR person would eventually say something like, "Well, we don't really hire agency people."

I decided to make sure that Bob did not leave this lunch without being convinced I would be perfect for this role.

I proceeded to pull out some samples of web case studies, and fired up my laptop. For the next 45 minutes or so, I would do the pitch of my life. Moving through his clearly defined wish list of skills, experience, and style one by one, I made the case that my value was clear. I discussed technology, strategy, tactics, execution, and challenges I had overcome. I showed him that I had grown immensely in the 10 years since he had worked with me.

Then, for good measure, I sincerely added my true feelings that because I had always respected him, it would be an honor to work for him, to help him look good, to help Countrywide continue the mission he had so passionately and compellingly articulated. I all but accepted a job I had not been offered. From my agency sales days, I knew my A-B-C's—Always...Be...*Closing*.

Of course, I knew it would never conclude like that, not in a large company. Even if he agreed, and wanted me to join his team, there would be other interviews with other players, background checks, applications to fill out, title and salary negotiations to be endured, but that was okay. It was, to this day, the best noninterview interview I have ever done.

As he got up to leave, we shook hands again. I was truly so happy for his success, and about the thought of maybe helping to support him. In the parking lot, he ended by saying, "I think this might be great. Call my assistant tomorrow; she will set up some meetings with people you need to meet."

LIKE PREPARING FOR a military deployment, interviewing for a job at Countrywide was an exercise in "hurry up and wait." It would be four months before a final offer was presented to me by Bob, but when I was in his shoes years later, I would finally understand why. A shrewd politician as well as a warm mentor, Bob knew instinctively that if I were to achieve success after joining such a huge company, I would need to be unofficially "green-lighted" by some in the organization, as well as formally approved by some higher-ups, namely, his boss, Andy Bielanski, the Chief Marketing Officer for all of Countrywide. Andy would be my last interview before the offer, but that would not be until May 2003, three months later.

Countrywide Corporate Marketing was essentially an internal ad agency, a company within the company that was Countrywide, serving all of the business units, including (obviously) Home Loans, the Bank, Insurance, and various other minions.

Corporate Marketing made no loans, took in no bank deposits, fielded no sales calls—they were a pure expense, only servicing the rest of the firm so that (hopefully) all of the folks within the business units themselves made their sales numbers and got their bonuses. And as a pure expense—both for the marketing costs directly as well as the overhead required for its huge staff (at its height Corporate Marketing had hundreds of people)—it was very vulnerable to scrutiny, ridicule, and charges of bloated uselessness.

This is often true in any sales organization with a centralized corporate marketing structure. From cars to technology to financial services, I had heard this again and again while working on the agency side. The riff was, when sales are *great, those sales guys are doing a great job.* When sales are *bad, those marketing people are driving the company straight into the ground.* So, it was best to make nice and make sure that the business units gave tacit approval to any marketing talent you wanted to bring on board.

This, of course, was not mandatory, but I believe that in any organization, soliciting input and approval before you hire for any senior role is wise. Typically that marketing person's success becomes a self-fulfilling prophecy if your head of sales loved the guy or gal.

First up was the man who would be my partner in the E-Commerce technology group. Like someone right out of Hollywood central casting, Jerry Romano was a battle-hardened sergeant, an ain't-got-no-time-for-anyone's-crap genius technologist with a passion for fast boats. A big man with a pencil always in his ear, his sleeves were always rolled up like Lou Grant (which also allowed him to show off his new Rolex GMT Master II).

Within the first 30 seconds he told me how he was faring during this, his twenty-seventh new diet and fourteenth Diet 7Up. His giant glass desk was a pile of wires, circuit boards, schematics, and used coffee cups; he was a total techie.

"So why the hell do you want to work in *this* dump," he asked sarcastically in the first five seconds, as he seemed to be reprogramming some code on his screen simultaneously.

I began with my standard, "Well, I believe that my experience and skill set will be a great asset to Coun—" He stopped me cold by putting his hand up toward my face.

"Nah, don't give me the prep school answer. Tell me, really, *why* do you want to work here?" he said, shaking his head with a smile.

If fifteen years of agency presentations had taught me anything, it was to learn how to quickly read a room, or the person in the room. Jerry was a straight shooter, so I would be one, too. *Fuck it,* I thought, *if I am going to lose this job, I am going to lose it for being who I really am.*

"I need a job; there's one here. I am an expert at online marketing, all kinds of marketing, in fact. I've known Bob for years, I trust him, and he told me to impress you. And I hate when people work on their computer while I am talking to them. Oh, and I went to all New York *public* schools, thanks."

Jerry stared at me, blank-faced, for what seemed like forever. Then his grin widened into a bellowing howl of laughter, his belly jiggling like Santa as he slapped his desk in giddy glee. He stood up, and I did, too, and he extended his hand to mine while slapping my back with the other.

"I *knew* Bob would send me a good one!" he said, beaming. "We just might have fun together selling money online, kid."

I totally agreed.

The interview had lasted three minutes.

A few days later, Bob would report to me, "I'm not sure what you said to Jerry, but he loved ya. Good work."

Two weeks later was my second interview, this time with Ed McCoy, from the loan sales unit in Home Loans. A clearly conservative man with wire-framed spectacles and short, perfectly combed hair, Ed was a no-nonsense professional who took his job very seriously. This apparently had been a serious transformation, as almost 15 years earlier, he reminded me, we briefly crossed paths on the agency side, knowing each other peripherally as we both worked at the same agency.

Now, as a serious, senior corporate executive at the business unit, any signs of agency goofiness were clearly beaten out of him. He had completely *turned to the dark side*, as we used to say in the agency world; he was now really a *client*. Now he was essentially Bob's internal "client" whom corporate marketing served to help him drive sales.

I believe strongly that the manner in which a firm treats its candidates reflects directly on their value structure, and Ed was very "Countrywide"—he was welcoming and cordial. But unlike Jerry, Ed was all business. So he got the "Well, I believe my experience and marketing knowledge will greatly benefit Countrywide and your division's success" speech. It seemed to work. The next day, I got word from Bob's assistant that Ed had given Bob the thumbs up on my progression.

My next interview was with someone who would eventually become a nemesis at the firm. Denise Lewis was a product of the whirlwind dot com era, and worked in online production for the Home Loans division. While Jerry was the technology arm of the firm, Denise would become my direct counterpart at the business unit, being my day-to-day direct peer and internal client, just as Denise's boss, Ed McCoy, was Bob's day-to-day internal client. Much like the agency business, or on a football field, the servicing team was sometimes structured in a way that mirrored the hierarchy of the client's organization, one for one. This created a cleaner chain of command and made sure everyone knew who they were "covering," or responsible for keeping happy, on the gridiron of profit.

It is important to note here, however, one important distinction between the organizational dynamics of an internal marketing servicing group and a true outside agency handling a client.

Most agency-client relationships are like a marriage. And as with all marriages, each one is different, with its unique history and dynamics. But they generally fall into two categories: new passion or mature partnership.

New relationships can be fleeting and stressful, where the intensity of the love (perhaps for the creative) may be slowly worn away by the tedium of getting to know someone (bad account service can wear on a client like a partner whom you suddenly discover snores or is a slob). In this type of relationship, the client tends to see the agency as truly an outside firm, doing what they do, charging money for the advertising services the client must have. The relationship can be tenuous, adversarial, and difficult. Many agency-client relationships rarely last past five years. This can be due to poor sales, poor service, mergers, cut budgets, changing of client staff, or client just feels like firing the agency one day.

The longer, venerable, staid relationships are what most agencies dream about, are rare, and are envied in the industry. A mark of a great shop is its long-standing clients. While being trained at Ogilvy New York, I saw firsthand what it was like to have a client see an agency team as part of their family, their brand, and not an outside invader but a true extension of their own internal staff. American Express had come of age with Ogilvy for decades (*"Don't Leave Home Without It," "Membership Has Its Privileges"*). The relationship between Volkswagen and Doyle Dane Bernbach (DDB) was legendary. The Venice, California, agency Chiat/Day has built the Apple brand ever since the famous 1984 Super Bowl commerical ("1984", "Think Different"). And, of course, the western city of Portland, Oregon, had been put on the agency map by what was once a little-known shop called Weiden & Kennedy, creating one of the most iconic brands and one of the best taglines ever, Nike's "Just Do It." These relationships were known to be as powerful and comfortable as a decades-long marriage, where the agency and client could finish each other's sentences. And they were based on mutual respect, not an "us vs. them" mentality.

Internal marketing service groups, such as Corporate Marketing within Countrywide, walked a fine line between these two scenarios. It was kind of like long-term stable marriages, where the alpha partners have made it clear that if they are not happy with beta's partnership, they'll get their needs met elsewhere. On the one hand, there was a definite sense of camaraderie, as we all were working toward the same goal of company profit, success, and growth. All of our checks said Countrywide on them, we all utilized the same health care plans, we all drank the same awful coffee. On the other hand, this concept that Corporate Marketing was the default service (no pun intended), and internal monopoly, created a rich layer of resentment and lack of control, always bubbling just under the surface, at the divisions.

The business divisions were tacitly obliged to use Countrywide's internal marketing department, but not required to, technically, to reach their sales goals. And we were not free. Each business unit paid into a pot for the costs of the marketing overhead, services, salaries, and the media costs itself, just as they would for an outside agency. Corporate Marketing itself generated zero revenue for the firm; we were entirely dependent on cash from the business units' budgets. Whether this was cheaper than an outside agency would have been,

I never knew, but there was no denying the incestuous and delicate political stress of this necessary arrangement. Sometimes it felt like being married to siblings. But the concept was that Corporate Marketing handled the agencies and executed the marketing work, creative, and media, so that the business units would be free to focus on maximizing their operations.

The politically correct move was for all the business units to play nice, pay in, and quietly grumble about the service monopoly that Corporate Marketing enjoyed. In return, the marketing group professionally dedicated ourselves to the shared goals with the business units and worked hard and in good faith to make sure Countrywide exceeded its revenue goals, helped everyone get their bonuses, returned value to shareholders, and helped us achieve the omnipresent mission of helping all Americans achieve the dream of homeownership.

The latter principle was what held us all together. For like America itself, although we were all from different backgrounds, experiences, and places, we were inexplicably drawn together and bonded by the same vision. Even during the worst knock-down, drag-out fights in polished conference rooms, all someone had to do was remind the room of our collective mission, and suddenly we'd all have our red heart lights glow in unison like "ETs" standing motionless in the forest. The opposing sides would grumble, nod heads together, kiss, and make up.

Sometimes it worked beautifully. Sometimes the friction came to a boil. Often, my differing opinions with Denise Lewis, and our radically different styles, were the cause.

Confrontational and bookish, Denise was a know-it-all and had an especially annoying habit of suggesting new ideas by beginning with the phrase, *"Just for kicks and giggles, let's do* [this]."

Her aggressive and combative style made me feel like she just enjoyed being difficult and contrarian. Brilliant or not, in my opinion she never seemed to learn one of the most important rules of business, and especially of corporate life: *Always play nice with the other kids*. Within the first 60 seconds of my meeting with her, she let me know who was going to be the boss.

"Well, you know, I will be very demanding," she began, sipping her coffee nonchalantly, her lipstick smearing on the coffee cup. "Do you think you're up for it? This is not like agency life at all; we work very hard here," she condescended, even though I think I was older and more experienced than she.

"Well, even on the agency side, I always succeeded at helping my clients get their bonus. I am sure we could build a good partnership." I smiled. *What a bitch*, I thought.

I got through the last 20 minutes of the meeting by asking her an open-ended question about the future of the web, and just sat back and let her pontificate. It seemed to work, as Bob made no mention of our tension when he reported back to me Denise's input.

THINGS WERE GOING well. Bob was getting good or neutral feedback from the internal players, at least enough to keep the wheels turning. I would need to go to one last interview, this time with Bob's boss, the one with the power to give a yea or nay vote on my joining one of the largest companies in the United States.

Andy Bielanski had been the Chief Marketing Officer for all of Countrywide for as long as I could remember. He and I, like Bob, had worked together in the agency world back in the early 1990s. Andy was, at that time, already a top player in the ad world. Soon after, he would be recruited to run marketing at Countrywide, and he brought Bob with him.

I liked Andy as a paternal figure with marketing expertise. He always treated me with respect, courtesy, and trust in my abilities. He was tall and handsome, with a thick head of salt-and-pepper hair and the whitest teeth I had ever seen. He perfectly looked the part of the polished CMO of a Fortune 100. Andy was a calm, passive leader, and underestimated by some who felt he was a just a pretty face. I never knew if he truly understood the respect he engendered from his marketing crew, and the presence he exuded when he walked in a room. I never saw him yell or get upset; he simply articulated the vision that we should all rally around, set goals, assigned ownership of those goals, and empowered people to do their work. I observed him closely during my time at Countrywide, and much of my skill as a leader now, if any, I attribute to trying to mimic his style, which, for better or worse, *worked*. He would become the archetype I would study as I aspired to be a CMO myself.

The average tenure of a CMO in America is about 18 to 24 months; that's it. It can be a thankless job, as running marketing in a sales organization is like herding cats in a dog kennel. When things go badly, it is usually the marketing head whose head the sales guys want on a rusty spike. So I believe the secret to Andy's success, having been at Countrywide for at least 10 years, was a serendipitous mix of luck as the company soared on the wings of the marketplace; brilliant strategy and bridge-building in what could be a political snake pit; and good old-fashioned charm.

Ever the politician, he was always shaking hands, patting backs, listening closely to business units' concerns, and generally being a great ad man. The business units, for the most part, genuinely felt like he listened, understood their needs, and directed us to support them properly. And he did this without throwing himself or us under the bus; he knew when to push back, and they respected him. And, also like a great politician, it seemed like he had an uncanny sense of when *not* to be around.

This final interview itself was not at all monumental. In fact, it seemed to be merely a formality at that point. No; the truly profound impact of that day came solely from an environment I had never experienced before.

Andy's office was actually in the headquarters building. Tightly secured like a top-secret base, it had guards at every checkpoint, every entryway, every hallway. Security cards were required to pass through any new area, especially the third floor, the executive suite.

I was directed by the stern, burly guard manning the front street entrance to park my car in a visitors-only area. He handed me a car pass, which was to be kept in sight on the dashboard at all times. Another guard, at the front security desk within the main lobby, would assign me yet another security pass once my appointment was confirmed and reauthorized by Andy's secretary. I hadn't seen this level of security since my flight training missions at the now-closed Otis Air Force base in New England.

As I approached the main lobby doors on that scorchingly hot, bright spring day, I hoped that beads of sweat would not mess up my perfectly starched white dress shirt. In my dark pinstriped suit and purple power tie, I was determined to finish my Countrywide interview process with style, strength, and expertise regardless of the outcome. Every presentation I had ever done in my agency career with so many other chief marketing officers had trained me for this day.

I could not have been prepared, though, for the majesty of this lobby at Countrywide's headquarters, which reminded me of Radio City Music Hall, Buckingham Palace, or even the unsinkable *Titanic*. The perfectly ice-cold air-conditioning hit my face as the guard buzzed me in past the glass front doors. A huge golden atrium made me feel Lilliputian with its massive high ceiling and open airspace. This was surely a powerful symbol of the new financial gilded age.

It was intimidating. The ceiling seemed to be at least 50 feet high, with a twin set of richly dark-colored carpeted staircases facing each other in the back of the auditorium, leading to the executive suite; the staircases were flanked by thick and dark wooden handrails that appeared to be carved by hand. It looked like a gentrified mansion entryway, right out of *Gone with the Wind*.

The cavernous hall was flanked at each side with mysterious double doors, also requiring badges apparently as I watched worker bees enter and exit with papers, lunches, and purpose. And there, at the center of this financial airplane hangar, was a relatively small security desk.

"May I help you, sir?" asked the guard, a kindly old gentleman.

"Yes. I have an appointment with Andy Bielanski."

"Okay, sir. Please have a seat. I will call his assistant. May I see your identification, please?"

ID? What was this, the Pentagon? Kinda cool. I pulled out my driver's license.

"Okay, sir. You can go up to the reception area at the top of the stairs. Here, you'll need this," he said, handing me a security badge.

At the top of the soft-carpeted stairs, after what seemed like a hundred curved steps, I approached the wizard who solely held the key to the secret lair of the executives. A sweet-looking, older woman held the ultimate power of access. I can't recall her name, but she was dressed in a handsome suit, had perfectly styled hair, and had a glowing smile that made her seem like the favorite aunt I never had. She smiled at me, yet with an odd, zombielike expression like I was the ten-millionth visitor she had buzzed in on this, her ten-millionth day on the job. It was like a scene right out of a David Lynch film, strange, and otherworldly. I half expected to see a dwarf in an elephant mask start walking past us in slow motion while speaking French backward.

She sat at a small yet ornate wooden desk topped by a small flat-screen television, on which a soap opera was playing with the volume at a minimum. She, too, called Andy's assistant to confirm that I was indeed at the third-floor desk, waiting to be led into the glass doors that separated us from the senior leadership of a company that hovered at about $20-plus billion in value at that moment.

Because of her seemingly monotonous job, all alone out there in the plush hallway all day, I felt sad for her. But then I did some quick math in my head and figured that if she had buzzed people in since 1985, she might also be worth at least $10 million in stock options by now. No wonder she was smiling. She probably owned the building.

And this touches upon what was a core driver for me in the pursuit of this role; it wasn't about getting rich quick by quibbling over this exact salary number, or negotiating these many vacation days, or haggling over a certain bonus. No; working at a Fortune 100 was an opportunity—albeit a long-term, uncertain, volatile opportunity—at real wealth.

Because every year, senior executives at Countrywide would be granted *stock options*.

It is important to note that stock options are not free money, but they can be free stocks. But, as much of America knows, stocks can mean positive money or negative money (read: loss). They are literally what their name implies: they are granted shares of stock where you have the *option* to sell stock in your company at a certain price, set by the top level of the firm. This is called the *strike price*.

For example, let's say a stock in the company you work for may be trading at about $20. On a set day every year, you *may* be *granted* (not guaranteed, mind you) the option to buy, let's say, 1,000 shares of the stock for, let's say, $16 a share, which is the strike price decided by the firm. Most firms grant a block of options every year, so if you let them sit in your account, you may have 20,000 shares over 20 years. Nice. Now, you can *exercise*, or sell, those options within a certain time frame (the option to sell can still expire after a while). If you sell your 1,000 options, which you bought at the $16 strike price when your company is roaring and the stock is at $26, congrats—you just made $10,000 (1,000 shares times the $10 positive difference in price). (Don't forget to pay taxes on this money when you file, or your new home may be made of steel bars, and paid for by the government.)

If you are at a firm for a long time, and the growth of the stock has been seriously good, yes, you could hit real wealth. Countrywide stock was under $5 for most of its life. During the boom, it hit about $45 by 2006. For fun let's do some quick, oversimplified math. (Or, if you worked there for a long time and sold everything in 2006, pay one of your servants to do the math for you.) If your average price spread as a Countrywide employee was that $45 share price in 2006 minus your strike price of $5, and you sold your 100,000 options you had accumulated over time, you just grossed $4 million.

Of course, if you worked there your whole life, and had 100,000 options to buy the stock at a strike price of $5, and, well, now it is more like $4, then, take off your worn-out shoes and your holey socks and count your toes to zero—because those stocks are now "underwater"—worth less than their strike price. Their value is zero.

Just ask people at Enron. And Bear Stearns. And Lehman Bros. And Lincoln Savings (remember *that* one?). And, I would imagine, some people now still at, or formerly at, Countrywide. And a host of other debacles over the years.

But as I waited for my interview, things were looking good at Countrywide. As I waited those few minutes for Andy's assistant to come fetch me, I picked up a copy of Countrywide's 2002 annual report. I flipped through page after page of glowing profit reports, charts going up, up, up. Angelo's smiling face adorned the opening statement of boundless optimism for an even better future. The revenue growth was truly stratospheric, bordering on unbelievable.

After a few more moments I was led into the executive suite. I entered a long, wide hallway adorned with even more dark green carpet, and dark desks that looked expensive. At least eight desks manned by gatekeeping assistants, most of them handsome, well-dressed older women—clearly career professional executive assistants, seasoned for the top 1 percent of American C-level executives (CEOs, CFOs, CMOs, etc.)—lined the wall that housed the beautifully appointed private offices.

Now, *this* was a bank. Not a speck of dust anywhere. Dark woods, rich carpets; it literally looked like a movie set, where the director wanted the audience to actually be able to *smell* the money. Being a movie buff my whole life, I tend to see things in the context of how they may have been portrayed in film when I was a kid. And this day provided two immediate, jarring images: when the father in *Mary Poppins,* bowler hat in hand, goes to the marble-laden, brass and gleaming, monstrous bank's great hall, to be fired; and, the dark-green-carpeted and dark-wood-adorned, stuffy old men's club of old money portrayed so fancifully by Don Ameche and Ralph Bellamy as "The Dukes" in *Trading Places.* And now, me as Eddie Murphy, being led in.

Even the walls were impressive. The dark paneling was so rich that it may not have been paneling at all, but rather real wood over the drywall. And they were lined with many wonderful paintings, all apparently the work of some eighteenth- or nineteenth-century masters I am sure I had heard of before, if I had had the time to look closer at the small polished brass plaques at the bottom of each work. The huge canvases, some as big as several feet across, were all images of idyllic vistas—grand, impactful, American vistas—each depicting some kind of wonderful hills, valleys, and homesteads. People working the fields with the manor in the background, building homes in the forest; a lakefront with a lovely colonial home on the edge; pioneers conquering the wilderness. Also, occasionally I would see a naval scene, a powerful clipper braving an ocean storm, the brave sailors' home on the sea of the unknown.

Then it hit me. These were all American *dreams*, representations of power, strength, perseverance, cultivating, farming, building, living, being American. It was a breathtaking collection of what America, and what Countrywide, wanted to stand for. I was impressed as I was led into Andy's office.

"Come in, come in, Adam, good to see you," he said, getting up to greet me and extending his large, leathery hand. "I thought we could grab lunch together here across the hall."

Honored that my interview had just been elevated to a meal with the Chief Marketing Officer, I tried to contain my excitement at this positive turn with a simple, "Sure, that sounds great, Andy."

We walked the few feet across from Andy's office, where I was welcomed into a large conference room that glowed golden. Gold wallpaper and fine golden drapes allowed the sunlight from the massive windows to bounce all around the room like I was inside Versailles. A long, slim, polished wood conference table that easily sat 20 people extended the length of the room. I saw two place settings, one at the end of the table, the other just diagonally to it. White linen place mats were topped with perfectly folded matching napkins. Silver utensils complemented what appeared to be fine china and crystal drinking glasses. I felt like I was at a state dinner, soon to be sitting next to the ambassador from Countrywideland. Good thing I wore my best suit and tie. We would soon see if I spoke Countrywidean well; I heard it could be a challenging dialect.

Andy was warm and friendly, immediately making me feel at ease by first talking about the old agency days; about the people we knew, the clients we served, the other brands we built together as part of the same team. Even though back in those days I was a fairly junior executive and he was an agency kingpin, he was always cordial and nice to me. I never forgot that.

We also shared a common bond as Andy also got his MBA at UCLA in the 1970s, before it was even in vogue to earn such a degree. Not only was I learning the secret handshake, but we also shared the unspoken kinship of being fellow alumni brethren.

We talked about Bob, and how great he was. I told him straight that my respect for him was one of the main drivers in my seeking this position, and that having spoken to many people around the organization already, both he and Andy were well respected, and this meant everything to me. He seemed to appreciate this positive feedback.

As we continued down our mutual ad agency memory lane, just Andy and me, at this huge table, the rest of the room was bustling with the frenzied preparations of the waiters preparing lunch for us. I noticed that all the servers were Latino men and women, quickly jumping and serving the needs of this isolated floor of what appeared to be mostly wealthy white men. The dichotomy was striking as white gloved hands used sterling silver tongs from silver trays to carefully place perfectly prepared chicken on my china plate.

"Thank you very much," I said to my server, being extra sensitive to my manners in this cultured environment. I, too, had been a busboy once, at an allegedly mob-owned catering hall in New York as a kid, so I knew what hard work it could be—the aching muscles, the hot, greasy stench from the kitchen baked into my clothes after work. The server smiled, and they all whisked themselves out of the room as quickly as they entered.

"Well, Adam," Andy continued, "this meeting was just a chance for me to meet with you briefly as we move forward. I heard you met a few folks already?"

"Yes, they were great. Denise was an interesting meeting."

"Yes, we know Denise can be, um, challenging. She's one of the reasons Bob and I like the idea of a former agency person in this role. We need someone who can manage Denise, not just service her; someone with good client experience."

"Well, I think she and I could be...friends," I said, smiling back.

Andy then asked me for my thoughts and some ideas for improving the website, which, having studied it already, I was glad to do. As the conversation was going so well, I saw an opportunity to ask Andy a more probing question as the waiter refilled our iced tea glasses.

"Andy, so what do you think is the most important difference between being on the agency side and being on the client side?"

"Well," he said, dabbing his lips with his linen napkin. "Although we are 'in charge,' and the agencies take direction from us, we have great, honest relationships with them; they aren't afraid to push back on us when they need to. Our responsibilities are greater; the final decisions are ours to make. But since they know that *we know* how they work, I think this helps us get better work out of them." He paused thoughtfully, and then continued, "And, unlike the agency world, where we used to spend all of our time trying to sell *this* particular concept to the client, here, it is more about trying to simply execute work that builds the brand and generates sales, given all the opinions we hear internally. If you build trust with the agencies and the business units, and they know that you are truly committed to helping them succeed, you'll be fine. We'll all be fine."

I nodded. He continued, "Unlike some companies, I think you'll find that marketing and the business lines are not at each other's throats here. Here it seems like we are really all in this together. You know, helping people become homeowners. I think there are few things more noble that we can do as marketers."

I was beginning to understand exactly how he felt, and I was enthralled. It had been years since I talked to Andy. But at that moment I remembered his ability to calmly charm a room. If he had asked me to work for him for one dollar right then, I think I would've taken it. That iced tea may well have been Countrywide Kool-Aid, and I was drinking it. From the symbols of wealth, success, pride, and dreams surrounding us, I was woozy with ambition and optimism.

Within 30 minutes, our brief lunch ended. The eager waiters quickly cleared away all the plates and linens, clearing the crumbs from the table using sterling silver crumb scoopers, perhaps prepping the dining room for the next private executive meal. Then, like a fine restaurant, they offered dessert, which Andy politely declined with a gentle wave of his hand.

"Well, Adam, I have to run to another meeting. I will connect with Bob and I am sure he will be in contact with you."

We shook hands in the silent hallway in front of his office, the air an oddly mixed aroma of deliciously baked chicken and new carpet smell. I walked back through the glass passage, past the security buzzer wizardess with a million options, and headed out down the palatial stairs, dropping off my security badge as I walked past the security desk.

The blast furnace of the Calabasas dry heat hit my face as I exited and made my way back to the car. Getting in quickly, I turned my car air-conditioner up all the way, icy air pouring over my face. I breathed out as if I had been holding my breath the entire meeting. As the ignition turned over, the local rock station I had been listening to seemed to know what I was feeling—it blared Aerosmith's "Back in the Saddle"—I let out an exalted scream from within the safety and privacy of my soundproof windows. *I nailed it.*

TWO WEEKS LATER, I got the call from Bob. Their extensive background security checks were completed; Countrywide was offering me the position of Senior Vice President of Online Marketing. The package was fair, the opportunity was enormous, and the future was mine with a seat on the Countrywide rocket. Like they say, if you travel far enough, you eventually meet yourself; I would begin my new life as a client and punch the corporate ticket on June 30, 2003.

4

Welcome to "Countrywide 101"

In the business world, the rearview mirror
is always clearer than the windshield.
—Warren Buffett

JUNE 30, 2003

Prime rate: 4.00%

Foreclosure rate: 1.24%

CFC stock price: ~$17.00

EVERYONE REMEMBERS THE little bit of magic they felt on the first day of any new school year. The new clothes, the new notebook with that new notebook smell; everything was just perfect, ready for the hard work of the year ahead. Monday, June 30, 2003, would be my first day in corporate America—as a client, finally—at Countrywide. In preparation I bought a whole new wardrobe—new suits, shoes, briefcase, the whole nine yards. From experience I knew that first impressions—the way I behaved, performed, presented myself and developed relationships in the *first critical weeks* of my new job— would galvanize my internal reputation that, good or bad, I would live with for years thereafter at this company.

By sheer coincidence, my first day would coincide with a semiannual gathering of the entire Corporate Marketing group, called the

"Leadership Summit." It was as if they had built the entire agenda just for me, orienting me through each and every role and responsibility that Corporate Marketing handled for the business divisions. Bob was a wonderful host that first day, introducing me to a dizzying array of new faces and name tags from among the hundreds who were attending. I followed him around all that day like a new duckling learning the ways of the pond. I quietly felt grateful, knowing that many corporate drones never find a mentor like this.

The Summit was held in the grand auditorium of what was called the "Learning Center" at Countrywide headquarters (which we used to smarmily refer to as the *Earning Center* because of the political points a "Countrywide culture class" could earn you there). It was part museum and part conference center, and housed on the main floor almost directly over the Vault, which was in the basement of the same wing.

Depending on your point of view, the museum aspect of the place was a tribute to the genius that was Angelo, a teary-eyed, panoramic melodrama of the American Dream we provided to the wretched refuse from the teeming shores of apartment rentals, or a creepy, a-little-too-idolizing, totalitarian telling of the same story. Bordering on cultish, it was a mélange of dusty models displaying the finer details of the first Countrywide storefront (complete with equally dusty, tiny 1960s cars), and a Times Square–like, lighted news ticker that constantly flashed Countrywide news of what was then a soaring daily stock price. Along the high walls of the vaulted atrium, mounted images of the iconic history of Countrywide complemented the smiling images of Angelo Mozilo and new homeowners basking in the financial light we shined on them. The only thing missing was a statue of him (most likely in bronze to perfectly capture that amazing tan). It was arguably an engaging, grandiose telling of the true success story that was Countrywide, but could also be interpreted as being just one blackjack table away from the *Countrywide Wax Museum and Casino.*

Bob had saved me a front-row seat next to him in the presentation auditorium, and I sat back as I watched the entire corporate team walk me through their functions, one by one.

Like a master of ceremonies, Andy opened the day with a pep talk about Countrywide, the American Dream we facilitated, and Corporate Marketing's role in that noble enterprise. You could've heard a pin drop as he spoke about it; I looked back toward the full auditorium and saw mouths agape with wonder and adoration, followed by real applause. *These people believe,* I thought. And truth be told, it was kinda cool. Like a proud day of show and tell, one by one each department came up to the stage and trumpeted its achievements, their growth, and their value. And the unspoken goal among all that apparent camaraderie was, *you had better show value.*

Portfolio Communications was first. This group handled the herculean task of communicating with, cross-selling to, and maintaining wonderful relationships with the millions of customers who had a loan with Countrywide. Millions of monthly statements had to be all perfectly computerized, nice to look at, flawlessly printed and mailed, with large type (with the average age of a primary loan holder in the midthirties, and the average age of a Home Equity customer being in their midforties, it was important to make the statement clear, large, and easy to understand). The website page that, after logging in, would show a customer all of their Countrywide financial data had to be seamless, fast, and accurate. As in any company, existing customers were our best prospects for additional sales, so the call centers had to be manned, scripted, and operationally perfect so that we could offer customers great new financial products to help them with their lives.

The Portfolio Communications Group was run by a rising star within the Countrywide universe. We simply called him *Wonderboy.* He was a baby-faced wunderkind who had grown quickly through the ranks of Countrywide. Smart, capable, and calm, he was an easy mark for anyone in the organization who was annoyed by his fast growth, but truly, his only fault was being so great at what he did.

Never uttering a bad word about anyone, always showing respect, courtesy, and professionalism, constantly generating new ideas and overcoming tough challenges, he was the one who would sit in the front of the class and ruin the curve for others who knew their value was marginal. And some people were jealous of his growth and his professional perfection.

He got promoted so often and quickly over the years that one internal joke, although obliquely complimentary to him, was a hallway favorite:

"What's today?" someone would ask.

The other guy would say, "I dunno, but Wonderboy just made SVP."

"Oh, then it must be only Tuesday."

I never knew if he knew that we referred to him as Wonderboy, but he was the best of Countrywide, and whoever put him in charge of keeping customers happy made the right decision.

That person was Wonderboy's boss, and the next to speak. Emily Simmons was a leader in marketing finance, who would emerge eventually as a great mentor to me as well.

Emily ran the group that handled marketing and loan production analytics, set all product pricing, oversaw the portfolio group, managed all qualitative and quantitative research, and generally was the antithesis of the soft, branding side of the group, which Bob ran. I quickly came to believe that she was a financial genius.

Emily was a CFA—a Chartered Financial Analyst, which until I met her I knew nothing about. Being a CFA was apparently one of the most prestigious titles that anyone in finance could attain. Ethics, tenacity, rigor, and analytics are the focus of the little-known three-year program, which requires increasingly difficult exams to be passed each year. The certification has been around for only about 60 years, and with only about 100,000 CFAs in existence, the honor is notoriously difficult to attain. Months later, in my MBA cockiness I took a practice CFA exam and bombed miserably.

After some impressive charts touting her group's success in price management, demand projection, and detailed analytics regarding every aspect of the operation one could imagine, I was hooked. This woman was good, and it appeared that Countrywide was on an upward trajectory the financial world had rarely seen before. The endless stream of jaw-dropping growth charts and dizzying regression analyses filled the lenses of my new eyeglasses. The sky seemed not even to be the limit as the results I saw matched the legend portrayed in the outer hall museum.

As if to accentuate the left- vs. right-brained aspects of the group, Bob was next onto the stage. His purview was the softer, branded elements of Countrywide, including all advertising media, creative, and messaging, as well as the front page, or "portal" of the website (www .countrywide.com) and the online media that drove prospects into it.

It was called a portal because that's what it was, a gateway to all the other business unit websites, including Home Loans, Banking, Insurance, Customer Information, and Securities. The portal had the challenging job of presenting all of Countrywide's offerings quickly in an engaging, informative manner, yet it also needed to quickly move you through and get out of the way so you could apply for a financial product as fast as possible.

Nothing could be bought directly off the portal; no revenue could be generated there. The revenue was generated when the easy-to-see Login to the customer area of the site moved you quickly to pay your mortgage online; when the simple rate calculator motivated you to click through to the application windows; when the great CD rates inspired you to open a bank account today on the bank site. Managing the portal was a politically challenging responsibility because the business units saw it as a necessary evil, the price of being part of a corporate family. But if they had their way (which was driven by their sales goals), there would be no portal, but simply a series of websites for each of the divisions: CountrywideHomeLoans.com, CountrywideBank.com, etc.

But this, of course, would have created marketing bedlam. It was necessary to keep some semblance of centralized marketing order. The overall "look" and messaging needed to stay in one centralized group, to ensure consistency and quality, and also to make sure that the never-ending hunt for revenue did not devolve the site into a screaming, carnival-barking mess of tacky bikini-clad women holding signs with rates on them.

We were *Countrywide*. We had class. We were friendly, approachable, helpful, conservative, nice neighbors. And only a friend like that could attain the trust needed to help you with your pursuit of the American Dream.

A year later, research would confirm that consumers' perceptions of Countrywide were so positive and powerful that I would recommend to Andy that we consider investing in a series of *line extensions* for the Countrywide brand. Like the Eddie Bauer Edition of the Ford Explorer, or the Disney line of Behr Home Decorating Paints, my idea was to develop a line of Countrywide-esque homes, perhaps with a certain Countrywide look and feel, each with their own picket fence, of course. I suggested perhaps KB Home as a partner in this, although we could negotiate with several different home builders. I even suggested the possibility of testing the concept further, into the even more lucrative home fixtures category, imagining a line of Countrywide faucets, carpets, flooring, place mats, etc. The "KB Countrywide Home" line idea never made it past Andy's desk, and I watched with dismay as in April 2006 Martha Stewart announced a pact with KB Home to create a line of Martha Stewart Homes. *Dammit*. (In the summer of 2007, when the housing market began its collapse in earnest, newspapers were reporting that the Martha Stewart line of KB Homes was the only one that was still selling well.)

Bob walked the room through all of the elements of the online marketing, over which I would take command: online media, creative, offers, and messaging. My job would be a complicated exercise in finding the right banner on the right site with the right creative, message, and offer that created maximum click-through and applications. Search was a combination of "Organic Search"—the free automated listings provided by the search engines—and Paid Search, which was the daily buy management of thousands of keywords that prospects might search for, and then (hopefully) present Countrywide prominently in the listings.

Television had not been invested in for a while. Interest rates were so low after 9/11 that the firm already couldn't complete all the applications fast enough, and didn't really need to invest in the broadcasted generation of new business. But in the coming months that would change as our operational capacity was enlarged and the market grew.

Bob also espoused the brand that was Countrywide, showing research that confirmed that the public liked and trusted us, that we were considered friends, and this was good. As he presented the findings compellingly, charmingly, and thoughtfully, I was proud that I reported to him. I could hear from the whispers in the audience around me that he was respected, well-liked, and considered smart and paternal at the firm.

Next up was Subprime Marketing, which serviced Countrywide's Subprime lending unit, Full Spectrum Lending out in Pasadena, California. Countrywide separated the marketing functions of Subprime vs. Prime, because the tone, manner, and style of the communications needed to be very different, and the financial aspects of the business also were very different.

Much talked about in the news at the center of the mortgage mess, the segregation of Prime vs. Subprime was based on a prospect's FICO score. The concept of the FICO score is based solely on the premise that past behavior is by far the truest predictor of future behavior, and one's predicted credit-worthiness can range from a horrible credit score of 450 to the superhuman valedictorial score of an 850. (Many consumers in America do not even know what their credit score is, even though so much of their lives is riding on that number.)

People with bad credit (FICO) scores, typically under 650, are considered Subprime credit risks. This does not mean that they all sleep in vans down by the river. It simply means that they have in their history demonstrated behavior or made late credit payments such that the FICO formula penalized them and lowered their scores. They may in fact carry large debts, which can affect the score, as well as other factors such as length of history and type of credit used. Many of them are responsible people with only a few minor dings in their credit history.

Conversely, Prime credit risks are not all rosy, sure bets. Prime means that their credit score is generally over 650. A household may have a stellar credit score of 820 but may owe thousands in revolving credit card debt, make payments on two cars, pay a first mortgage and a Home Equity Loan, tuition, and much more. But they always pay their bills on time, and their score reflects that—as well as their total debt load. In reality, many times a Prime loan might be just as precarious as a Subprime loan. The overextended household may only be one bad event away from financial disaster. Prime loans simply *tend to be* more stable, but by 2008 data showed that foreclosures were seeping into the Prime segment faster than ever—implying that the overextension of American household borrowing and consumerism may have been finally catching up with us.

Prime prospects, because their credit was so good, could pick and choose which lender they went with based on rate, service, brand, whatever, because the banks would fight among themselves to get that so-called "A-paper," pristine business. (This is essentially the basis for business models for firms such as Lending Tree—"When Banks Compete, You Win"—where a single application would be courted by several different lenders.) When a Prime prospect would call Countrywide, *they* were interviewing *us* for the job of servicing *them*.

Conversely, when a Subprime prospect would call our Full Spectrum Lending unit to submit an application, *we* were interviewing *them*, to see if they were worthy of us taking a risk. This is why across the industry the *application* rate (converting from inbound call to completed application) for a Subprime prospect tended to be much higher than a Prime prospect—and why the *funding* rate of an application (the conversion rate for completed application to loan approval and money sent) for Prime could be much higher; the Prime applications would usually pass financial risk assessment more easily because they were generally less risky (or so they appeared).

Typically a Subprime prospect would need to apply to several lenders with the hope of getting just one approval, although the scale of this desperation would depend heavily on a variety of factors, including credit card and other revolving debt, FICO score, equity in the home (collateral) if at all, and financial records, if any. (Yes, at the height of the mania, so-called "Liar Loans" sometimes were granted with no documentation, and no proof of income. Absolute—total—madness.)

The Subprime Marketing group was run by a guy we called "Spanky." I never learned how he earned this nickname, but it apparently stuck long before I had arrived. I personally felt that his style could be so abrasive that there had to be some other reason why we hired this guy; some said it was simply because of some family relationships with senior management. Such whispers were never confirmed, but he ran Subprime Corporate Marketing for the largest mortgage company in the United States. I never saw him do anything wrong or unethical, and indeed he worked within the same strict legal and regulatory rules we all did. I believe he tried his best; but in my humble opinion, it just seemed that his people skills sucked.

Spanky walked the room through the scale of their marketing operations and the marketing machine that serviced Full Spectrum Lending was truly awesome in its size and reach.

They sent out truckloads of direct mail every month, with hundreds of different sizes, shapes, messages, and offers. They managed a giant call center. They tested and ran Subprime-targeted online media, and also ran the site that was yet another door from the portal: FullSpectrum Lending.com. It was impressive and profitable. Industry-wide, Subprime loans typically yielded greater fees and higher rates than their Prime cousins, which is why our free-market, capitalist system generated so many new Subprime firms during the boom. Like the Forty-niners of old, they all sought gold when word spread that it was there for the taking.

To those in the media who seem to enjoy pointing out, as if it was some evil conspiracy, that rates for Subprime loans were higher and fees were greater, I submit that this was to be expected, as in any a risk-based business model. If corporations were not additionally compensated for the additional risk they were assuming by underwriting these Subprime loans, the marketplace would cease lending to those with less than perfect credit—and that would prevent those people from the "fresh start" chance to demonstrate their new, Prime-like payment discipline. So I vote that giving people second chances, and lending people money even though they may have had a bad day or two in their past, was indeed a noble and needed offering, if managed thoughtfully and diligently, and if it is well regulated by government forces not motivated by profit.

Devoid of any quantitative brain-wracking, like a nice, light sorbet after a huge meal, the day ended with the intrepid Public Relations group. After hours upon hours of charts and graphs and endless PowerPoints, the PR women, led by Susan Martin (known informally as "Suzie"), walked onto the stage with a handmade mobile of paper and sticks; there were some awkward giggles from the audience as the preschool demonstration was brought out.

Slim, attractive, and charming, Suzie was the perfect camera face for any and all public relations appearances, and could easily engage a room. She was more seasoned than the other members of her team, and was said to have been a former stand-up comedienne years ago, before she joined Countrywide. Perhaps this contributed to her seeming to be so comfortable on stage, more so than the others.

The group huddled around the mobile, as the signs hanging from each of the extended sticks became clearer. Up on the stage, I thought they might all break out into a big musical number from *Gypsy*, but instead they used their time to walk the audience through each of their core functions, each drawn onto one hanging part of the mobile, including *Media Relations, Investor Relations, Executive Appearances and Speeches*, and, of course, *Crisis Management*.

Public relations can be defined as achieving any positive mention in the media that does not cost discrete media dollars to place; it is essentially any free advertising. When a newspaper reader sees "Countrywide" in a news story, it is supposed to be a positive impression—just like a paid ad also creates an impression. (When I say "impression" here I refer to the imprinting on a reader's retina, rather than assessing how they *feel* about the brand.)

Most people think that public relations is primarily comprised of staff who make sure to "get the word out" about a company, its goodness, products, support for the community, etc., and this is partly true. Their relationships with reporters and their publications can get your company name mentioned in a news story, and the depth of those relationships can be critical. But the reality is, the far more important role that public relations plays is the power to call upon those relationships when it is important that the company stay *out* of the newspaper.

Although it has been said that "there is no such thing as bad publicity"—in that, any mention raises *awareness* for your brand—for every good story you may have ever read about Countrywide during its height, there were probably ten other stories you never saw, because the PR team did their job of keeping (for the most part) negative references or stories out of the press as much as possible.

But that was back in the boom. The torrential flood of bad news—financial, emotional, nationwide—that Countrywide endured by the summer of 2007 was arguably as monumental as Enron. No PR team could possibly have kept the downfall of Countrywide, as well as the emerging housing and mortgage crisis, from becoming front-page news on every paper in America almost every day. It would become an unenviable position, I am sure, and the worst confluence of soul-crushing bad luck and awful happenstance that any PR person should ever have to endure, and yet it was mercilessly out of their control.

But on the stage that day, all was well. They presented their hand-crafted mobile and demonstrated their role to the room. Unlike all the other groups that had presented that day, there were no quantitative accolades for their achievements; PR was almost impossible to quantify, and this was a challenging place to be in a quantitatively driven firm. How does an entire department justify its costs when it was impossible to lay out its monetary value to the firm on a white board? *Easy*. Make sure Countrywide was written about as much as possible in as many papers as possible, focused on how Countrywide was bringing the dream of homeownership to America. Like when I used to throw a fun ad concept on the table at one of my old agency-client meetings, nothing silenced and inspired a group of skeptical executives more than to show them their positive mentions in the *Wall Street Journal*.

As the PR group began concluding what would be the final briefing of this first day of Countrywide school, I began to realize just how vast this firm was. Yes, of course, Countrywide was a financial services company. But through my own prism of experience with so many other types of business categories, I grew evermore in awe of just how many kinds of business models were encompassed within this sprawling megafirm.

Countrywide was a service business. Unlike a company that sold widgets—razors, peaches, pens, etc.—Countrywide sold an ethereal concept; customers could not actually hold the money in their hands. The entire brand that was Countrywide, like most commodity and service businesses, came down to the quality of customers' experiences during the process, both pre- and post-sale. How long you were kept on hold when you called customer service; how informed and nice the agent Peggy was in solving your problem, and more importantly, being empowered to solve it and take personal ownership of its resolution; how consistently clean were the branches; whether the loan package arrived on time and correctly. This is the DNA of a service brand, and, like many performance-based judgments of quality, every service brand is *only* as good as the customers' most recent interaction with that brand.

Countrywide was a capacity business. Any service business is also a capacity business in that the front end drive to acquire customers is limited by, or capped by, the true, finite capacity of its service operations. For example, I am frequently correcting clients when they say that I am in the customer *acquisition* business. Yes, my Countrywide title stated that I was in the customer acquisition business, but, more accurately, I was in the customer *load management* business. When I worked on the GTE account years ago, the worst thing I could have done would have been to generate 50,000 calls on a particular day regarding some new long-distance plan if their call center capacity was only 5,000 calls. Similarly, hotels and airlines had finite numbers of beds and rooms and nights, or plane seats per day, and the marketer's job was to fill those systems to *capacity*, not to burst the dam.

Much of my time at Countrywide was spent managing that very narrow optimal flow of customers per day, per hour, per agent, through the call centers and website, to maximize efficiency but not overload the system. We had only so many phone lines, so many call agents, and so many man-hours with which to process applications.

Countrywide was a "click and mortar" business. This meant that it offered both a robust online experience as well as retail and call-center channels. Countrywide not only had a prolific website where you could pretty much get anything you needed, but it also had a very large network of retail storefronts where customers could go see Sally to discuss their loans in person. And this was critical, as Countrywide was indeed a "premium lender." This meant that while its loan rates may not have been the lowest rates in town (although they were typically competitive), customers who were "old-timers or first-timers"—seniors used to the personal relationships, or first-time home buyers needing a little extra hand-holding—appreciated being able to fill out an application at three o'clock in the morning in their jammies while the blue light of their computer screens shined in their home office, and then being able to go see Steve in the Santa Monica office to ask a few questions about it. This optimal mix of choices for the customer—call us, come in, or go online—was truly a model that was customer-centric, that is, focused on the customers' comfort and style and chosen, preferred method of engagement.

Countrywide was first and foremost a sales organization. This is an important distinction, although, frankly, its semantic relevance is arguable. Yes we did marketing. But *sales*, not how customers *felt* about us, was the most important priority in the firm. We were a public company, and as a senior officer of this public company, it was my duty to return value to shareholders as quickly and as profitably as possible. That's it. Most of the "finance jocks" on the upper floors didn't give a damn about how our brochures looked, or how fast our website functioned, or how emotional our television ads were. To them, the only thing that mattered—and one could argue that this was rightly so—were the sales numbers. Every week, every month, every quarter was a nerve-wracking recap of how many loans were sold, how many Certificates of Deposit were opened, how many Home Equity Loans we signed, and what the amounts on those loans were. And, like a true sales organization, we were all only as good as our last reports.

Countrywide was a technology business. Behind the websites and the storefronts and the call centers, Countrywide was an operational marvel. In a genius bit of foresight, back in the 1980s it was one of the first financial firms in the country to invest in computer and database technology to streamline the speed and efficiency of loan processing and management. As I learned while working on the larger financial services clients in my career, as well as other operational masters such as Microsoft, Nissan, Bank of America and others, technology made all of it run smoothly, such as it did. While I did not market this technological expertise directly to consumers, the broad and deep understanding of database development, modeling and analytics, call center and web systems, web programming, and tracking systems that I acquired during my time at marketing agencies was critical to help manage it all.

Countrywide was both a Brand Marketing and a Direct Marketing company. Branding alone is best used for products and services that are so ubiquitous, so widespread, that large-scale messages to as many people as possible may be the most efficient path to maximize sales. Driven largely by emotionally connecting with the customer, most Super Bowl commercials represent great examples of this, from Pepsi to pretzels, from computers to cars; everyone needs one, everyone has one, everyone has these products in their daily lives. And indeed we used emotional connections wherever we could to separate ourselves from the commoditized pack of financial services companies.

But unlike soda, not everyone needs a home loan or a money market account. That's where the Direct Marketing methodology comes in. From response-driven television to direct mail to targeted online web banners and management of online search keywords, Countrywide created engaging, informative, and motivational messages and used legal and readily available prospect information to deliver them directly to customers who needed them most. Countrywide's success or failure at that time rested greatly on this. And with so many types of customers and influencers for customers, both in the consumer and business areas, including not only homeowners but also builders, brokers, agents, and even employees and former customers, at any one time we were not running one giant marketing enterprise but, in fact, hundreds of smaller ones, all synchronized in a ballet of profit. In our business, for example, there was no such thing as "junk mail," only mail that is the wrong offer sent to the wrong person at the wrong time; our job was to send the right offer to the right person at the right time. This is the essence of great Direct Marketing, and most of what I did there.

Countrywide was a powerful, aspirational brand. Like a delicate flower, this required careful and thoughtful nurturing and handling. At its height, Countrywide proudly proclaimed, and most of its employees felt, including me, that we were doing something most noble and important for America. We were helping all Americans achieve the dream of homeownership. What could be more wonderful than that?

And during the great housing boom, for which Countrywide was in fact partly responsible, the firm began to enjoy iconic status through the use of certain images that appeared to perfectly encapsulate what we felt about what we were doing. In many brochures and other marketing materials, we would frequently use a powerful image of a beautiful curbside home, typically a colonial or Cape Cod style, against a deeply rich dark blue sky, and inevitably there it was—the charming, white picket fence.

Resonating as a financial colossus with the welcoming charm of a small-town Wal-Mart greeter, Countrywide was designed to be, and was seen as, a personality of a wonderful, helpful neighbor—an advocate—who you wanted in your financial corner, who you wanted to live next door to and borrow sugar from, who you liked chatting with at the post office—who you *trusted*.

Throughout my agency career I came to understand and revere the awesome power of the aspirational brand. A power never to be underestimated in its ability to break through the clutter of millions of other messages, these were brands that enticed you with images of things you could have, things you could be, things you could aspire to: lives that were better, safer, healthier, happier, younger.

And in America, there have been fewer aspirations more powerful, more central, than becoming a homeowner. From the earliest days, land meant wealth, power, status, and privilege. From the new America that was founded by wealthy landowners, to the pioneering courage of western settlers and beneficiaries of the Homestead Act of 1862, even a modest homestead meant you were an upstanding member of the community, of society, worthy of the responsibility and *privilege* of home ownership. And if the home incurred a debt, only those worthy of such trust would be allowed to assume such a debt. But if your credit was good, if your word was your bond, and if the entire community knew it, you were trusted to pay back that debt, in good faith.

AS THE GREAT auditorium began to empty out, I began flipping through the pile of Countrywide materials Bob had given me to help me get up to speed on the Countrywide brand and messaging. Within this pile was a curious brochure titled *The American Dream of Homeownership: From Cliché to Mission.* It was part of a speech that Angelo eloquently gave in February 2003 in Washington, D.C., on behalf of the Joint Center for Housing Studies at Harvard University and sponsored by the National Housing Endowment.

Partially written by the PR group, I assumed, it was a passionate and compelling expression of the mission of Countrywide's and Angelo's beliefs, focused on bringing the dream especially to the underprivileged in our country, through access and opportunity in the mortgage and housing systems.

On one of the pages of the brochure there was a beautiful shot of Americana to accentuate the theme of the piece: a large American flag hung vertically on what appeared to be a farmhouse. The picture was shot upward, so that the deep, rich blue sky was the majestic backdrop.

Well, you can take the boy out of the Air Force, but you can't take the Air Force out of the boy—I immediately saw that in the picture, the flag was hung improperly. It showed the vertically hung flag with the blue area (the "union") on the *right*, when I knew that the blue area was supposed to be hung on the *left*. Perhaps I may have been the only Countrywide marketing person to ever have served in any way, I didn't know, but I turned to Bob as the all-day meeting ended and pointed out the error to him. Perhaps being slightly obnoxious on my first day, I told him that especially for a Washington, D.C., appearance, I wondered if anyone had checked for such errors and for proper imaging of the flag. It would not be the last time that my patriotic programming would conflict with the culture of Countrywide.

"Are you sure?" he asked. "That speech already occurred back in February, and I didn't hear about anyone else noticing that, so don't worry about it."

"Well, don't tell anyone then," I responded, perhaps with unintentional foreshadowing, "because I think that to show the union blue on the *right* usually signals...*distress*."

So ended my first day at Countrywide—with an omen of future distress.

IN NOVEMBER 2007, Sally Ridgeway, 44, tried to kill herself because Countrywide had decided it was going to take her home.

She and her disabled husband, Steve, had fallen behind on their mortgage payments because Steve's medical bills were consuming almost all of their income. She reported to me that she had done some research and believed that in Colorado there was a law that allowed life insurance policies to pay out for suicides if the policyholder had held the policy for a certain number of years. With her death, she believed that her ailing husband would be able to afford payments on the house, pay for his medicine, and be able to live an unburdened life. But the pills didn't work, and she survived, she said with pangs of desperate regret in her shaking voice.

Sally had rented for most of her life, until her first marriage. Her husband owned that house, and after their divorce she rented again.

In 2005 she met her second husband, Steve, who had been injured in a construction accident in 1999. Eager to give both herself and her husband the pride of homeownership, Sally told me, she "got caught up in the frenzy" of the home-buying boom and decided to buy a two-bedroom condo in 2005 in Lakewood, Colorado.

The Ridgeways' condo would sell for $118,500; they qualified for a $120,000 loan. They had been married recently and spent their honeymoon moving into their new home. Their first loan ironically came through a broker named American Dream Mortgage.

They got the loan based solely on Sally's income, which then was about $2,200 in net take-home pay every month. Her credit was poor (although she did not know what her FICO score was), so she qualified for a Subprime, two-year Adjustable Rate Mortgage at the high rate of 8.50%. This made her monthly payments for those first two years $821 per month—a manageable sum, about a third of her net monthly income.

Sally worked in construction, so work was not steady. And when Steve was injured on the job, he was not part of a union, nor did he have health insurance, so his injury and recovery since then has been through the state's workers' compensation system. During the two years of their steady $821 monthly mortgage payments, Steve's medical and drug costs rose, but they still were able to make their mortgage payments.

Then in June 2007 the loan finally readjusted, as they knew it would. The letter from Countrywide, which had been servicing their mortgage since 2006, alerted them that their readjusted mortgage payment would now be $1,240, a 51% increase. They could not afford this new amount. Over the next year the amount would readjust again twice, slightly downward, but they still could not afford the new amount of $1,040 in June 2008. That year they started falling behind on their payments.

Sally had first reached out to Countrywide because "their website told me that they wanted to work with distressed homeowners to find solutions." Instead she sent letter after letter, being transferred from department to department, then having to resend document after document. Even with some guidance and support from the Colorado Foreclosure Hotline service, nothing was happening. Finally, after a few months she got word that her case had been sent to the foreclosure department, and the process had begun. That was when she decided she was better off dead. But the pills didn't work.

With foreclosure soon to be upon her, I asked Sally what she would do then. She replied that she had no idea, as her history of bankruptcy and foreclosure would have ruined her credit badly enough so that even obtaining an apartment might be difficult. Also, she would not be able to afford the escalating local rents. "I don't know what we'll do then... We may be homeless," she said somberly.

I asked her if she blames anyone.

"I bear partial responsibility, yes," she said.

But she also said she blames a mortgage industry that initially wooed her, then abandoned her when she needed support. Noting that at first she found Countrywide's website comforting and seemingly eager to help, she now curses a system that makes no room for negotiation or compromise. She also blames the government for not regulating the mortgage industry more forcefully, implying that somehow the government should have seen this coming.

"They can bail out Bear Stearns but not regular Americans?" she asked rhetorically. "We don't want a handout, just a way out of this hard time."

Like all my interview subjects, I asked her what she would say to the new president if he were reading her story. What should he do for the future?

"Get rid of all Adjustable Rate Loans," she said as she began to cry.

5

A Corporate Dream Factory

Let us all be happy and live within our means,
even if we have to borrow the money to do it with.
—Artemus Ward, American humorist

JULY 2003

Prime rate: 4.00%

Foreclosure rate: 1.24%

CFC stock price: ~$17.00

D URING THE NEXT few weeks I discovered just how far and wide Countrywide reached, with thousands of employees and specialties far beyond the cloister of Corporate Marketing. There was a massive loan servicing operation, processing payments and services every day for our multimillion customer count. There was a large legal group; a sprawling real-estate management area, which handled all the office buildings and people space; human resources; loan underwriting; and numerous other departments that kept the entire machine running.

One curious reality of the Countrywide universe was that the company was so vast, and its tentacles so far and wide, that many of these folks worked miles away from each other. It was like a small government unto itself, it was so big, and yet it had no single Microsoft or

Lucas-like massive, centralized campus. Yes, there was a headquarters building in Calabasas, but the true reach of the enterprise had long ago outgrown its confines. At its height Countrywide was said to have leased and/or owned more than 50 different buildings and parts of buildings across the entire Southern California region, including Woodland Hills, Thousand Oaks, Westlake, and many other local cities. That did not even include the call centers and other administrative offices in Plano, Texas (ironically on a street called Legacy Drive), nor the local service branches for the Bank or Home Loan divisions, which spanned the entire country. And their hubs, whether 30 to 50 miles north of Los Angeles or in Texas, were always, always hot, and I don't mean warm—I mean like Phoenix-Vegas-Sierra Leone hot. Maybe the rent was cheaper because in the summer it would hit 110 degrees outside, but it motivated us to stay indoors and keep working to sell loans.

Within my area, managing the website and generating new visits and applications through it constituted more than a full-time job. Like most of us, my typical days lasted 10 hours or more, not including my one-hour commute each way. It was grueling fun.

When I came on board I was assigned only one midlevel staff member, a smiling, bubbly woman named Sue Laski. She was an energetic woman who had been on Bob's team for more than a year by then. With a glint in her eye she would help me handle the needs of our online search efforts, the site, online media, and anything else I asked her to focus on. Our relationship quickly became productive and cordial, and she was especially helpful in acclimating me to the processes and procedures of such a large organization.

My first stumble was solely based on my urgent desire to impress Bob and validate his confidence in me. The website had not been redesigned (or "refreshed," in the online marketing vernacular) for at least a year, and like a newly elected official zealous to make a difference within the "first hundred days," I was eager to lead this most visible charge within the first weeks of my tenure, boldly and ferociously. But

I would quickly learn that at Countrywide, with its long-standing and entrenched bureaucracy and culture, nothing happened ferociously or quickly.

Refreshing a website with so many business units as constituents is like chasing chickens. They all know where they want to go (only in the self-interested direction of their own bonuses), and don't care where you want them to go. The portal was the front door to the chicken coop that housed the Home Loans, Bank, Insurance, and Securities websites, and as the new SVP of Online Marketing, I would need to keep all those chickens from running off in all different directions.

With Bob's oversight, I set out to improve the website. "Improvement" would be defined both qualitatively and quantitatively. The quantity goals were easy to articulate, with a charter to increase the conversion to application rate (from site visit to click-through to completed loan or bank product application), lower the site Drop-off rate (the rate at which site visitors would drop off, or exit the site in the first few seconds of coming there without doing anything), and a host of other trackable actions that could use improvement.

More subtle were the qualitative aspects of any new site refresh; the "look" of the site, the placement of key elements, the speed and ease of use that the backroom technology provided, and every conceivable detail, right down to the exact size, color, and words on any "Click Here" buttons.

I used the site redesign project as the reason for me to make the rounds and set time for meet and greets and lunches with all the key players: Ed McCoy, from the Loan Production group and with whom I had interviewed, who welcomed me nicely; Peter Blume, the then–Chief Marketing Officer of Countrywide Bank, who quickly reminded me with his angry finger pointed in my face at lunch that he "didn't want any of Andy's staff to tell the Bank what to do"; Seth Steinberg, the friendly and smart team player who ran Countrywide Insurance Services; and of course, Wonderboy in the Portfolio Communications group, who was so respected that Loan Servicing anointed him to be their ambassador to this impromptu site redesign committee that I was creating.

Although I was technically in charge of marketing for the site, I did not handle any customer communications, including the site experience after a customer logged in with his or her private password. I focused on the generation of new customers to the site; once they became customers I handed them off to Wonderboy's group. Truth was, I was glad to leave that to him. My plate was completely full, and he was exceedingly capable of caring for, and upselling, cross-selling, and reselling those customers additional products online and via mail.

I approached the site redesign in what I thought was a thoughtful, analytical way that I had learned at agencies, and how I had seen many clients do it. We pored through traffic data and identified areas for improvement and spots of heightened drop-offs. We asked customers through online surveys what they wanted more of or less of in the site. We studied the "best practices" of the competing sites, looking for patterns we could emulate, from Wells, Bank of America, DiTech, and at least 20 others. When we presented our recommended site changes to the committee, we would need to have airtight rationales for each and every one that would need to stand up to rigorous cross-examination of how and why it would lead to more profits. Nothing was done whimsically at Countrywide, and this was an element of their smart culture that I took to quickly.

With all of the research completed, we set to work with the online agency to begin conceptualizing new designs for the site—some radical, some subtle. Having presented hundreds of new creative ideas in my agency life, I always showed up with a few wild ones—always give the decision makers something radical to kill, as it typically elevates the surviving concepts.

Site design is a Rube Goldbergesque puzzle of creative elements, technological constraints, resource challenges, and time, all of which must fit together. For example, at one time we wanted to move the Login area for customers from one side of the site to the other—where most competitors had theirs (they must have had data showing this was more conducive to flow-through)—but our technology design would have required a total upheaval of computer systems at all the other divisions to make that simple change. So our Login stayed where it was.

The online agency was directed to explore not only new designs but also to show them in what are called *wireframes*, which are essentially blueprint-like box layouts of the proposed site designs using simple shapes. Wireframes are to online site design what sketches are to cartoons. This allows us to check all the technological and other "is this realistic?" constraints before investing in creative progression. Sometimes this can lead to simple yet powerful changes.

One in particular, which would have a far-reaching positive impact, was to raise some on-site tools "above the fold." An old newspaper term, it refers to making sure that the most important or customer-preferred tools and information appeared in the top half of the screen (like a newspaper's front page), which appeared first when the site loaded (when you scrolled down, that was equivalent to being "below the fold," as if you turned over your newspaper's front page). Research showed that many people were more likely to apply for a loan after they used certain online research tools that were helpful in informing their decision.

Once the wireframing process was completed, we set out to create a series of optional design overhauls as well as minor tweaks to the existing site, and worked for weeks to prepare the presentation to the committee. Using the great power of Outlook's Meeting Invite, I then pushed the Send button and exerted some leadership. The Invite for Corporate Marketing's presentation of New Site Design Recommendations would be the first big meeting Invite to go out from my desk as I began to solidify my sea legs in this new role.

It was a disaster.

My first big meeting fell somewhere between a prison riot and a public flogging; what started out as a cordial review of our recommendations devolved into chaos and contention.

"Why is Insurance the last to be listed?" Seth asked, predictably only concerned with his Insurance business.

"Did you know that our Bank is the twelfth largest in the United States? Why aren't we first up top?" barked the CMO of the Bank.

Everybody chimed in. Ed, from the Loans division, simply "didn't like it." *Great, that's helpful, Ed, a real productive comment.*

Spanky chimed in and argued that the Subprime message should be "front and center," suggesting that even though this was the *Countrywide* website, it should shout loudly up top, *Full Spectrum Lending.*

"But that would confuse the millions of people who come to this site for Prime loans, seeking Countrywide," I responded.

"No, it won't," he stated decisively.

Then with the large rejections out of the way, they all jumped into the subjective nitty-gritty.

"Why is that button blue?"

"What about showing a video?"

"I think Angelo should be on here talking."

"Are we having lunch brought in?"

They all talked over one another as I slowly slunk back silently into my chair. I wanted to crawl under the table. I even thought about trying to wave my hand and use Jedi mind tricks. *These are the web changes you have been looking for…* Nope. Didn't work. They kept bickering and yapping. I wasn't a corporate Jedi, yet. No rationales mattered, only their personal opinions did, and some were not at all trained in marketing backgrounds. But, it was I who serviced *them*, so I had to listen.

I had been too aggressive, too bold in my assumption that I could just waltz into this culture with its politics and its opinions and its personalities and change the world in a day. With rates still near all-time lows, Countrywide was beginning to crank out more applications than it could handle. Housing values were just beginning their stratospheric rise, and Refis were flowing through cubicled hallways paved with gold. Who was I to suggest changing anything that might upset this spigot? Maybe I was too cocky. Maybe I should not have worn cuff links.

Yes, cuff links. Since starting at Countrywide, I tended to "overshoot the runway" on attire. I wanted to be known as a professional, a client now, no longer an agency flip-flops cliché. I always wore a tie. And many days, I would wear crisply starched shirts with French cuffs, and accompanying cuff links to clink on the conference tables as I presented some critical marketing data. I wanted to be taken seriously, and during my New York training, I saw that dressing the part could make the difference.

But through this experience I would slowly learn that when in Rome, be mindful of which Romans are supposed to wear cuff links. Like eagles, stars, or stripes on military uniforms, there is also a subtle rank system in the uniforms of corporate America. Depending on the culture of the firm, these can be unspoken yet critically important to heed, lest ye be judged as being *too big for thy britches*.

I came to learn anecdotally later that some folks at the site redesign meeting thought my wearing cuff links at Countrywide was pretentious. Even as a senior officer of a Fortune 100, rank is relative. Apparently no one copied me on the memo that only Executive VPs and their bosses, Managing Directors, were *qualified* to wear them. After a few more weeks of childish Alex P. Keaton–esque bravado and continued cuff linkery just to protest (and demonstrating extra loud clanking on conference tables for good measure), I quietly retired my little badges of self-aggrandizing—my silver knots, my round opals, my tiny Mickey Mouses—to the depths of my sock drawer and slunk back into buttonland.

Likewise, my grand proposal for a newly redesigned Countrywide website was quietly shelved. We had agreed to some simple, obvious tweaks to maximize application rates and some other small things, but under Bob's shrewd political guidance, he recommended and I agreed that this could wait until my tenure at the firm was more established with smaller, highly visible "base hits" in the online space before I would swing wildly and reach again for a grand-slam homer. After some time I would use some newfound clout and stronger internal relationships to lobby for broader site changes, would do a better job of preselling the changes before the meeting (best to make them think *they thought of*, and partly own, these changes, as opposed to appearing to dictate the changes *to them*), and, of course, would quietly not wear cuff links.

I would, however, continue to speak my mind and, I think, show guts when needed. A case in point was the high-profile Internet Committee on which I sat. Like the sprawling efforts of a government, Countrywide was so huge that it was sprinkled with hundreds of large and small committee structures, each assigned specific tactical tasks or strategic oversight. The Internet Committee was comprised of me, the online people at Full Spectrum Lending (including Spanky), my argumentative website management counterpart in Home Loans, Denise, and a myriad of other technologists and analysts.

Meetings were held quarterly, and it could be a nerve-racking experience—not for the subject matter, in which we all felt fluent—but because every 12 weeks or so we would need to present our progress to the head of the committee, Dave Sambol, the head of all loan production. Dave was a quantitative wunderkind and "king of the finance jocks" who led Countrywide up through the boom and eventual bust. (At the end of May 2008, Sambol would quietly leave Countrywide, which was now owned by the new power at Bank of America. The press would report that he would walk away with millions.)

As we on the Internet Committee presented our quarterly results and business plan to Sambol, it provided me with an opportunity to study him. The first, most visible trait, which I believe was both a blessing and a curse, was how young he looked. I was not sure of his true age, but he looked no more than 35 years old, which was a powerful contrast to the elder-statesman image of Angelo, or even the COO, Stan Kurland, who, in his fifties, had your standard-issue face lines that could only be earned through years of weathering experience and survival through many storms.

Sambol's youthful face, combined with his slim frame, clearly brilliant mathematical mind, and smooth, confident presentation skills in public forums implied that he might eventually be the heir apparent to this empire, if anything ever happened to Stan (who left the company in 2006).

People were intimidated by Sambol's obvious intellectual power, his even greater political power, and these realities motivated all of us to make sure that we provided him the respect and, frankly, subtle fear that he deserved.

And unlike most other senior executives I had known at Countrywide and throughout my marketing career, he had a unique ability to ask questions that were at once important, pedantic, and brilliant, and seemingly out of left field. It was common knowledge that if you were presenting to Sambol, you had better have your shit together, or he might grill you—in front of everyone in the meeting. Exposing stupidity or sloppiness of an overvalued team member was considered sport by some at Countrywide, although no one ever said it. However, I must give this cultural trait some credit; it did push everyone, every day, to study harder, be more diligent, more buttoned up, and more driven to show our own value every day, as if every day was our final interview. Nothing wakes up a class faster than the threat of daily exams.

I can recall seeing others present to Sambol, taking turns one by one walking the plank of scrutiny and cross-examination. But the diversity of his questioning was truly amazing, and he was right to ask the questions he did. It was his job to make sure the company was running right. Someone once told me, *"Always assume that everyone is stupid, and nobody cares, and you'll be all right.*" From my point of view, Sambol seemed to live this credo as well.

As the nervous midlevel manager might be stuttering through page 12 of his financial report, or nervously showing the new web site designs for testing, Sambol would sometimes keep his eyes down, studying the document, as if the presenter were not necessary. This, too, reminded me of my agency days, when I would present to Japanese clients. Frequently they would listen with their heads bowed and their eyes closed, making it appear as though they were sleeping. Then at the end they would seem to wake up and ask a very specific question about slide number 84, paragraph three, item six.

And, of course, as was the case in every single Countrywide meeting, out came the Hewlett-Packard engineering calculator. Or, even better, Texas Instruments. Like calculating light sabers whipped out from the belts of financial jedis, those little ubiquitous supercomputers would slide quietly out of their little black leather–holstered sheaths, where Sambol and usually every manager in the room would start calculating and recalculating the numbers they were being presented. Every year proud finance jocks would show off their new X75-DL prototype or whatever the model was, having just arrived from the HP or TI factory. This was a wonderfully dorky and charming part of the "finance jock" culture, where the power of math intersected with the unspoken "gotcha" culture.

But it wasn't just about "gotcha" and weeding out incompetence. Yes, even at Countrywide, it "took a village," via peer review. Actually, it was a way for those of us inside this Countrywide family, those of us who knew the secret handshakes and commonly believed in the great mission we were on together, to do what most great companies do: have our work critiqued by our peers such that a dozen set of eyes review it as well to make sure it is correct.

Done to great effect in medicine, law, science, and, yes, financial services, peer review is critical to making sure that objective confidence is created, mistakes are eliminated, and, because the group has seen it, questioned it, and vetted it, it then has a much greater chance of support and success. For chrissakes, this was people's *money* we were talking about. Money for our customers, money back to our shareholders, budgets we were assigned and seriously responsible for. Every penny had to be identified, and every return needed to be maximized.

Pity the poor manager who attempts something important or who spends real money on his or her own; it will lack the support needed for it to succeed, then it won't succeed, then all will tell you, "I told you it wouldn't succeed." Success, or failure can be a self-fulfilling prophecy. In a peer review culture, make sure any sizable effort is blessed before you launch.

As the frantic clicking of dozens of numbered buttons on the squad of HP calculators created their numerical symphony in thoughtful silence, equally awkward moments of silence would ensue as the perspiring, slightly shaking presenter would pause and, looking at Sambol buried in the data, perhaps panic, that he had *no* questions so far. This could also be bad.

Then, as Sambol slowly looked up at the screen projection, his questions would begin. *Uh-oh, here it comes*, I would think. *Poor bastard better know his stuff, or I may just see this guy cry in this very room.* Note: these are not exact words from the meeting, but I recall it went something like this:

"Steve, walk me through your mathematics for page 12 of this forecast," Sambol might begin benignly.

"Steve" would walk him through the equations, the variables, the regressions, and the calculus, piece by piece, careful not to make a wrong move, lest the buzzer in this tense game of financial Operation would go off. *BBZZZZ!*

"Okay, I see," Sambol would continue. Then would come the first bullet.

"I noticed that one of your numbers is wrong, cell D-37 on page six. Am I calculating it wrong?"

Calculators would all click together again, frantically all checking cell D-37 at once, each jockeying to be the first to call out "Yup, it's wrong," like in some sadistic race.

"Um, I guess there is a mistake in there," the crushed manager would say, crawling back to his chair like a dog that had just been run over by a car. Now all of his data, all of his presentation, were suspect. Just like that, his value was diminished, and more so, the notion that perhaps his value to the firm was *negative* may have been placed into everyone's mind.

At Countrywide I was drilled and trained—and compelled actually—to always be buttoned up to perfection. With a precision and a professionalism I had not seen since the Air Force, the mechanisms of Countrywide processes, procedures, checking and rechecking, and attention to perfect, verifiable detail had to be on a par with or exceeding that of NASA. I loved it. And although I, too, could make a mistake, like anyone, I also had no patience, ever, for consistent sloppiness, laziness, or people who didn't have their material memorized and perfected, and weren't fluent in it. This was where my style and Countrywide's culture aligned perfectly. I was constantly proud of the culture of perfection that surrounded me, for what we were doing was important, large, and meaningful. *Don't screw it up.*

But occasionally Sambol would throw a holistic question out there that would truly impress me. Remember, in my agency life I had presented complicated, strategic, creative, and analytical ideas to dozens of CEOs and their skeptical sycophants who surrounded them. I had heard every question from them, smart ones, dumb ones, scary ones, lame ones, even ones that demonstrated that they weren't listening. But besides his uncanny ability to find the one numerical mistake in one cell in one spreadsheet in a binder comprised of 347 pages, sometimes Sambol would transcend all that, and bring us all back to why we were there.

"Okay, Steve, these numbers, *while partially incorrect*, are still compelling. But more importantly, why are we doing this at all?" Sambol asked, seemingly out of nowhere.

[Awkward pause.]

Sambol looked around the room at mouths agape, and seemed incredulous that no one understood the question, or was afraid to answer. "C'mon, guys—how will this effort help our customers achieve the dream of homeownership and directly accomplish our mission?" he said, obviously becoming frustrated, as if he knew the answer himself, but wanted to test the group to see if they would get it right.

It's an odd sensation to hear 12 supercalculators suddenly stop calculating.

A few managers would look at him as if they really didn't understand the question, or, of course, were scared that it might be some sort of trick question. Some of the finance guys would revert to their comfort zones and start talking about standard deviations and the "green" levels of projections and so forth.

Sambol put his hand up, shook his head, and asked again, "No, guys, you're not getting it. Never mind the numbers. *Why* are we doing this? Who can tell me?"

This would be one of those moments when I would be glad not to be part of the clique of finance jocks. I decided to go for it.

"Because this will make us easier to do business with," I said, timidly. "Customers will get into their loans easier, faster, and more comfortably." I paused. Sambol nodded a little.

Having spoken up, I was half convinced I would be fired on the spot when he noticed I had a lame-ass dime-store Ronco calculator with giant keys like a second grader.

He took it in, paused for a moment, nodded silently, and after a few terrifying seconds where my career perhaps hung by a thread, finally said, "Good answer."

He concluded, turning to the now-petrified presenter, and said, "Fix these numbers and let me see this again next week, correct this time."

The meeting adjourned. When Sambol exited I could see a few of the attendees exhale visibly, as if they had been holding their breath the entire time. We would all live to fight another day.

Except the nervous guy with the wrong numbers. He disappeared after that meeting. I never found out what happened to him.

That was the last time I was in a meeting with David Sambol, and the awe I developed watching him grill us in that meeting has stayed with me to this day. He believed in what he was doing, what we all were doing. He demanded perfection, diligence, stewardship, and smarts, and he got it. I respected his unique ability to analyze the smallest microscopic quantitative detail, every assumption, and then immediately jump to the macro esoteric *meaning* of and *reasons* for what we may have been doing on his watch. From that day on, as I was so impressed by him, a little part of my own style is based on what I witnessed that day.

Hailed as a wunderkind quantitative genius who helped steer the ship during the boom (some ballsy internal players even gave him a whispered nickname, *Doogie Howser*), he also was vilified by some who suffered losses from the bust. Yes, he was part of the machine, but I believe that may not be fair. Exactly how personally responsible for the boom he was is, of course, arguable, and yet I do know the ambitious pride we all felt that day when he proclaimed to us that our mission, our strategic goal for America, was to ensure a "Loan for Every Customer," so that every American would have the ability to realize the dream of homeownership. Like Angelo Mozilo himself, I think he truly believed in what we were doing. I did too.

THAT AUTUMN OF 2003 I continued to grow more comfortable in my role, and made some good progress toward my goals and Countrywide's online goals as well. With Sue's help and Bob's guidance, we created new Paid Search methodologies, hired some new agency talent, and generally did a better job of seizing the fast-growing opportunities in the Paid Search space. At that time the major players were Yahoo, MSN Search, and a little-known newcomer to the search engine space that we had just begun testing, called Google.

We began testing more online banner placements, where a Countrywide banner would appear on a site with some groovy rate, and then we would watch the number of clicks to discrete, trackable landing pages, then see how many of them would convert to completed loan applications. The banner testing had two major components: one was fully controllable; the other was, well, not.

In placing banner ads in the Wild West of online media, generally speaking you have two basic options: the specific site placement, or the affiliate network. Specific site placement is buying a certain amount of banner space, for X dollars, on a specific site, such as Yahoo, CNN, or whatever suits your fancy (and profits). This ensures that your banner winds up in the proper environment that may be conducive to selling your product (like a bank may buy space in Yahoo Finance, for example).

The affiliate network is a less controllable spiderweb of thousands of sites that all agree to be part of whatever affiliate network you buy on, where you throw your banners into the pot and pay for whatever spaces or clicks you get, sometimes randomly. The downside of the affiliate networks is the frightening loss of control in some cases, but this can be balanced by incredibly cheap deals. The nightmare scenario, especially for a respected brand, is that your banner ad for that Disneyland vacation randomly goes through the affiliate tentacles and somehow winds up on a website for something inappropriate, such as alcohol, gambling, or, *gawd fawbid*, porn.

Like all businesses, there are great affiliate networks that have solved this problem, and there are other, cheaper ones that are a bigger gamble. But you pay more for this better affiliate quality, and I made sure that whatever testing we did on any affiliate, we had the rep print out a total list of all the sites in its network (sometimes in the thousands), and Sue and I would go through and mark out any sites that we judged Countrywide couldn't be on—ever. We would insist in writing that we would be assured, through severe financial penalty to the network if necessary, that Countrywide would never wind up on any of those sites.

But sometimes even the most exact placements on the most respected sites caused embarrassing problems as Countrywide online advertising evolved with the still evolving world of the web. Yahoo especially, with its endless tentacles and site pages, would accidentally cause one very serious situation two years later, in 2005.

One day our call center received a complaint from a customer that they had seen a Countrywide banner ad appear within a Yahoo chat room that featured *child porn. WHAT??!!* was the general reaction internally and swiftly. Back then, Yahoo, like many sites, allowed so-called "user-generated content" within chat rooms. This meant that anyone could designate and open any new chat room about any subject, including some shocking and disturbing themes such as child porn and other unmentionables. Like many other online portals at the time, I suppose Yahoo also felt that the need for free-dom of speech on the web outweighed their moral authority to censor it. When a new chat room was created, Yahoo also would serve up a few banner ads to pay for this free service. Well, apparently something was up, because then we received another call. And another. Then hundreds. Within two hours I had called for an all-hands-on-deck conference call immediately with our Yahoo media representative and all of the business unit leaders who depended on online media, as well as Suzie, our head of Public Relations; we would need her on this one.

At first it seemed odd that we received so many calls on one day; something specific must have happened in medialand. I found it very unlikely that all of the nation's pedophiles decided to rise up one day, identify themselves as going on these chat rooms, and then decided to all call one of their advertisers in protest. No; it was something else.

Ironically, a quick web search identified the source of this PR brush fire that morning. An enterprising reporter at Houston station KPRC had done an investigative story for their newscast about these user-generated chat rooms, using Yahoo as an example. When the camera took footage of how easy it was for the reporter to see these shocking chat room topics, such as "Girls Twelve and Under for Older Guys," there was one of our Countrywide web banners front and center. *Jeezus.* Other ads were shown as well, from other venerable, wholesome family brands. *A PR nightmare come true.*

Of course, to add to my stress of the day, the first question from the business units was, *"Adam, why did you put our ads on there?"* Good question. Truth was, I didn't. The Yahoo buy was a large one, consisting of specific placements as well as promises to run the ad through the thousands of other pages as appropriate. But Yahoo was a good, professional partner. Although I can't recall specifically, there most likely was standard language in the Yahoo contract to ensure that our ads would not wind up on any questionable or inappropriate areas of the site. Apparently this didn't happen.

As we all huddled on the conference call, tensions were high. The Yahoo representative apologized profusely and offered to give us free media credits. But Suzie pushed harder. "What is Yahoo's policy on allowing these chat rooms at all?" she asked. I added, "Yes, frankly, with this kind of offering and lack of quality control, Countrywide may consider purging Yahoo from our media buys altogether." Now remember, Countrywide spent a lot of money on Yahoo, so this woke her up.

The only funny aspect to this story, if there was one, was to sit on that call that day and listen to eight senior corporate executives, in my opinion, all make believe that they had no idea what a chat room was.

There seemed to me to be an extra need for them to distance them-selves so far from the seediness of the issue that it became a real eye-roller when one of them asked Yahoo, "Can you please explain to us exactly what a chat room *is?*" It was the equivalent of a meeting about a porno magazine and having the senior officials look quizzically and ask dumbly, "Hmm, er, what's a magazine? Never heard of it."

As it turns out, this call would become a historic turning point in the Wild West of the web. The story was so far-reaching, and the nation-wide response so angry, and the advertisers' response so repulsed, that Yahoo decided to pull the plug forever on any user-generated chat rooms and Countrywide was partly responsible. To this day, you can-not go on Yahoo and create your own chat room to share pictures of frogs in lingerie smoking cigarettes.

THOUGH LIKE MANY other accidental stumbles along the way, none of it mattered during the heyday of the amazing Refi boom under way that fall of 2003 to the spring of 2004. It was the Roaring Twenties all over again. Both the Prime Rate and the 10-Year Treasury Note—both of which affected various loan rates—hit new lows, fueling the mad rush to refinance what seemed like every home in America. Calls for Refi applications were coming in faster than we could process them, and home values were rising, creating higher appraisals for even higher cash-out possibilities on the homes during the Refi process.

Things had never been better; for Countrywide, for homeowners, for America, for me. We were fulfilling dreams every day; dreams of homeownership, of paying off debt, of sending Junior to college, of new cars or that long-awaited vacation. We were a corporate dream factory like no other, facilitating the fulfillment of life, liberty, and the pursuit of happiness, through money.

Countrywide, just like all public companies, and I, as a senior officer in that public company, had only one reason for existence: to return maximum value to shareholders as fast and as much as possible through the products and/or services we sold. The assumption was that we would do just that, and also as a public company, we would do this within ethical and legal frameworks to do *what was right*.

But in the frothy frenzy of that Refi boom, we felt we were doing what was more right than anything else in business—helping more and more people achieve the American Dream by lending them money to do so. When the boom ended, and the mortgage and housing crisis became acute in the summer of 2007, suddenly calls were made for the heads of financial services firms to be placed on rusty spikes. The "evil corporations" had once again duped America and caused this mess. *Let's kill this horrible animal—this hunter of customers, this gatherer of revenue—because it bit us.*

Why should we euthanize financial services corporations for simply enabling us to get *ourselves* into this mess? True, one can never speak to every single action at every single company—and there were some predatory lending practices and mortgage fraud perpetrated during the boom, to be sure (although I never saw any evidence of that at Countrywide)—but that is no reason to convict the entire *system*. *[Insert overused "Don't throw out the baby with the bathwater" idiom here.]*

Context is a powerful force. The context that this book is providing—*What were we thinking?*—will hopefully help future generations avoid the same mistakes. And the context of the actual data inside the mess is critical as well. Yes, the foreclosure rate at the time of this writing is more than 2%, a new all-time high in America. This is bad. However, this also means that 98 percent of all mortgage holders are working hard every day to pay their monthly bill and keep the promises they made to pay back that debt in good faith to the financial institution that lent them that money based on their word.

Financial services companies loan money to credible people for appropriate fees and a reasonable return on that investment; this is what they were created to do. Like we do with tigers, we should and do confine corporations seeking profit into controlled environments (regulations and laws) so they can be themselves yet not hurt us. Unless of course, we decide not to listen to the rules of engagement, and stick our arms into that cage. Then we will get bitten. So let's not shoot them if they bite.

But that fall and winter of 2003–2004, we could do no wrong. I wish I could take credit for the extraordinary growth of Countrywide loan production, but frankly, this was primarily driven by the unbelievably low rates being offered by the financial system. As our site traffic grew, applications soared, and my internal relationships and reputation blossomed, Bob began to become more hands-off, requiring fewer and fewer status meetings and less and less micromanaging. This trust he showed in my abilities just made me want to do a better job, for me, for him, for Countrywide.

I used this time to take slightly greater risks within my own area, such as investing in new Search keyword tests, new minor tweaks to the Countrywide website to enhance efficiency or application rates, and new online media banner placements (like sifting for gold, online banner testing is a never-ending search for newly profitable placements, creatives, and offers across hundreds of appropriate sites). Of course, I did not do any of this in a vacuum, and much of it was done in handicapped situations.

Sue, my intrepid middle manager, was becoming a challenge. Often sick, she would call in at midday, after we would spend the morning wondering where she was. When she would take vacations, like clockwork she would call in on the day she was due back and provide some story about how the plane was broken and she was stranded in her island paradise, or some other such drama. This escalated over time, getting to the point where HRs needed to be consulted.

Being a manager in a Fortune 100 required a keen understanding of the rights of the employee, of the firm, and of the rules regarding private matters. For example, I could ask her when she would return, but I was not allowed to directly ask her what her ailment was. Now normally up to that point, with any team member I had ever managed, I honestly didn't care about how often they were in the office as long as things were getting done. But with Sue, she would simply disappear for days, even weeks at a time, and nothing was getting done, even though she promised that "nothing would drop." It was becoming embarrassing to me when a senior business unit manager would ask me why he had never received a critical call back from Sue.

I was incredulous at this point. The two possible scenarios in my mind were equally disturbing. Either she was a liar of some kind, who somehow got off on the sympathy of the illness when she would return, or, there was some other health or behavior issue that was so serious, she did not even feel she could share it with the company. If she had, I am sure Countrywide would have offered to help her, somehow.

Human Resources jumped in, advising me not to question her motives, her reasons, or her stories, but to simply begin keeping a log of any and all duties that were not being fulfilled by her. This was terribly disappointing, and it killed me to have to do it, as I had built what I thought was a trusting relationship with Sue. But I had either misjudged that trust, or she was taking advantage of it.

After weeks of HR warnings to Sue, even more absences, pleading by me for more conscientious, professional behavior on her part, and a meticulous log showing all of her behavior on paper, Sue was quietly let go from Countrywide. We never discovered what the real issues were with her.

Sue wasn't my only problem. While most of my working relationships with my internal clients at the business units were profitable, professional, cordial, and fun, there's always one to ruin the curve. Denise Lewis had been a pain in my ass from the very first day I interviewed with her before I came on board. Male or female, every company has a Denise. To me she seemed arrogant, distrustful, and just generally annoying, but I had to work with her. I, in Corporate Marketing, supported the needs and goals of her Loan Division just like I did for Bank and Insurance. But I felt like Denise never believed in the value Corporate Marketing provided, and she acted like she thought that she was the only one who knew the web, knew marketing, and knew what customers wanted. She had never managed agency services before, so she had no framework of experience to call upon to motivate agency partners to do the best work for us.

I can recall one time in particular that was seared on my memory. An outside online agency, hired by me, was presenting concepts to us via conference call for some new creative online banner ideas. The concepts were bold and interesting. But like all creative, judging how "good" it was was a subjective exercise. Yet unquestionably, all the concepts were "very Countrywide."

Whether talking about creative, culture, or people, it was generally known that Countrywide had its own way about it; a mythology directly derivative of its powerful brand and of Angelo. A candidate for a job at Countrywide who was wholesome, honest, hardworking, helpful, and friendly would be referred to as "very Countrywide." A call center representative who went the extra mile; a branch manager who always had a smile—such were the stuff of Countrywide. We were Wal-Mart. We were Mr. Rogers. We were hot dogs, apple pie, and Chevrolet—Countrywide was the best of America. And the concepts we reviewed that day all were inviting, warm, and friendly, complete with white-picket-fenced images touting the beauty of the American Dream.

In cases like this that involved the subjectivity of creative, I would call upon my Direct Marketing background and, maximizing the power of the web, try to pick just two or three concepts to *test*. By rotating two or three banner concepts into the same media buy space, within one day I could clearly see which banner would be generating the greatest number of clicks, or responses. When in doubt of subjective creative choices, always let the marketplace—your customers— tell you which one will be most profitable via their response behavior.

Only a fool or an inexperienced marketer makes sweeping projections about the future success or failure of any concept without discrete testing or at least some kind of data to back up that assertion.

"These suck," Denise spouted on the conference call as the *agency folks listened*.

"What do you mean, 'These suck,' Denise?" I snapped.

"They just suck. How much did we pay for this crap?"

"Don't worry about agency fees, Denise. These costs were planned and are well within the creative budgets that *Corporate* manages," I scolded.

There was an awkward silence on the agency side of the call as they listened to us argue in front of them about the work they had just presented. My professional and military programming had taught me never to argue with another officer in front of enlisted folks. And this agency had been enlisted to help us generate powerful banner creative. This fight looked bad, very bad.

"Denise, why don't we take this discussion offline? That way I can get a better sense of what your concerns are?" I asked, so as to end this embarrassing call quickly.

At that point Denise went into a tirade while the others were still on the call, chastising the agency and generally saying everything she should not have. Although I pushed all of the agencies hard during my tenure there, partly because I, too, shared an agency heritage and partly because I wanted to motivate them to do great work for us, I always tried to be fair, cordial, understanding, and appreciative of the services and hard work they were providing. I also knew how the agency gossip network worked. Once a client was flagged as being irresponsible, abusive, or otherwise impossible to work for, that company ran the risk of agencies no longer offering their services. Now Denise had potentially put Countrywide in that position due to her outrageous behavior. Like any poorly behaved toddler, it was time that Denise got a *time-out*.

I was enraged by this nutjob. As she ranted I emailed the agency person who I knew was online with a simple header: "Hang up on her." They did, which just infuriated her more. Then I did, too. For the next few weeks, partly through childish rage, partly because I could, I completely shut down any contact with Denise. This was unheard of, as Denise was supposed to be my main internal client, the one I serviced the most with Corporate's online marketing engine. But I had had enough. This was not the first time she had behaved outrageously.

A few weeks passed, and I heard through the grapevine that Denise's anger had turned into concern as I continued to ignore her completely. Her alienation of her critically needed partners in Corporate could drastically affect her success and thereby her bonus. I went out of my way to bring the case, and my reasons for my own behavior, to the attention of Denise's boss, Ed McCoy. The one phrase I said to Ed that changed everything was my comment that during that call, while hearing Denise yell at those agency people, "was the only time I had ever been *embarrassed* to work for Countrywide." In our culture of *being Countrywide*, that's all I had to say.

Finally, a few days later, Denise showed up at my office door, hat in hand, and apologized for her behavior, promised to be a good partner and allow us to use our expertise to manage the creative process. Apparently her boss had spoken to her. It was the first and only time that I had used the power of my relationships and credibility to put someone else in her place at Countrywide. Thereafter, Denise behaved.

FLUSH WITH WHAT seemed like never-ending success and infinite profit, it was shrewdly appropriate for Bob to begin lobbying for some good old-fashioned brand spending, via television. Research had shown that while our brand personality was well regarded by those consumers who had heard of us, it turned out that not many consumers had heard of us at all, relative to our competitors. While we were very visible in California, Texas, and other western states, the data showed that our brand awareness, compared to other top banks, such as Bank of America and Wells Fargo, could be improved. This mortgage boom also would give us the opportunity to "spread the word" about Countrywide and what it meant across the national television airwaves.

Countrywide, although acutely aware of the power of its brand, had not been on television for a long while, simply because the revenues were so good, so the argument went, they didn't need to. They had tried doing some television for Home Equity Loans in the late 1990s, but it did not generate a lift in loan applications great enough to warrant further spending. Like I had seen at many client meetings during my agency career, if a single television campaign or ad didn't magically generate a torrent of new business, the sales guys would simply reach the sweeping, generalized conclusion that "TV doesn't work."

Of course, that depends on your goals, timing, budgets, message, creative, and offer. If your goal is a million new sales by Friday, then yes, it is possible that TV won't do the trick (unless you give away a free house with every loan). But keep in mind that Countrywide, and all financial services companies, were selling a *commodity*: money.

Marketing commodities is especially challenging. Like bottled water or bleach, any lending brand may fall victim to consumers feeling that they are "all the same," and simply go with the cheapest one. This can threaten revenues; just ask Procter & Gamble, fighting for Tide against generic, supermarket-brand detergents; that's where branding comes in.

As mentioned, branding is an ethereal power that must be delicately and deliberately cultivated, driven toward the greatest emotional bond possible with the consumer. If you ever doubt the power of brands, try to explain how we have more than 300 different brands of cars out there; they all get you where you need to go.

When times are good, and many people are buying your product, it is an especially important time to maximize the branding effect. At that time Countrywide was approaching the funding of almost one of every six mortgages in the United States (eventually handling, at its height, one of five mortgages in the United States). With this great reach into so many households, and so many loans being funded, fulfilling the dreams of so many people every single day, the opportunity to demonstrate that value to both new customers and potential customers was great. Those customers who had already been funded by us would be able to feel as if their lender decision was being validated and praised. Prospects would be able to share in the success stories and feel *aspirational* toward them. Wall Street would get all warm and fuzzy about the magic we created in the fabric of America.

After weeks of lobbying, presentations, projections, and generally charming half the company, Bob finally received approval to begin development on the ad campaign that would signify the height of Countrywide's promise, the "Realize Your Dreams" campaign.

"Realize Your Dreams" would not only be the new ad campaign for Countrywide, it also would become the new tagline. I had assisted in the development of many advertising slogans in my career, but for Countrywide, at that exact moment, this line was one of the most perfect I had ever heard. There were endless meetings about this issue, as so many internal constituents would have to agree to it, so there were an equal number of line explorations. But unlike the research necessary for other elements of advertising, I had learned over the years to trust the "punch" of the tagline. If it instinctively *hit me*, then *that* might be the one. It's one of those things you just learn to know. And "Realize Your Dreams" hit me immediately.

It was a strong call to action to prospects, especially "fence-sitters" who had yet to join the craze. It was a message to existing customers to take even more money out of their house to fund other dreams. It was perfect for the army of Human Resources recruiters on the hunt for the 30,000 new positions Countrywide was rapidly trying to fill as the firm expanded to meet increasing demand; it challenged candidates as well—especially great sales people—to "Realize Their

[Career] Dreams." It was short, a great lapel button, a great lunchroom poster. It worked for the Bank, where savings for retirement, or maximizing the existing retirement of the Bank's seniors audience, was paramount. It worked for Wall Street, where starry-eyed investors could realize their investment portfolio dreams as the stock began to soar. It spoke to builders, brokers, and bartenders. It was about homeownership, about Angelo, about America. It was aspirational, inspirational, flexible, and delightfully vague so it could mean different things to different people. It was *It*.

The tagline would be especially poignant for the millions of historically underserved or ethnically diverse prospects for first-time homeownership, which was a core audience for Countrywide. Baked into the ethos of our mission from the start, helping everyone achieve the American Dream meant a special emphasis on "lowering the barriers to homeownership" for African Americans, Latinos, and other minority groups who could face potential challenges within the existing lending system. Countrywide took great pride in the strides it made in reaching out to these audiences and making a difference in their rates of homeownership. I even heard once, proudly mentioned by one of our ethnic marketing specialists, that we had the highest number of Native American customers in the country. Of course, one could also argue that these underserved segments offered the greatest marketshare *growth* opportunity.

And so Countrywide's first television ad campaign in a decade would begin the massive effort to be developed. Bob was at the helm, but, of course, like iron filings to a magnet, nothing motivated everyone to give an opinion more than doing television ads. Bob would listen to hundreds of suggestions, large and small, from every level of the firm, with his intrepid and renowned patience that only he possessed. Watching this campaign develop internally allowed me to observe just how perfect he was for this role; empathic diplomat, shrewd charmer, powerful salesman.

Our longtime ad agency, the Los Angeles firm of Dailey & Associates, had the assignment, and they dove in with their usual gusto. These guys were smart; they knew Countrywide from their years of service on the business, and that alone saved us weeks of having to get any new agency up to speed on what "being Countrywide" meant. And they understood clearly the main message that would need to emerge from this campaign: that Countrywide was the solution to your homebuying challenges, especially first-time buyers or those in special situations.

This television campaign would be a media mix, bought using both "traditional television" media and "direct response"; these are generally the two types of media buying on television (there are others, but I don't want to bore you).

Traditional media are specific placements where you decide that you want your commercial to run on *Friends* at an exact time. You pay for that exactness—a lot, in fact—because you want to reach your exact best audience just as Joey is immersed in his buffoonery. This represents much of prime time TV and the major networks.

But Direct Response TV buying is different. Generally reserved only for those commercials with an 800 number or some other response mechanism, they can be "short form" or "long form" depending on the spot lengths (anywhere from 15 seconds to two minutes or more, even for infomercials). These media buys can be considerably less expensive per spot to place, but you give up the ability to place the spot in an *exact* time spot. Instead, direct buys are bought in what are called "dayparts." With fancy names such as "early prime," that simply means that for your much less expensive cost, you tell the station to run your spot somewhere within a typically four-hour time slot. And then, your 60-second, response-driven commercial pops up somewhere during CNN's *Situation Room*. Good enough targeting for your product, at a much smaller media cost.

Bob led the process by which we brought this campaign to life, but as the manager of many ad campaigns, I was a close adviser to Bob on its development. My input would also be critical from a response perspective, which was my expertise, and he knew that I would never be afraid to hold back on any opinions or thoughts I had that could make the commercials more engaging, informative, or motivational.

Being in charge of the website, I also would be responsible for making sure that these spots would be easily accessible and presented properly to anyone who wished to view them: customers, employees, investors, and, most importantly, Angelo. It would have been a political disaster to get the millions approved for this campaign and then have the CEO struggle to see them easily on the website. One glitch and the whole thing would be tainted, as well as marketing's reputation for getting things done flawlessly. Each spot would end up being huge digital files, which normally would be a piece of cake for our enormous site pipes. But during one meeting I did some back-of-the-envelope math and quickly discovered the potential for a problem.

There were three spots in the campaign. In addition, Angelo himself was to record a brief video (essentially a fourth spot) articulating the meaning and purpose of our new advertising and how it would demonstrate our mission and our passion for it. This Angelo video would be seen by employees, investors, etc. Each spot was a large file, but all four together was an enormous amount of data, but still manageable. No sweat. Oh, wait—on the day this campaign breaks, it was conceivable that all 60,000 or so employees would want to view them all on the website, not even counting the thousands of marketing and financial journalists who may want to view all four spots. Even if only a portion of the total potential audience viewed them that first day, this would require the site to be able to handle a much larger load than usual. Even before the concept tissues of the campaign were completed, I was hard at work with Jerry, our genius head of our technological web "Q branch," making sure that the only person who really mattered (Angelo) would be able to pull up these spots flawlessly and seamlessly on launch day, or we...*buffering*...would...*buffering*...be...*buffering*...dead.

When Dailey presented their concepts to choose from, there was a clear winner. "Realize Your Dreams" would come alive through a series of "slice of life" vignettes that showed first-time homebuyers who either had their problems solved by Countrywide, or would. There would be a few different commercials within the same campaign, but two of them stood out.

One starred an African American couple who were just moving into their new first home via the magic of Countrywide's ability to get them a loan. It was charming and sweet. In it, the script implied that the wife had handled the problem-solving, that the husband was contrarian but now contrite.

A recent (and in my opinion, disturbing) trend in advertising is something I call the "dumb-husband syndrome." It seems that from paper towels, to financial services, to vacations, American commercials have been invaded by families of brilliant wives and of husbands that are dumber than a bag of rubber hammers. Men, grown men, who can't operate a toaster, who don't understand all this retirement planning stuff, who only care about football and beer. I find these types of spots annoying at best and offensive at worst. If the roles were reversed and the helpless wife needed her man to survive, I am sure the complaint calls would ring off the hook. So in consistently pebble-in-the-shoe fashion, I brought up this concern to Bob, thinking I was defending the manhood of millions of American males who could indeed operate the toilet all by themselves and who might need a loan. My concerns were quickly silenced via a slight Bob eye-roll, and that was it.

The spot opened on a front door establishing shot (the spot was called "Front Door"), showing only a hint of what was probably the proverbial Countrywide home. (It was smart to not show the actual house, as "dream home" can mean different things to different people; from farmhouses to suburbia to an urban townhome, it was better to leave it up to each individual's imagination.) The husband approaches the door, and the wife opens it, stopping him in the doorway like he was some kind of unwanted Amway salesman. Then she begins playfully reminding him how doubtful he was that they would get a loan, but then makes him admit that, due to Countrywide's help (as hinted via a Countrywide logo and a "First Time Buyer Loans" graphic appearing below this scene), she turned out to be right, and he turned out to be wrong. They smile together as she says, "Welcome home" as she opens the door for him.

Then came the voiceover read, saying "Realizing *Your* Dreams, at Countrywide Home Loans...Call or visit your local branch today." The screen showed the website, phone number, and "or visit your local branch."

Fade out.

The spot was good, effective, and warm. It showed the hope every young couple feels. It showed Countrywide as the expert solutions provider for their needs. It was warm and fuzzy and Americanesque. I hope that in 2008 this couple is not suffering foreclosure because they put no money down and got an Adjustable Rate Mortgage that they could never afford when it reset....

The second spot showed two women, one a mom in a park playing with a little boy, obviously the son of one of the women. One woman was white, and the other was of vague origin, maybe Italian or Indian. This is often intentional in ads, because if an actor is of an unknown ethnicity, every ethnicity may then relate to them. (Also, redheads always work—just watch tonight's commercials on your TV. Lotsa redheads; art directors love the color.)

The women are clearly friends, and it opens with one talking about her skepticism that she, with her single income and lack of time, would actually be able to qualify for a home loan. The friend tells her that she accomplished this, with the help of "them," and encourages her to call *Countrywide*. The same logos, graphics, and "Call Now" appeared below this scene, as the little boy slides down a slide as the women laugh together. Nice.

In America back then, the streets were lined with gold, and easy home-ownership seemed possible even for single mothers with small salaries.

Advertising both mirrors our culture and partly defines it. And looking back now on these commercials, as they were created in early 2004, the tone of these spots will forever be a time capsule, a frozen sample of the hubris of the boom. Back then, homeownership was not a privilege earned by years of saving for a down payment and ensuring you could afford the monthly bill. No, back then, homeownership had somehow morphed into a *right*, where anyone and everyone could and *should* get into their own home, with one of the plentiful exotic loan products available from not only Countrywide, but an array of banks and lenders just dying to give you their money. No down payment. No income. No documentation needed. Even if you had poor credit. No chance of paying the mortgage when it reset? No worries, you can always refinance, because home values would never stop rising.

Wrong. Now these television spots, which seemed perfectly emotionally compelling and real back then, are a creepy testament to the madness of the time, almost ripe for biting *Saturday Night Live*–like parodies:

Countrywide Spot 1 Redux: SNL-like Parody Concept: "Front Door"
The husband approaches the door, the wife opens it, stopping him in the doorway like he was some kind of unwanted Amway salesman. (Note, they can easily be white this time, it doesn't matter.)

"You said we couldn't afford this place," she says to him.

His eyes darting like he had been caught in an error, then responds, "Yeah."

She continues, "You said we'd actually have to document and prove our income, to somehow find $50,000 for a down payment...*Now* what do you say?"

Copy appears below him with the Countrywide logo: *We're experts at getting you into homes you could never afford, for free...*as he says, "I was wrong, wasn't I?"

Countrywide-Foreclosure-Waiting-To-Happen Loans.

She says, "Welcome home."

[Fade out.]

Countrywide Spot 2 Redux: SNL-like Parody Concept: "Playground"

The women are clearly friends, and it opens with one saying skeptically, "Like *I* could buy a home..."

The other responds, "You *could*..."

"But I owe $50,000 on my credit cards and only make $21,500 a year..."

Up comes Countrywide logo, type at bottom reads:

We're experts at getting you into homes you could never afford, for free...

Getting even more skeptical, she responds, "Yeah *right*, with *my* murder conviction?"

"You'd be surprised..."

Countrywide's No-Way-You're-Ready-To-Own-Your-Own-Home Loans.

[Fade out.]

AFTER DECADES OF economic Darwinism, the system had purposely designed through natural selection that getting a loan was *intentionally difficult*. To demonstrate that you could be responsible enough to be worthy of signing those promissory notes, you were *supposed* to have already struggled and succeeded in securing a good job, generating a certain level of income, and working your fingers to the bone to have saved up enough for the down payment. It showed something beyond the numbers; it demonstrated *character*. The system naturally weeded out those who were either not ready to embark on that commitment, or had demonstrated previous behaviors implying that they were not financially mature enough to keep that promise to pay the money back. The new system of loans, and Refis awarded to anyone with a pulse was, in retrospect, long-term madness driven by short-term profit.

Today as I write this, my two young sons are having their last elementary school day of the year. They described to me how they felt both happy and sad at the same time, so this morning I taught them a relevant new word: *bittersweet*. These commercials now have become quaint, bittersweet reminders of the years when money fell from the sky, when times were good. Countrywide was fulfilling dreams on a scale never before seen in American financial services. We were a corporate *dream factory*, completing application after application, funding loan after loan, with a vigor and a spirit driven by a shared mission to do *good* for America, with a proud founding father, Angelo, who still walked the halls and encouraged us all.

By the time the "Realize Your Dreams" campaign was launched in the autumn of 2004, I had never been prouder at any point in my career. The work was compelling, emotional, and effective at raising our awareness, but more importantly, I was now fully immersed in helping Americans *realize their dreams*. Yes, I was a diehard romantic trapped within a profit-driven, pragmatic corporate world, but I also was achieving my own dreams of being an effective client—helping to maximize one of the fastest corporate rises in history. This was the height of my career, this was the height of Countrywide, and each perhaps helped create the other. I was part of Countrywide, and the spirit of success that was Countrywide would always be a part of me.

Then, something started to happen. Rates began to rise.

———————

LISA BARNES WAS a healthy, vibrant mother of two in Santa Monica, California, who unexpectedly found herself inside a mortgage "help program" or so she thought. Unlike other troubled mortgage stories of formal and complete default and/or foreclosure, Lisa was one of the many well-intentioned homeowners who, during the crisis, wound up floating somewhere within the purgatory world halfway between homelessness and the happiness of good standing, adrift in a sea of uncertainty and soul-crushing worry.

Whereas some of the other stories of troubled homes were triggered by overspending, illness, job loss, loan resets, or other factors, Lisa was suffering an affliction affecting millions of other families, especially women: divorce.

During her marriage she enjoyed what some would consider to be a wealthy lifestyle, as her entrepreneur husband bought and sold companies that provided an income easily close to a million dollars a year. Lisa and her two daughters lived the affluent lifestyle that Santa Monica provided, and things were good. This allowed Lisa to continue her work part-time as a counselor and therapist to autistic children, which provided her with rewards far beyond what any income could.

As the divorce proceeded, the relationship turned violent. Lisa grabbed her two daughters and left her husband, renting a small place in order to gain her footing. Things were so bad and the legal wrangling so venomous, that she decided to completely walk away from the riches that they had acquired as a couple; she was determined, perhaps out of spite, perhaps out of pride, to make it on her own. With grit and guts, she set out again as a single woman with children to rebuild her life.

Child support would supplement her income such that she could afford to buy a home for her and her daughters to resume a secure life. Lisa's father would live with them in exchange for child care while she was at work. She had figured that, along with that critical child support, she would be able to afford a monthly mortgage payment of $4,500. Through a friend of a friend, she was referred to someone in the local Santa Monica office of Countrywide for her loan. She had found a charming cottage, built in 1922, in Santa Monica for $950,000. It was within the school district that the kids loved, was in familiar surroundings, and near Lisa's family.

While the price of this freestanding house was way beyond the national average sale price of about $165,000, it is important to note that Santa Monica was, and still is, one of the most expensive neighborhoods in the nation. Adjacent to the Pacific Ocean, Santa Monica is a town where one could easily see Brad Pitt at the local Starbucks on occasion or Meg Ryan at the supermarket (I myself once picked up a cantaloupe she had dropped in front of me), so that location and lifestyle made home values very expensive.

Countrywide provided her with two loans to cover the cost of the house. First, a 30-year-fixed for a portion of it, and then, a second "piggyback" loan that covered the other portion. "Piggies" were a popular method of "covering the spread" between the cost of a home and the limits of a conventional first loan, and, of course, were completely legal. Lisa stressed to the salesperson that her monthly budget limit was $4,500, and she claims she was assured repeatedly that her monthly payment would not exceed that. Lisa was able to put zero money down on a home that cost nearly a million dollars. She and her daughters moved into the house and tried to begin their new life, providing a new sense of normalcy for her girls. Then, two events hit at the same time.

She received her first mortgage bill for the promised $4,500 amount. But then the monthly bill for the *second* loan arrived; it would be another $1,600 per month, making her total monthly costs for her home $6,100, way beyond her budget. On top of that, the divorce had become so adversarial that Lisa's ex had decided to stop making child support payments. Her housing costs had soared at the moment her income had been cut. When I asked her why she was surprised at getting the second loan bill, she responded that she had thought that the salesperson understood that her total monthly budget should not exceed $4,500. Either he did not understand, or he really did, but wanted the extra loan sale; we will never know. She could not recall seeing any clear explanation within the inches of stacked paperwork she would sign for the loans, stating the exact amount of her monthly payment. "I should have read it more carefully I guess, but I did not expect a $6,100 per month mortgage payment."

I asked her why she did not call Countrywide right then to complain and fix it, but, perhaps echoing a theme prevalent throughout many of these cases, she felt stupid about her own misunderstanding; she did not want to call Countrywide to argue about papers that she herself had signed, afraid of her own embarrassment. Instead, she resorted to the only backup plan that most people have; she used her credit cards to make her housing payments, reaching her credit limit within six months.

She sat at her kitchen table one evening after the girls had gone to sleep, and sifted through her bills. Her credit cards were maxed out. The monthly housing bills from Countrywide totaling $6,100 stared her in the face. There was nowhere for her to turn, nothing she could do; she could not pay her mortgage. As the tears came, she sat there, feeling more alone in this life than she ever had before. The overwhelming, swirling abyss of hopelessness, confusion, and frighteningly real possibility of homelessness came crashing down on her, silently, at the kitchen table that night. She quietly laid her head down into her folded arms on the table, and wept until she drifted into the only salvation she seemed to have left: sleep.

Rays of the warm dawn touched her face in the kitchen as the new day came. The tears all drained, and with children to care for, the prospects of a new day strengthened her resolve to figure something out. She called Countrywide for help.

At that moment Lisa entered a world of "customer service" that appeared to be designed by Lewis Carroll. She proactively and courageously explained to the pleasant customer service agent that summer day in 2007 that she had not yet defaulted on her mortgage, but was about to. Lisa asked what programs were available to help her, as she explained her divorce and sudden lack of child support. She was then transferred to what had by then been euphemistically deemed the "Hope Department."

On the line with another agent, she was told that all of their existing programs at the time only applied to people who were able to pay at least a portion of their mortgage due, and that the excess, unpaid amount would need to be piled onto payments when her situation improved. While she stared at the tissues on the table, full of tears from the night before, Lisa told them that she was not able to make any of the $6,100 payment, and when she would start getting money from her divorce, it was unlikely that she would be able to pay more than that anyway. At a dead end, the agent told Lisa to write a letter and fax it in, explaining her situation, and that her case "would be reviewed." Lisa followed up, confirmed that the fax had arrived, and also confirmed that her case was indeed in review. She was told she would be contacted soon.

Five long months went by, and no word. That same year of 2007, Countrywide entered into its implosion period, when they would tap out their credit line, hemorrhage huge losses, and eventually be swallowed by Bank of America. Perhaps Lisa's case review suddenly fell from their priority list, because Lisa never received any call, e-mail, or letter, ever. Not even did any mortgage bill arrive. She was floating in a purgatory space of *presumed* default, and not yet foreclosure, but she had no idea what was happening. All she knew was that no one had come to evict her and her children from her home. She filed for bankruptcy during this time, and got out from under her other debts just as her divorce support began to finally flow in.

Then, one day, she got her mortgage bill, again. Same old $6,100 total from the two loans. There was no mention on the statement of any late fees, penalties, or even any acknowledgment that she had missed five payments. Although in financial straits, Lisa was still honest, so she called Countrywide again to inquire about this regular bill, wondering what had ever happened to her "case review." She simply wanted to know where she stood.

Lisa asked the main line agent to transfer her to the Hope Department with whom she had spoken before.

"I don't know what that is," stated the confused agent, continuing, saying, "and I see no record of any late payments or default on your account."

Lisa, although pleasantly surprised, was still in need of answers to this apparent mystery concerning her financial reality. Had it all simply been a bad dream over her kitchen table that night? Finally, the agent transferred her to another department that she felt "could be" the so-called Hope Department that Lisa was asking about.

They had no record of her call, her letter, or her case. It was as if the entire recent episode had never happened. Lisa could not believe it. They told her to "write a letter and we will put your case into review." She said okay just to get off the call, and hung up.

She stared at the receiver, astonished that her default had entered some kind of quasi "don't ask, don't tell" mortgage twilight zone. Since that call she told me that she has been able to make the monthly payments, barely. Convinced and calm in the fact that she tried to do the right thing, she had become resigned to not knowing what had happened or how the missed payments had affected her financial history.

Every day since then she has faced an uncertain future, wondering if the sheriff might one day come knocking and take her house away.

6

Idol Worship

The nation is prosperous on the whole,
but how much prosperity is there in a hole?
—Will Rogers

NOVEMBER 2003

Prime rate: 4.00%

Foreclosure rate: 1.29%

CFC stock price: ~$26.00

ANGELO MOZILO SEEMED lost.

The CEO of my employer and one of the largest companies in America, Countrywide—who also was my boss's boss's boss—stepped out of a long black limo, complete with darkened windows, right there in front of me as I walked down a street in San Diego. He walked alone, no "handlers," which struck me as odd for a true icon of American entrepreneurial success, a gazillionaire, and one of my idols at that time. This man *was* Countrywide.

Since starting my role as Senior Vice President of Marketing only a few months earlier, I still felt like a rookie, still learning the ins and outs of the company, but beginning to get more comfortable in my new corporate responsibility. During that time I had heard so much about Angelo from everyone there—the vision, the charisma, the legend.

In March of 1969 in New York City, as my parents began dreaming of owning their own home, the same Angelo Mozilo, a feisty, charismatic, gifted salesman, and the son of Italian immigrants who began working in his father's butcher shop at age 12, together with his paternal and quantitative partner David Loeb, began a small company that would change the world. They had a dream that they could build a new kind of mortgage company, and one day be in a position to help all Americans achieve the dream of homeownership. Looking forward to the dreams of future growth and success, they, with the unique, arrogant gumption that is the stuff of many an American success story, named it *Countrywide*. It was truly inspiring. Even though I worked for Angelo, the sight of him, alone, on that street stopped me short. I felt like I had just bumped into Mickey Mantle at the grocery store.

Attired in his now famous stylized banker's dark suit with pinstripes, crisp white shirt, and bright yellow power tie, his perfectly polished precision in dress was the stuff of legend for us "Young Turks." We used to huddle around the televisions in the conference room to "see what Angelo is wearing today" during many of his newsmaking interviews on CNBC, bantering with Maria Bartiromo about the new mortgage boom that he helped create.

A trim and fit man in his sixties, Angelo Mozilo stands only about five feet, six inches tall—*about my height*, I proudly thought—and he had a palpable presence. His small stature, impeccable tailoring, and silver hair also reminded me of my dad. The combination of blindingly white teeth and deep, dark, been-in-Aruba-for-six-weeks complexion made him "pop" on the television business shows, sometimes in an orangelike glow, but this was balanced by his aura of paternal warmth that usually put people at ease. He was slick, rich, famous, reassuring, and full of charm—and packaged with the precision of a U.S. Marine.

Now, here he was in person, standing on the street, alone. And it was an ugly street. The homeless people stared from the sidewalk, as surprised by his presence as I was. It stank of urine and garbage. One guy with no legs was in a wheelchair, with all his worldly possessions in an old, beat-up baby stroller. His home was a cardboard box.

Angelo and I were both on our way to the same evening party, as part of the same trade show—the annual conference of the MBA, the Mortgage Bankers Association of America. There, the many players in the mortgage industry, including lenders, agents, brokers, and other secondary beneficiaries of this quickly growing segment of American business mingled, networked, partied.

I had met Angelo face-to-face for the first time only a few hours earlier. When I entered the palatial pavilion where the show was being staged, I saw the giant Countrywide "booth"—a small movie set, really—where connections were made, Countrywide products and services were touted, and "new carpet smell" wafted. Large-screen televisions played videos espousing the growth of Countrywide, the smiling faces of its employees, and proud families on the front porches of their first homes, complete with the ubiquitous white-picket-fenced-montages of the American Dream that would make any capitalist proud. Bank of America, Washington Mutual, Lending Tree, Fannie Mae, Freddie Mac, Citibank—the giants of American personal, commercial, and mortgage finance—as well as hundreds of other smaller names were all there, contributing to the sensory overload. I loved it. It was a loud, glitzy symphony of capitalist financial propaganda, part Vegas, part Disneyland.

Angelo had been standing right there at the center of the booth. I walked right over to him and introduced myself.

"Excuse me, Mr. Mozilo?" I asked cautiously.

"Yes?" he answered and turned toward me. This was my chance to meet him and maybe even get on his "rising star" radar. I never stopped to think if that was actually a good thing.

"My name is Adam Michaelson. I am your new Marketing SVP…?" I uttered it like a question. Gimme a break, I was nervous.

For a moment he looked at me but seemed not to engage with me. *Awkward moment*, I thought, as panic set in.

Just then he stretched out his small hand, and said, "Welcome to Countrywide, Adam. What are you working on?"

Unlike many other Fortune 100 firms where employees are working for the faceless corporation, Countrywide was one of the few companies left in America where the young executives were also working for the charismatic leader who embodied the essence and character of the firm. My MBA heart was aflutter at personally talking to the *founder*. Imagine being a young, ambitious executive talking alone to Sam Walton, Lee Iacocca, Ray Kroc, Walt Disney. That's how I felt. Angelo Mozilo of Countrywide was one of the last of this "Hall of CEOs" that I aspired to become. In my head I could faintly hear my dad reminding me, "Never idolize people too much, they may someday disappoint you."

As Angelo asked me about my work for the firm, it seemed like he was not simply being polite; he really wanted to know what value I was bringing to Countrywide.

I couldn't believe it. This titan of finance, this hero of thousands of MBA geeks had just asked me about *my work* that I was doing for him. This was real rock-star stuff, and suddenly I felt 12 years old.

Uh-oh, I thought, *I better get the answer right.*

"I'm working on developing new online channels in which to drive new Prime customer leads," I said. *Good grammar*, I thought—so far so good. *Stay focused, stay poised....*

"Ahh," he responded.

Crap, I'm blowing it. So in usual fashion, I dove in deeper.

"Yes, we are working on developing new ways to drive lead production using organic and paid search test methods. We're also doing some new online banner testing, and then working on enhancing conversion of those leads to application through the website experience alone."

He nodded, still shaking my hand like a political candidate gunning for office. It looked like he was thinking about what to say, really pondering it.

"I was also in charge of the web launch for our new 'Realize Your Dreams' brand campaign," I continued.

He again nodded some more.

Awkward pause...Is he going to call security?

Then all of a sudden he began to smile broadly as he uttered the few short sentences that would drive my life for the next three-plus years:

"Well, that is very exciting new technology for us. Any new way to help bring homeownership to our customers is very welcome at Countrywide. I am counting on you to help us with our mission, and I am looking forward to seeing you do a great job."

His words sunk into me, and the noise of the pavilion faded from my ears. Just then, as his sentence was finishing, a group of senior executives came over to escort him to another meeting. Not exactly a security detail, but the "entourage effect" I was expecting had finally occurred. I responded with a simple "Thank you, Mr. Mozilo" as they whisked him off to what was obviously one in a long line of personal appearances, meetings, and CNBC interviews that day.

I stood there for a moment, dumbly looking at my own hand. I took in his words about value, dedication, and being part of the Countrywide mission. It could have easily sounded scripted, the words he spoke to me, and maybe it was what he said to every employee he met, but the *way* he said it, with earnest belief in what he was doing, I, too, *believed*. We weren't selling soap, or beer, or a hotel stay, or even money, really. We were selling the ultimate American Dream. We were selling—indeed, *facilitating*—the realization of the oldest dream in America: owning one's own home.

Private land and home ownership was at the very core of the ideals of Anglican society, the society from which America evolved, dating back to the Magna Carta and the very essence of freedom, self-determination, and "the pursuit of happiness." It was, and still is, the bedrock of communities, civil organization, and the family unit. This was the stuff that truly brought quality to people's lives and neighborhoods, and I was reminded at that moment with Angelo what it was all about. I was never prouder of my career than at that moment, and I decided to redouble my efforts to help this wonderful mission, to help Angelo, and to help *people*.

BACK ON THAT seedy street in San Diego, several hours later, I grew concerned. Maybe it was having grown up in working-class neighborhoods on Long Island, but I decided that Angelo required an escort immediately. He looked like an easy mark out there all alone. I sprang into action, walking briskly toward him.

"Mr. Mozilo?" I asked.

"Yes?" he asked me.

"I'm Adam Michaelson, we met earlier at the show...?"

For a few seconds he seemed to be searching for my face in his memory.

"Are you looking for the NAR party?" I asked.

"Yes," he responded. "Where is it?" There were no signs to indicate where the party was.

The NAR was the National Association of Realtors, a powerful lobby of real estate agents in the United States, and a key element of the mortgage business, obviously. I was a little surprised that such a powerful group would hold an industry party in such a depressed section of San Diego, with no clear signs of where to go. *Knuckleheads*, I thought.

We walked and walked, past row after row of shanties that reeked of human suffering. I wanted to use these precious minutes alone with him to engage him again in a familiar chat to build a relationship to broaden my career—about Countrywide, marketing, life—or simply to learn more about him and how he got to where he was in business. But it didn't feel right. *Just get him off the street*, I thought. We kept walking in silence.

"Well, my itinerary says it's number 2147," I said. Looking around, I heard the *thump-thump-thump* of club music as we walked closer to a steel staircase like a subway entrance. I saw the little hand-drawn "NAR Party" sign, finally.

We walked into the exuberant technobeat of the loud music. The moment we entered the smoky, basementlike room, executives came over to Angelo and pulled him into the crowd. There were no thank yous, no acknowledgments of our two-minute adventure together on the streets of San Diego.

I never again personally met with or talked to Angelo Mozilo in the years I was at Countrywide. The last time I was with him, the richest and most powerful founder of the largest mortgage firm in the United States, Angelo Mozilo of Countrywide, was dressed in what looked like a handmade suit, surrounded by homeless people lying in boxes on a seedy street in San Diego.

SOMETIMES I AM so disgusted with our vapid, celebrity culture; I think maybe we are getting what we deserve as a nation. Leave it to a country where we have news stories of celebrity "baby bump updates" to let a celebrity foreclosure bring the deep and real crisis to life.

To paraphrase Stalin (as CNN commentator Glenn Beck also cleverly did on his blog), one foreclosure is a tragedy, a million is a statistic. Apparently, historians may have accidentally left off the last piece of this quote, "and Ed McMahon getting foreclosed is a cataclysm!"

In June 2008, Ed McMahon became the celebrity poster child of the mortgage mess. Johnny Carson's ubiquitous shoulder parrot apparently had gotten himself into trouble on his Beverly Hills mansion, and was behind more than $600,000 on a $4.8 million loan through a firm called ReconTrust, which just happened to be a unit of Countrywide. (I could envision Countrywide PR people slapping their own foreheads when they saw *this one* coming over the wire.) Ed reported that he had broken his neck and was unable to work.

Ed went on *Larry King Live* to tell his story. When asked why he went public, he responded that he "wanted to give people hope, give them optimism, give them some kind of guidance....I speak for all of them, as far as I'm concerned."

Asked how he got into this mess, he simply said, "If you spend more money than you make, you know what happens." Thanks, Ed. Of course, this pitchman for many useless products and services you didn't need to buy was not the only celebrity earning the special-attention treatment.

As Ed's plight galvanized a riveted nation, candlelight vigils were held as crowds held hands and sang "Ed will oooovverrrcommmm," and rock stars began planning a live worldwide concert from Yankee Stadium to help raise money for Ed ("Ed Aid 2008"), the press became flooded with other well-to-dos who got into trouble. Of course, many were not your typical homes, your typical homeowners, nor your typical reasons for foreclosure.

Baseball star José Canseco, a gazillionaire, simply and voluntarily walked away from his $2.5 million, 7,300-square-foot home as the value of the place descended below the mortgage amount. I wonder if he threw the keys back to his lender, bulls-eyeing the mitt all the way from the outfield.

Boxer Evander "the Real Deal" Holyfield defaulted on a $10 million dollar loan from Washington Mutual Bank for his 54,000-square-foot estate with 109 rooms, 17 bathrooms, 3 kitchens, and a bowling alley. *Waaaaaa.* Oh, and of course, it is located on Evander Holyfield Highway in suburban Atlanta. The news of the impending foreclosure was front-page-worthy all over the nation, another symbol of the trials and tribulations of poor souls who may lose their mansions. Holyfield responded, "I'm not broke, I'm just not liquid." *'Kay. Sounds like America.* More interesting was the follow-up story that most of the press did not put on the same front pages, that the Real Deal apparently TKO'd the payment problem and the home was quietly removed from the foreclosure process. *Thank goodness Evander is all right.*

Then, of course, there was the most fun story for antipoliticos: even a Congresswoman had her home foreclosed. The Sacramento home of Southern California Representative Laura Richardson (D) was sold at auction in May 2008 for $388,000; she had paid $535,000 for it (with no money down) in January 2007. In an eerie coincidence, the number 535 is also the number of all the people in Congress (435 representatives and 100 senators), and also at the time of this writing fairly represents a recent foreclosure statistic as reported by the Mortgage Bankers Association: in America about 1 in every 535 homes is in the foreclosure process.

Like any demographic group—even the wealthy—some are smart; others, well, are not so smart. Many of them delegate their bill-paying and finances to "trusted advisers." *Especially* if I had millions of dollars, I would be *more* likely to watch over every transaction. Many studies I've seen of financial defaults do show an interesting bump in the number of affluent professionals such as doctors and lawyers. Maybe because they do trust others to handle it for them. I once had a boss who was very wealthy, but had to run to the gas company to pay his $5 bill, which he had not paid in months, before they shut his gas off. It happens.

Maybe that's why the Ed McMahon story struck such a chord. While, yes, he will most likely not be living on the streets, and his veiled call for public pity and assistance by calling in a favor with Larry King may not have totally been for "all of the people he said he speaks for," his drama had all the ingredients of many of the stories one-tenth his financial size.

He spent more than he made. He assumed that his then-current level of income would go on forever. He didn't plan, didn't assume anything would happen. He got hurt and couldn't work. *Whammo.*

These are elements consistent with foreclosures happening to many of the regular people out there. And for that cautionary part of the tale alone, Ed may have pushed some people to proactively check their finances, plan ahead, not sign for that new risky loan, and stop spending more than they made.

And for that wake-up call alone, maybe we should thank him for coming forward.

In the end, someone eventually did buy Ed's house.

7

Building a Better Housetrap

A bank is a place where they lend you an umbrella
in fair weather, and ask for it back when it begins to rain.
—Robert Frost

FEBRUARY 2004
Prime rate: 4.00%
Foreclosure rate: 1.29%
CFC stock price: ~$29.00

IN THE SUMMER and fall of 2003, everything was humming for me, for Countrywide, and for the mortgage and housing business. The boom was on. Mortgage rates had hit almost an all-time low, and the entire nation rushed to refinance their bloated mortgages from previous years. A good refinance into one of the available so-called "exotic" loans could mean a much cheaper monthly payment, sometimes saving hundreds or even thousands of dollars. But it is arguable if Countrywide truly knew that these refinancings would turn out to be millions of small financial nuclear weapons they were planting all throughout the marketplace, with detonators set on varying times, which would eventually cause a cascading implosion of the worldwide economy.

*   *   *

THE REFI BOOM had several causes, but some are more obvious than others. Yes, mortgage rates had dropped, offering homeowners the chance to *apply* to refinance. But the trigger was the other side of the equation. Banks decide whether to refinance a home based partly on what is called the Loan-to-Value ratio, also known as LTV. Most loans require an 80/20 LTV in order to be approved. This simply means that the loan should not exceed 80 percent of the appraised value of the home, so the risk to the bank will be tolerable. If the run-up in housing values had not coincided with the dropping of rates, and consumers' crazed search for new ways to *spend*, the Refi boom may not have happened. It was the perfect storm of lower rates, the consumer demand to refinance, and the newly found value in the increasing price of homes that created a false sense of lower risk with the banks.

The other reason why it was a boom speaks to a marketing concept that not every financial-quarter-focused finance jock may have thought about. Any push of a new product, service, or other beneficial offering to an eager marketplace will sometimes cause an early and heavy surge of activity, as the "low-hanging fruit" beats a path to your door. This marketing term refers to the easy pickings—those homeowners who would be first in line for these new loans and are typically the cheapest to acquire. Over time, after the rush has passed, it becomes harder and more expensive to acquire new customers. This dynamic is what often happens when newspaper Food Section readers pack the house of the new restaurant in town, then that same restaurant empties down to a trickle a few weeks later. The initial level of activity can be misleading in managing operations, and it can wreak havoc on projecting the capacity needs of a service system.

Let's say a company is used to doing a hundred Refis a week. With rates at near lows, and home values approaching near highs, maybe that load moves to a thousand Refis a week. *Wow, good for you—you're now a mortgage kingpin.* But now you also need to hire more people to answer the phones, write the paperwork, and approve the loans, as well as to find the space, the computers, and the paper clips to make that all happen at a level of a thousand loans a week. Well, a few weeks go by, and most of the people who were running to your door to Refi have now *already* Refi'd. Guess what? The number of new loans is going to drop and you now need to find other ways to fill up your capacity so you don't have to fire people. This initial surge of interest, activity, and customers is normal, as is the eventual decline, and these speak to the broader issue of financial *sustainability*. We've heard a lot about the concept of sustainability in recent years, much of it in the context of global resources and our gluttonous consumption of just about everything on the planet. The same opportunity, as well as dangers, also can apply to financial products.

Long ago, some smart folks in the lumber industry—or in the early colonies, hell, I don't know—were sittin' back with a cold ale on some fresh stump and surveyed the hard work they had accomplished that day. *Wow*, they thought. *Look at all the amazing trees we cut down today. What a great job we did.* Then they took another sip of ale, surveyed the panorama all the way down to the river (let's assume there was a river— humor me), and then looked at each other blankly as they all suddenly shared the same thought. *Oh, no, Jeremiah—where art all thy trees?*

So, slowly but steadfastly, they started planting lil' baby trees everywhere so they would have a sustainable forest in which to cultivate a never-ending cycle of planting and cutting. (Well, at least that's what was *supposed* to happen. Al Gore would argue about how good a job we did.) The same is true of fishing and a host of other industries. Financial services, too. Or so we thought.

Every time someone refinances, the firms associated with that process generate fees as revenue. The lender, the appraiser, the escrow company, the broker—everyone. But usually those fees are rolled up into the new loan so the customer may not have to lay out those fees in cash up front. So, people refinancing their loans was good for all. The assumptive sustainability would come from never-ending rises in home values, where, hypothetically, the forest would regrow cycle after cycle, and through new Refis we would recut and recut, achieving eternal financial bliss for all. *Yup, good luck with all that.*

Some thought that this Refi boom was sustainable. Others simply thought of the Refi cycle as a *durable good*. Like a computer or a washing machine or a car, durable goods are designed to last only a few years, either through the technology becoming obsolete or the manufacturing designed to fail after a few years. *Why doesn't a car company make a car that lasts forever? (Believe me, they could if they wanted to.) Because then you would never have to buy another one.*

This creates a built-in cycle of rebuying, such as a car every five years or so. Marketers think of this as the *Lifetime Value* of a customer; GM does not simply want you to buy one car for $20,000. They hope you buy six cars from them over 30 years and they make revenue of $120,000 from your household. The same was true of Refis. If Wonderboy did a good job of servicing you when your loan was funded, you might Refi through us again and again.

But then again, didn't we all—customers, lenders, government, the markets—didn't *we all* know truly in our hearts and minds that it would be unsustainable? What *is it* with our culture, as a civilization, that has us continually pillaging resources and leading to systems' own demise? The mortgage and housing boom combined with our nutball urges for *stuff*—to consume endlessly—consumed us so that we have almost depleted any equity we built in our homes.

Finance is a lot like physics, ecology, and other sciences; what goes up must come down, and systems that have had their resources depleted will eventually fail. So why did all financial services assume that trees would always keep growing from the forest floor after we had cut them all down?

Refinancing especially turned out to be a dangerous "get out of jail free" card for overspending, and it is a big part of our problem. It can be like letting a financial toddler play with a loaded debt gun. Let's take a simplified example. Say a homeowner has a two-year-old $400,000 mortgage. He also owes $30,000 in credit card debt. If the value of his property has gone up to, say, $600,000 (verified via a new wacky appraisal—completely legitimized by the other recent, wackier sales in the local neighborhood), the owner can apply to refinance the house, getting a new loan that resets to another 30-year term. The homeowner would then get a new 30-year loan for $430,000 and pay off the credit cards. Sound good? Sure, a 7% bundled refinanced loan is way better than 18% on a credit card, right? *But he now owes $430,000 over another 30 years, a $30,000 increase over his original principal.*

But let's say then his credit card bills run up again (and data suggest people usually do this), and the value of the home goes back *down* to $400,000. The bank will not grant another refinance because the loan amount ($430,000) is already *more than* the home is worth ($400,000). Maybe he falls behind on payments. He can't sell the house because the neighborhood is overloaded with houses for sale already, with many families in the same tough situation. Whammo: default, then foreclosure, and a great part of the debacle. *Welcome to America, 2009 and 2010.*

Lenders, including Countrywide, created more and more exotic loan products and lent money to anyone with a heartbeat so that everyone could Refi. For example, Countrywide alone offered almost two hundred different loan products. This enabled homeowners to get into larger homes and to use their increasing home value as a personal ATM.

There were three types of loan products in particular that mostly comprised the poisonous soup of refinancing during the boom— (offered to both Subprime households and Prime households): Adjustable Rate Mortgages, so-called PayOption (Negative Amortization) Loans, and the new threat of Home Equity Loans. They are at the center of what will continue to be a further mortgage meltdown in 2009 and beyond; in fact, we as a nation could be paying for the proliferation of these loans for decades.

First on the list of infamous products is the Adjustable Rate Mortgage, or ARM loan, the first destructive wave, especially in Subprime markets. An ARM is like those "Introductory 0% Interest Rates" on credit cards that deluge our mailboxes every day. Your credit card might be at 0% interest for six months, and then suddenly become 18% or more after that. Your credit card minimum payment might go from $100 to $1,000 overnight. *Better read the fine print before you buy that new plasma TV.*

An ARM loan is still usually a 30-year loan, but this can be misleading. For a simple hypothetical example, let's say a normal 30-year fixed rate loan at 7% interest would require a steadfast monthly payment of $2,000 per month for 30 years—that payment amount would never change. You love that you can plan your family's finances around the never-changing monthly payment, but you don't want to pay $2,000 a month. You can afford to pay only $800 a month. Well then, an aggressive lender or broker might get you a low introductory rate of only 2% for the first three years, then it would reset to the higher rate of more than 7% after that three-year period (a "3/1 ARM"). So your payment for the first three years on this ARM loan, let's say, is only $800. *Nice.* Now you can shop and buy more and more with that extra cash—that is, until the introductory rate ends after the thirty-sixth month, and the loan resets. That was all fine. You'd just Refi and get a new ARM at the reset point. After all, housing values were always going up and interest rates were going to be forever low, right? But that, as we know now and should have known then, was a fallacy.

ARMs can wreak havoc on a home's finances if people don't plan for the reset. Maybe the owner did not plan for the higher monthly payment even though he or she should have known it was coming. Maybe they really didn't know, or maybe unforeseen financial hardships hit the family. Maybe they just believed the hype about our overheated housing market. This nightmare is occurring across millions of kitchen tables *right now.*

It doesn't matter why, but in the thirty-seventh month of our hypothetical ARM loan, as sure as the sun will rise, the huge new mortgage bill arrives. Maybe now it's $3,500 per month, a $2,700 increase. That's because the loan, having reset, now must re-add the monies you did not pay in the first three years. It is not a penalty; it is simply the monies you really owed. That money must be paid off eventually, so it gets re-amortized across the rest of the life of the loan.

The financial chaos occurs when the owner experiences an ARM reset, and then tries to go refinance the loan in a declining housing market. The lenders will not approve them, and now the owner can't sell the house. Now multiply this scenario by 10 million homes. *I don't know about you, but I'm worried about the Second Great Depression.*

There was, and is, a tidal wave of Adjustable Rate Mortgages resetting in 2008 and 2009 and beyond. More than $300 billion worth of ARMs reset in 2008 alone. We could see hundreds of billions in ARMs resetting during 2009, 2010, and 2011. *So fasten your seat belts.*

Typically there is a time lag of a few months from the time the ARM resets to the failure of the owner to refinance, and then to foreclosure proceedings. The time period data of ARMs due to reset does not reflect the time-lag effect of such post-ARM foreclosures. Nor does it show the ripple effects that such events have on the broader economy, a blast wave that can be felt months or even years later.

People who suffer the loss of their homes through foreclosure do not buy new cars. They do not buy new appliances or shop at Home Depot. Homes in foreclosure and owned by banks typically add to the blight and crime in neighborhoods, hurting local businesses, and in turn putting additional pressure on local and state tax revenues. And all those homes sit there on the balance sheet of the banks, which then need to drop prices even further to sell them quickly, which in turn pulls down on the values of other homes in the area. A glut of housing inventory pushes builders to stop building, and they are forced to cut jobs, continuing to fuel the fire.

The bottom line is that we could be seeing the fallout from these resets for years to come, even after the latest wave of bailouts seemingly "ended" the problem.

A new, more sinister version of the ARM was developed in mid-2004, and I would hear about it in the infamous Vault meeting: the PayOption, or Negative Amortization loan, which I described in the first chapter. This loan type, with its option for a "minimum payment," which may have been *less than* the interest and/or principal owed, could have easily put borrowers further and further underwater each month as the loan actually increased, piling on unpaid principal and interest. Yet this product offering was totally legal, and these types of loans were being offered by many financial institutions.

The third leg of this unholy financial trinity, and arguably a market bomb still waiting to go off in 2010, was the increasingly popular Home Equity Loan, or Home Equity Line of Credit (HELOC). A simpler concept to sell than either the PayOption or ARM, the Home Equity products allowed you to pull cash out of the perceived value of your home and use it for other nifty things, typically (and ironically) the consolidation of other forms of debt, usually credit cards, cars, home improvement, tuition, vacations, etc.

This type of cash-out product was essentially taking a loan from your own home, and thereby your own net worth. A Home Equity *Loan* was defined as a fixed amount, say, $50,000, that would be added to your overall loan. If your mortgage Refi gave you a total debt of $400,000, and you got a Home Equity Loan of $50,000, well, congratulations; fifty grand would magically appear in your checking account, but now you owed $450,000 in total, plus ever-growing interest, of course.

A Home Equity *Line of Credit* was not a set amount, but rather a Line of Credit you could pull from if you needed it. If you got a HELOC for $50,000, you would not owe $50,000. You would get a cute little checkbook and you could write yourself checks, only using what you needed, up to $50,000. If used wisely, this could be a smart option for those in up to their necks in credit card debt. Better to pay off that card that charged you 18% interest and instead pay off a HELOC in the 5% range (and the interest paid may also be tax-deductible).

Yes, HELOCs were smart and powerful "rainy-day reserves" if you needed quick cash, but the worst thing for any bank would be for you to open a HELOC, and then never draw any money from it. Banks loved it when you carried some kind of draw balance on your HELOC. The account was active, and you were more likely to draw more.

In one classic moment of minor political self-destruction, I can remember recommending that we test a HELOC offer touting it as this amazing emergency fund to use only if you need it. The premise would be, *Open it now, don't use it 'til ya need it*. Most people did not know that if you lost your job, that was when most banks probably would *not* approve a HELOC account for you, even though that's when you may need the cash the most. The idea was, open it while you still have a job, and get it approved, just in case. I can still recall like it was yesterday the finance jocks around the table, looking at me like I was from Mars.

"Why would we tell people that?" they asked.

"So we could open more accounts, and give people that flexible, emergency fund if they needed it, right?" I said, marketing simpleton that I was.

"But their draws will initially be zero, probably. That's bad, Adam. That costs us money." (They probably envisioned me in diapers with a rattle at this point.)

"But isn't that what HELOCs are supposed to be for? Peace of mind, just-in-case, yada yada? They'll draw eventually," I pushed.

"Well, yes, but we also want them to draw at least X dollars so that these accounts can be profitable." They rolled their eyes at the marketing dweeb and continued onto another topic.

And so went a classic example of how Countrywide, although a strong believer in its own advocacy brand, helping people, blah blah, was still a sales-driven, profit-focused public Fortune 100 that usually only thought one financial quarter ahead at any time.

The fallout from Home Equity products may be the last domino to fall in the crisis over the next 24 months. Many Home Equity Loans are done by different banks than the first mortgage holder. If a home goes into foreclosure, the first bank dumps the property on the market, typically at a loss, and the first bank gets paid back first. The second bank, the one that may have granted the Home Equity Loan, gets paid back only after the first bank is covered, and only if there is any money left over.

So here is a hypothetical that shows that particular element of the nightmare scenario, and why it is potentially worse: A house once worth $600,000 but now worth $350,000, with $450,000 in total debts ($350,000 mortgage and $100,000 Home Equity Loan) gets foreclosed and dumped for $300,000. The first bank loses $50,000 on the deal, but that's not that bad, all things considered. The second bank, however, using current laws (according to press reports) gets nothing. The $100,000 HELOC becomes a total loss. In mid-2008, data began showing a slow but noticeable increase in the number of Home Equity late payments as well, which could be an ominous sign of further waves of meltdown.

BUT BACK IN the second half of 2003, during the greatest Refi boom *ever*, no one was thinking about such things. Everyone was getting paper-rich. Like the billionaire receptionist at a 1997 dot com, we were basking in the glow of virtual value, and loving it. And there I was, just having happened to wind up right in the middle of it, partly responsible for the security and growth of one of the largest firms in the world, responsible for online marketing, driven and incentivized to help people borrow more, and more, and more....

Then rates slowly started going up.

Mortgage rates—generally based on the yield of 10-year Treasury Notes—as well as the Prime Rate set by the Fed (which directly affected Home Equity rates), began to creep up from their 2003 lows. Suddenly the mad rush of Refis began to taper. Actually, it wasn't a collapse or anything of the kind, in fact, the spectacular rate of growth had simply *slowed*, But it was just enough to freak everyone out.

One of the things I loved about Countrywide was its focus on winning. We were the best, the biggest, the first, the leader. Well, *leadership is action, not position*, and this was a core part of Countrywide's culture. So in the early weeks of 2004, things started to move quickly in another direction. As a new mortgage company seemed to be popping up on every street corner, as the wave of frenzied Refis began to crest, and as our capacity and product offerings grew, it was time for a new mantra.

Down from on high, Dave Sambol emerged from the mountaintop with tablets proclaiming that Countrywide would now strive to provide *A Loan For Every Customer*. A lofty, noble idea, this was simply an expansion of the concept that every American should be allowed to achieve the dream of homeownership, and Countrywide was the only one powerful enough to do it. While this was an internal directive, eventually it would morph into the consumer-facing "Nobody Can Do What Countrywide Can"—a popular slogan that was developed in 2005 and lived on until the Bank of America takeover.

As a student of history, I can remember what hit me first about our new mantra. It had an eerily similar cadence to another lofty, noble, and aspirational slogan of yesteryear—*A Chicken in Every Pot*—Herbert Hoover's 1928 campaign slogan. And we all know how *that* one turned out. Interesting parallels like this—the Roaring Twenties and this time of unprecedented growth and riches, just before the onslaught of a storm we had never experienced before—were just beginning.

ONE DAY IN February 2004, Andy came by my office. While he was familiar and paternal, it was rare for him to visit my office personally, usually delegating direction down through Bob to me as needed. The whole meeting lasted about 60 seconds, but would forever change my role at Countrywide. "We need to start our own Prime-focused customer acquisition group," he said.

As mentioned, Countrywide already had a robust Subprime marketing operation, housed within its segregated Subprime group at Full Spectrum Lending. Keeping them separate was intentional for many reasons: different financial metrics, operations, and marketing styles, and probably about a thousand government regulations mandating that separation. But one unspoken reason was that we didn't want the sometimes tacky and cheesy marketing messages to Subprime customers to tarnish our snooty and pristine Countrywide brand. It was a smart move. Contrary to the press's portrayal of Countrywide in the last year as a "Subprime lender," the truth was that Full Spectrum Lending (FSL) was a Subprime lender; Countrywide Home Loans was a Prime lender. Yes, Countrywide owned FSL, and maybe the distinction was just semantics, but this was a critical aspect to elevating the Countrywide brand to where it had gone. We could not have made "Realize Your Dreams" believable if we were known as Crazy Angelo's House of Subprime Lending, complete with a *Three-Day Parking Lot Sale, This Weekend Only!*

On a brand basis, Countrywide was a classy neighbor you wanted to live next to, and we kept our yard perfectly pruned. FSL was our kooky cousin who lived in the other part of town. For *National Lampoon's Vacation* fans, Countrywide was Clark W. Griswold, and FSL was our cousin Eddie.

FSL already had an internal Customer Acquisition group, but now the powers-that-be wanted an initiative focused on Prime customers, within the Countrywide brand style. And Andy wanted me to start it up.

Andy knew that much of my background was in Direct Response marketing, and any new group dedicated to the large-scale finding, engaging, informing, and motivating of new customers to come to Countrywide would require expertise in many different media, way beyond just online, including a ton of direct mail, a specialty of mine.

"Do you want me to engage with FSL resources?" I asked, being careful to outline the political boundaries of this project.

"Well, go ahead and learn from what they've done, but this is going

THE FORECLOSURE OF AMERICA

to be strictly for Countrywide—to Prime prospects only. You've done a good job with our new customer growth online, and you have the mail experience, so I want you to run it. This is going to stay within Corporate Marketing, but go see Ed, who will be running the call center and operations in Home Loans. Also, your product offerings will now be a Home Equity focus, talk to Ed about that, too." He spoke fast, obviously on his way to yet another meeting.

This last reference to the shift to Home Equity mining, which Andy said almost in passing, was huge. As Refi applications began to taper off, the finance jocks at headquarters smartly sought out new financial forests to decimate, and this, naturally was the trillion dollars of mostly untapped home equity that had built up in the value of American homes over the past couple of years. The edict that soon made its way through the halls and accompanied Sambol's recent "A Loan For Every Customer" was the ominously foreshadowing "Home Equity is Countrywide's Next Frontier." Ed's production group would offer prospects any kind of loan they wanted—Purchase loans and Refis (in all of their exotic forms), as well as that small little addition to the application script [paraphrased]:

"Would you also like to pull some money out of your home for debt consolidation, home improvement, or other? It's so fast and easy to add that as we have your application for the other loan done already, and I can see on your application that you have at least a hundred thousand dollars in equity just sitting there doing nothing for you…"

Andy continued. "[Wonderboy] is up to his neck in customer communications and doesn't have the time. You handle it. Go ahead and write up a plan, and send it to me by end of the week. I want you to work with both Bob and Emily on this."

"You got it, Chief," I responded quickly and respectfully. It was like the general had come to me, one of his lieutenant colonels, and offered me a special mission. I was eager to build the best damn new customer acquisition group he had ever seen.

"Oh, and Adam—this is *important*." With that one line I understood that this directive was coming from the top levels of the company, and would be high profile, and high responsibility. I was determined to make it great.

But by mentioning that I would need to work with both Bob and Emily on this, Andy, perhaps inadvertently, immediately muddied the waters. Bob was my boss; he handled all Brand and Online for the firm, and was focused on the right-brain, creative aspects of the marketing. Emily Simmons, a powerhouse of marketing finance, was a left-brained, quantitative genius who was more focused on the numbers, results, and metrics. Any powerful new customer acquisition plan would require both branding elements as well as a hard-core focus on the metrics, so I understood why Andy did this. Both of them were smart, dedicated, talented professionals, but it was totally like mixing oil and water. With that one statement, Andy set the stage for months of my having to walk a tightrope between these two, separate but equal masters of Countrywide's powerful marketing team.

Still, I was excited to have been given this assignment by the CMO. Minutes after Andy left my office, I cleared my schedule, cleaned off my desk, closed my door, and placed a crisp new yellow legal pad in front of me. Staring out my office window at the horses running free on the ranch across the highway, I pondered what this new operation could mean for my career and for Countrywide if done right. This would be my marketing plan symphony, my masterpiece, utilizing every shred of knowledge and experience I had ever accumulated across hundreds of ad accounts, at tens of agencies, across thousands of different and varied marketing meetings, messages, and campaigns. I would use my newfound knowledge of operational systems, organizational structures, financial projections, and timing assumptions that I was acquiring simultaneously during my MBA studies at UCLA Anderson (which I would complete that summer). I would check and triple-check every possible outcome, every variable, and every assumption. It would tangibly, visibly, personally add new value to Countrywide beyond just Online.

I couldn't possibly know at that time that my plan would help create, within a year, a huge, profitable new operation generating tens of thousands of new loans, worth billions in lending amounts, mailing tons of direct-mail pieces every month, airing new television commercials all over cable television every day, employing hundreds of new people in both Texas and California, directly adding to the next, and last, wave of the boom.

I set pen to paper and began.

One month later, after countless revisions and endless meetings to sell it to the business divisions, it was approved by Andy.

(NOW IS THE part where I need to delicately balance my need to tell this part of the story compellingly and truthfully, without providing you with any proprietary information about this marketing plan specifically, so I don't get clubbed and torched by Countrywide lawyers—if there are any left by the time you read this. So here goes.)

LIKE NATURE'S BRILLIANT design of the brain, a great marketing plan is a balanced mélange of the analytical, quantitative side and the ethereal, qualitative aspects. Neither alone can accomplish the goal, but rather only the perfect synchronization of both together. And Bob and Emily would carefully review this document specifically to their own perspectives and strengths.

All great marketing plans have a "front-end push" (the resources, creative pieces, and messages we are sending out) that is actually determined first by the needs of the "back-end pull" (the number of loans needed, at what amounts, over what time frames, using what capacities). So first I needed to find out what the quantitative and financial goals were before I could draw up the front end of the darn thing. After a series of meetings with Emily, and doing some other hallway detective work on my own, I learned what the strategic goals would be for this new group, by when, and how much. This was a critical cipher in the calculations, for like a financial services Rosetta Stone, this would allow me to determine the *waterfall*, and back into the scale of the operation.

The "waterfall" is called that because when drawn up on paper it resembles a series of waterfalls, each one defining the goals tighter and tighter as it moves through time. Here is a hypothetical example using a similar business model, insurance.

Let's say your boss comes to you one day and says that your company needs to generate 100,000 new insurance policies next year that pay premiums of $6,000 a year, at a total marketing acquisition cost capped at no more than $300 to be spent for each new customer. (In reality, total acquisition costs are much higher, because you also need to pay for salaries, buildings, computers, 401(k)s, etc.) If you achieve your goal, the company will make new revenue of $600 million ($6,000 premium per new customer times 100,000 new customers). *Wow, that's a lotta moolah—good work.*

Okay, then we need to subtract what you spent to acquire those new customers, which would be $30 million (100,000 new customers times a capped cost of $300 each). So your simplified *profit*, also known as your *margin* (I won't bore you with all the other dizzying array of real-world accounting rules and tasks to determine true margin, which typically allows some firms to profit only a few cents for every dollar they take in) would be $570 million in marketing profit ($600 million premium revenue minus $30 million in marketing costs). *Sounds easy, right? Well, not so fast, cowboy/girl.*

You also need to understand and know the average rates of *conversion* for each step of the process of getting an insurance policy, and then you must *back into* the plan numbers. Nobody gets a policy lickety-split with just one phone call. Let's use some simplistic (and fake) assumptions and put them up on our imaginary whiteboard. For now let's assume that the insurance company does only Direct Mail to solicit new customers. This way we can build this insurance policy marketing plan together:

Goal: 100,000 new policies

Assumptions, or internal data from your insurance marketing analytics department, based on years of marketing insurance policies:

- Only 1 percent of direct mailers historically get a response to the website or the call center. (1 percent is your *response rate*)

- Of all callers, only 20 percent *convert* from a call (sales lead) to a completed insurance application. (20 percent is your *lead-to-completed-application conversion rate*)

- Of all completed applications, we know that only 70 percent *convert* to an approved policy (70 percent is also your *application-to-approval conversion rate*). (The 30 percent that drop off could be due to underwriting not granting the policy because the customer once had the sniffles, or the customer dropping out because he got a better offer with another company—whatever. Marketing the broken healthcare system could easily be my entire second book.)

Now you can *back into* your numbers, like so (imagine a pretty little backward waterfall here, falling upward).

- If your goal is 100,000 new policies, then you will need about 143,000 new completed applications (only 70 percent will become policies).

- If you need 143,000 new completed applications, you will need about 715,000 people to call the call center inquiring about insurance (remember, only 20 percent of those callers will convert to a completed application).

- If you need 715,000 people to call the call center over a year, then with a typical 1 percent response rate to your mailings, you will need to send out about 71.5 million mailers over the course of the year, or about 6 million mailers a month.

- If your mailers cost about 50 cents each to create, print, post, and mail, then your marketing budget would need to be about $36 million.

Now we need to back into the maximum marketing cost mandate we were given. Remember, your boss told you that the maximum marketing cost per new policy could not exceed $300. Well, a $36 million marketing budget divided by 100,000 new policies equals $360 each in marketing costs. You are over budget by a cool $6 million, or 20 percent. Or, spending only $300 each, you will attain only about 83,000 new policies and will miss your goal. Congratulations—you're fired.

You had better think of something. And yes, each conversion point or flexible cost in the system is a chance for you to save your job, and generate 100,000 new policies at only $300 each, either by increasing the rates or lowering the costs.

To lower your costs of mailing, you could rebid the entire year's worth of printing costs, competitively, across three new printers. You could cut colors, use only black ink, and do away with that cheesy gold seal. You might try printing several months' worth of pieces in advance, to save printer set-up costs. You could maybe lower the weight of the mailing, or even test sending it using third class postage, although this would increase the travel time from send point to in-home from only three days via first class postage to up to 14 days or more for third class.

To increase your 1 percent response rate, maybe you can create a new offer in your mailer, or make your envelope more compelling so it has a higher *open rate*. Maybe you can add a limited-time offer so urgency will boost the response rate. Maybe you can make it larger, smaller, more colorful, less colorful, with a window, or no window, with a stamp, or no stamp, just an "indicia" (what they call that little postage-paid box). Or even make it look like a bill.

To increase your call-to-completed-application rate, you can review the call reps' script and try to make it more effective. You can partner with your sales director to develop some sales contests, boost morale, or hire better people. You can talk to finance to see if the rates can be lowered, compared to the competitive "mystery shopping" you will have done with other insurers. Perhaps you can make the process of applying simpler and easier, because after you did some research and listened to some calls, you realized that most customers want to complete the application but drop off after the fourth *hour* of questioning. Or maybe you can work with technology and make sure that the 5 percent of callers who accidentally get hung up on, or who are stuck waiting on hold for more than 30 minutes, can be lessened. Yes, sometimes the simplest things work.

(One time I worked with a client on an application website, and they couldn't figure out why application rates were so bad. Going on the website myself, I saw that the programmers had allowed only two digit spaces for the five-digit zip code. *Duh*. Every application was ending right there, of course. Simple things matter. And, it also reminded me of just how many clients never tested or used their own products or services, never "flipping their own burgers" to experience what their customers were experiencing.)

To increase your completed application to granted policy rate, you need to redesign the entire health care underwriting system. Better stick with the other conversion points.

Of course, for this example, I am leaving out a great many elements, many of which created a mind-numbing list of system details that would need to be considered and perfected in your insurance marketing program. In Countrywide, we had almost two hundred different loan products, and each had its own profit margin targets, requiring almost two hundred different waterfalls. Call tracking numbers had to be "deduped," as what might appear to be 100 calls could turn out to be 50 prospects calling twice, or even three times. We had hundreds of different mailers, some we knew worked well, others were being tested for new responses—different sizes, shapes, messages, offers, everything. At one point the matrix tracking the results of the cross section of the many mailing types across the huge array of different product messages took up my entire office wall. The total mailing quantities eventually were astronomical, every single month.

Then there were operational waterfalls as well. If your insurance company needed to generate 715,000 calls over the year, some back-of-the-envelope math might create some alarm. If you had only one shift of 100 agents working per day (vs. a 24-hour call center), and an average agent could handle only 16 calls over an 8-hour shift, then you might be in trouble. They would be able to handle 1,600 calls per day. If the center was open 7 days a week, that would be 11,200 calls per week. Now let's assume 51 weeks in a year (they need holidays off). In one year, those 100 agents might be able to handle only 571,200 calls. *Oops.* You're short a couple hundred thousand calls in your capacity. Congrats—you're fired again.

This is where the "front end vs. back end" culture of your firm comes in. Some firms have a finite set of resources—maybe those 100 agents, and that's it—and they don't want or are unable to invest in increasing their capacity. Then you will need to slap the chiefs' heads around and tell them that per their own systemic constraints, the company is physically able to handle only 571,200 calls, and they need to rework their sales goals to max out at only about 70,000 new policies.

Other firms, such as Countrywide was then, saw the humongous opportunity to maximize new revenue, achieve never-before levels of market share, and carpe diem in the new world order of Refis and

HELOCs. They were eager and willing to invest huge sums in new people, systems, buildings, and all forms of operations to maximize the production capacity of their dream factory.

Many firms in the real world play a never-ending game of hot-cold-hot-cold, keeping their fingers on the production knobs, ready to turn them up or down and recalibrate the system, carefully monitoring the delicate balance of demand and capacity every day, week, month, and year. Some do this on a macro scale, such as car companies, who need to achieve the seemingly mystical task of producing the projected exact number of cars the public will buy in a particular year. (My hat goes off to those projection wizards; truly amazing work.) On a smaller scale, if you owned a bakery, you would need to figure out exactly how many loaves of bread you usually sell per day not to waste resources.

Increasing capacity is difficult. If your insurance marketing plan requires the hiring of another 50 agents, well, you had better get to work. You'll need more office space, 50 new workstations, new computers, more server capacity in your technology, and hundreds and hundreds of labor hours of interviewing, screening, hiring, and training.

Because the loan process, laws, regulations, and certifications required for any new Countrywide sales agents were so rigid and complex, a new agent would typically spend several months as a trainee, listening in on hundreds of other calls with a mentor before they were allowed to fly solo and walk a customer through an application process alone. Although supervisors frequently listened in on agent calls to ensure quality, every one of those calls was also recorded to make sure everything was on the up-and-up.

Of course, sometimes things didn't always go as planned. I can recall one period in 2005 when reviewing the call data, we noticed a precipitous and unexplained drop-off in our application rate among one group of newly minted agents. People were calling in at normal levels, but for some reason they didn't finish the application process.

So I scheduled a "listen in" where I would literally be patched into the calls so I could hear exactly what was going on. Jeff Stone, my cherubic-faced, anxiety-ridden buddy and head of the call center operation, listened in as well. Within seconds I realized what was wrong. I heard a typical caller get patched through to the agent.

"Yes, I was calling about refinancing my home," a nice-sounding lady asked.

"*Ya, mon, we kin help yoo wit dat, reet awee,*" replied the Countrywide agent.

The thick Caribbean accent, combined with occasional static on the line, made it sound like the prospect had been connected to the Trinidad office of Countrywide.

"Um, is this Countrywide?" asked the suspicious customer.

"*Yaa fa shaw it eezzz! New worries maaam, we gonna git yoo a greet loan tooodee.*" The prospect hung up.

I didn't know whether to laugh or get angry at whoever decided that this guy would be a good phone sales agent. For years I had worked with call centers, and through experience and seeing data I knew that agents with minimal or no accents tended to generate more sales. This isn't a racist statement, it was a business fact. This is the reason why many of the largest call center companies in the world who service major corporations (yes, many call centers are outsourced, as it is a specialized operation) are in the Midwest, in accentless states such as Nebraska, or in Utah (at least they used to be before outsourcing to other countries became more efficient for some). Also, the large office space needed for call centers tends to be cheaper in the Midwest, and young, eager labor was generally more available from the local labor pool, especially in college towns.

Our call center was in Plano, Texas, where the local talent pool was a rich mix of different cultures and talent. And there were a lot of accents in Texas, but this was not what I was expecting. I immediately got off the call and called Jeff. We agreed quickly that anyone with a sharp accent of any kind should be moved into other areas, such as servicing existing customers. Once the heavy accents were removed from the new customer acquisition call center, application rates quickly rose back to normal levels.

At the height of the boom, within a year of the plan being approved, we had indeed expanded our operations, our call center and our entire marketing enterprise. But every day came down to a hot potato dance of getting the call volume *just right*. Sometimes too many calls would flood the call center (Monday mornings were always the heaviest), causing long wait times on hold, potentially losing business. Jeff would call me, yelling, as only he could, "We're dying over here, cool us off!" Then on other days, calls would be down, and agents would be sitting around with nothing to do. The same red-faced Jeff would call me, yelling, "We're dying over here, heat us up!" Every day was a search for that holy grail of just enough calls to keep everyone crazy busy but not have wait times of more than a few minutes at most. It was like making sure a spacecraft hit that thin window of reentry just right—too shallow and they bounce back into space; too steep and they burn up—every single day.

So it was up to me to design a flexible, scalable, profitable marketing engine, with multiple pistons, that would keep Jeff's group at peak levels of efficiency, as well as maximize web traffic and loan applications through our large network of nationwide branches. I took this responsibility very seriously, in part because this is what the company needed and it would create new shareholder value. But also I honestly felt good about being able to reach out to more and more homeowners and offer to lend them money. Many people would Refi and ease their monthly payment expenses. Many would pull money from their newly found home equity to improve their home, pay off crushing credit cards, send Junior to college, or take that dream vacation. *What could be more good than that?*

I also felt a responsibility to feed the thousands of salespeople that Countrywide had with as many new sales leads as possible. Many of the army of sales professionals worked at least partly on commissions. They, too, had mortgages, kids, bills. If I did not do my job well and keep new leads flowing to their desks, these people would make less money, or even worse, be laid off. And not just salespeople, but also all of the administrative people, the underwriters, and the thousands of other jobs that ran the Countrywide machine would be at risk if the volume of loan production waned.

I would rededicate myself to building the best new customer marketing engine I could.

AS THE OPERATION grew, it was clear that this new marketing force would have three distinct yet equally critical elements driving it forward: Online, Direct Mail, and TV.

First would be the existing online efforts I already controlled, but just expanded. A certain percentage of total loan leads would be driven into the website every month through Paid Search, Organic (Unpaid) Search, Affiliates, and Online media (banner click-throughs). Also, various areas of the Countrywide Home Loans site (vs. just the front-door portal that was Countrywide.com) would get new, more robust application tools, fun little Home Equity "what is it and how does it work?" web movies, and an array of other bells and whistles I would need to work on with my favorite nemesis, Denise. Like a military arsenal, Online would be the fast and recallable "Minutemen" fighter planes or ground troops with which to quickly modulate the flow of leads into the call center daily. Within hours we could dial down, or up, our search listings, our banner placements, even our presence on Bankrate.com, the top rates listing site for all the players in the lending industry. Experience and common sense would confirm that Online recalibration, unlike TV or Mail, would be the fastest weapon for optimizing flow at the call center, to either cool it off or heat it up as necessary by hundreds of leads per day.

The second new area would be Direct Mail. Mail was the submarine-launched ICBMs, the large-scale missiles that could not be recalled once mailed; that could be targeted down to the household or neighborhood, and that, like submarines, could most likely not be readily seen by the competition (at least not as visibly as web banners or TV).

The Subprime division, Full Spectrum Lending, already had a massive direct-mail operation, so I would first mine their response data to determine what were the most winning pieces they had, and then I would "Countrywide" them so that any FSL cheesiness would be replaced with Countrywide class and higher tone. (Remember, these pieces would go to the Prime prospects with top credit scores.) But our group would still start out from scratch.

For example, just because a yellow envelope of an FSL mailing may have worked in driving in new Subprime loan applications doesn't mean that the same piece, even with less salesy language, would work for Prime. I had many salespeople sending me tens of mailers from all sorts of competitors with notes saying "This worked; let's mimic it." Bob wanted more "branded" pieces, with full, rich colors; smiling faces; picket fences; and other Countrywide icons. Emily didn't care, just ordering me to "make sure it makes money." Some people said I should only mail postcards. Others said oversized envelopes were the way to go. And I dutifully listened to every opinion, then decided not to listen to any of them; I would let our customers decide. I can remember the day I had to look Bob in the eyes and say, "With all due respect, your opinion, my opinion, means nothing on Direct Mail; the only opinion that matters is our customers' response behavior." But then again this kind of in-your-face pushback was partly why he hired me.

I would need to test every conceivable size, shape, color, message, offer, and targeting scenario I could using "test cells"—mail quantities small enough to be low-risk, but large enough to generate statistically significant response results. Then I would need to remail the exact same tests to replicate the results of the experiments and validate our conclusions. Much of Direct Marketing is based on the Scientific Method, where we create a hypothesis of what we think customers will respond most to, then we test it for response results (mail it, put it on TV or on the website); then, to make sure we don't get false results, replicate the experiment exactly. If we get the same results, only then would we feel comfortable enough to move forward with a potential "roll out"—either putting the TV spot all over the airwaves with many more media dollars, or printing 10 million of the winning direct mailer, or keeping that same web banner up. Remember, if you see a direct-response ad in any medium, and then you see it twice, or more, chances are that that mix of creative, offer, and message was their winning test.

But Direct Mail, as mundane as it can appear, is the precise and thoughtful application of data analysis. "Junk mail" is just the wrong offer sent to the wrong person at the wrong time. Well, data helped us find the right person at the right time, so it was at least 60 percent of the success of the effort.

There were two types of mailings. Those offers that you get for credit cards and loans that say you are "preapproved" means that they have legally looked at your credit score; that's how they deem you preapproved. Generic offers without preapproval did not involve searching your credit score. We had two groups of resources for each of these prospect types. New prospect lists without "preapproved credit" were generally pulled from the massive databases of all U.S. households that are legally and readily available for purchase by any direct marketer for anything from exercise equipment to catalogs to financial products. Credit scored lists would need to be rented for one-time or multiple use from one of the three credit tracking firms, Equifax, TransUnion, or Experian.

Although my group focused solely on the Prime prospects (those with FICO scores over 650), even within these Prime prospects, we could build database models that could more finely tune these data.

For example, if we wanted to push Home Equity loans, we could target people who we knew had a child who would be soon entering college, or had just bought a new home and might need to do some remodeling, or a household that for whatever reason had attempted to get some new credit cards in recent months. It did not take a brain surgeon to think that maybe, just maybe, those types of people might be more likely to respond to an offer for a Home Equity loan. Of course, they would never receive an offer unless we knew also from home sale vs. home worth data (either via publicly available information or our own data, if their first loans were with Countrywide) that they indeed *did* have equity in their home to use.

Much has been made in the media of evil corporations using public, legal, and completely legitimate and accessible credit, financial, and household data to send offers to people. This is done every day, in most every business category, to every household in the United States. Just check your mailbox if you don't believe this. From the earliest days in the mid-nineteenth century when the first frontier-worn catalogs of little companies called Montgomery Ward and Sears Roebuck offered a pioneer family just about everything it needed, and new mail services and railroads invented the newly booming shipping industry, direct marketing has been helping people get what they need long before any web came about. And even today, with our ever-increasing over-70 population exploding, direct marketing in mail and the web still helps people get what they need, easily, quickly, and relatively cheaply without having to ever leave their homes. It is up to consumers to be cautious, make smart decisions, and throw out the junk mail if they don't want it. Nobody has ever been forced to buy anything. But, America keeps responding to it, and sending money for products and services. *If y'all didn't respond, there would be no direct marketing industry.* Of course, you could ask not to be mailed. Here's the web address to get on the national "Do Not Mail" List: www.dmachoice .org/MPS/proto1.php.

Television would be the final leg of our marketing triad. To extend the military metaphor, TV was our "air cover," carpet bombing the airwaves and softening the prospect with a wholesome, welcoming, clear, warm message of expertise, support, and advocacy. That softened prospect could then also get a direct mailer, the "boots taking the hill." The TV message would first become "No One Can Do What Countrywide Can," then in later months would morph into a stronger statement, of simply "Countrywide Can" when it began to become harder to get loans as rates slowly rose.

As Direct Response Television began development, Bob and I were both involved because it was so visible; Bob was a bonafide expert in the Countrywide brand, and I had the stronger Direct Response TV experience. Together we would make a powerful team in the creation of this response-oriented follow-up to "Realize Your Dreams," which had since been stopped due to budget constraints. We thought we were all set to develop these TV spots on our own.

Then, entered *Slick Rick*.

One day word came from Andy that he wanted us to work on the TV concepting with a friend of his, a consultant whom we quickly dubbed Slick Rick. We called him that because Rick was as smooth as they came in the agency world. He was a financial services Direct Response TV expert with a rich background, had a friendly, gregarious manner, and was absolutely *nice* to everyone. His tailored, charming, "Mr. Perfect" style initially drove me totally *batshit*.

Naturally, being still somewhat immature and cocky at this time, I immediately bristled at the thought of an outside consultant being assigned to us by Andy, to teach us what we thought we already knew how to do. Bob, being much more seasoned and mature, and politically savvy, immediately embraced this newcomer and welcomed him into our family, eagerly asking for and absorbing any large and small suggestions he had in the new TV concepting.

Why would he so readily hand over any power to this new guy?

Because he was smart. And at the end of the day, he simply welcomed any extra value that would further the goals and the messages of Countrywide. Maybe he did resent Rick's presence, but he never showed it, and never shared these feelings with his team. He always seemed to put brand and firm before personal ego and ambition; it was one of the things I so admired about him. He rose above most petty politics, and in so doing, taught us all how to get along, and taught me how to grow up a little more. To this day I still encounter many top-level senior executives who do not have this wisdom that Bob so readily projected to his team.

Within a few weeks, to my surprise, my initial perceptions of Slick Rick would give way to a deep admiration and respect that I did not anticipate. I misjudged him. He could have used his relationship with Andy to barrel through the organization, taking control of everyone and everything related to TV. Instead, he was a true professional, and obviously experienced in those common mistakes that inexperienced consultants often make. He was always there to help, not own the process. He showed respect for those of us not as senior as he. He, like Bob and Emily, nurtured and inspired all of us to do better work, with a firm hand, yet with a smile and a joke when needed. He listened, studied, engaged, and encouraged all of us to do better. In the end, I had Rick all wrong, and to this day I consider him among the very best marketing professionals I know. In later years, as I would move onto other things, he would eventually take a greater role in the development of all Countrywide DRTV, staying as a consultant until the end.

Unlike Brand TV, which may run for weeks and weeks on air, Direct Response TV, like Direct Mail, was a never-ending search for the most profitable mix of message, creative, and offer. DRTV never settled with one spot and hoped for the best. No, DRTV was considered *disposable advertising*. Spots would be tested and retested, and even when a winner was found, the profitability and response of those winning spots would typically die off after six to eight weeks, as the low-hanging fruit of responders to that TV spot ran out. So DRTV spots needed to be disposable, coming on and off with regularity as response conditions fluctuated. This required the unique skills and sensibilities of DR creative people. Unlike Brand creatives, who may fall in love with their own work, DR creative people understood that in their business, they may create 10 to 20 spots, and maybe one of them will work and the other 19 will never again see the light of day.

This also required an intense and inexpensive process of ongoing commercial development and production. Unlike the extravagant, multimillion-dollar, minimovie production budgets for ads that featured helicopter shots in Australia and hundreds of people dancing and that might appear once during the Super Bowl, DR spots for an operation this size needed to be cheap, fast, and to the point. No spot would be able to exceed a cost more than the low five figures, and the message was clear and simple: *Money is your problem, Countrywide is your solution, here's how, and call now.* That's it. That's the secret of DRTV marketing. Show a good rate, too. And we would need to crank out a few new spots every few weeks. Most Brand TV spots take three to four months of concepting, prep, and production before they get on the air; our DRTV spots would go from paper to airing within four weeks.

This was the time when I pushed harder and took more thoughtful risks. There comes a point in every career where your confidence and abilities rise to where you can stop asking for permission in favor of asking for forgiveness. Many times I would approve and release new test mailings and web tests without financial approval from Emily or creative approval from Bob. Granted, it was a small amount of money, but I felt it was important to take some risks to establish trust and elevate confidence in this new division quickly. Luckily for me, we started to find some winning combinations that were beginning to drive new leads and new revenue.

I took some political risks on building a staff for this new group. I had to walk the delicate line of not brazenly poaching the best talent from other areas in marketing, but, frankly, I put the word out that I was looking, and they came to me, wanting to join this new adventure.

One person was named Julia Lee. She was known as a rising star in the marketing group, and would grow to become one of the most talented, loyal, dedicated, hardworking managers I ever had the pleasure of working with. She got things done, had great relationships within the firm, and having come from Wonderboy's Customer Communications group, was an expert in Direct Mail.

Soon I was able to add a more senior guy who was an expert in other areas on which we would focus: data modeling and tracking analytics. Brian Egan was a quiet, reserved family man who rarely spoke in meetings, but when he did, it was something brilliant. The hiring of Brian became a political hot potato. Using the smart Bob method of securing preapproval, I had Brian meet with Denise and with many other internal people as well. Everyone gave Brian a big thumbs up—except Denise, ever the contrarian.

Brian had been hard to find. I went through hundreds of résumés and interviewed tens of candidates; some were not who they said they were, some didn't make it through the array of internal meetings I would put them through; some were "just not very Countrywide." But with Brian, we knew that his skill set, temperament, and experience were exactly what we needed, so I extended the offer to Brian anyway on my own authority. Denise was furious, of course. Truth was, given my own combative style when annoyed, I actually made the move to hire Brian on my own *because I knew* Denise hated him. In the end, Denise calmed down and realized it was a battle not worth fighting, and Brian, too, became a valued member of my new customer marketing SWAT team.

I was still working to find a replacement for my former troublesome Online manager, and eventually found a candidate that I had interviewed years earlier in the agency world and saw as a star. Sam Goodwin flew through the Countrywide interview process with flying colors and I told Bob and Andy I was going to hire him to be my new First VP of Online Marketing. (Countrywide officer ranks went like this: Assistant VP, VP, First VP, Senior VP [me], Executive VP [Bob and Emily], then Managing Director, then Senior Managing Director [Andy was SMD and CMO], then Dave, Stan, and Angelo.) In one of the most embarrassing moments ever for me at Countrywide, I made Sam an offer at four P.M. one day, only to get a call from Andy at five P.M.

"Did you make Sam the offer yet?" Andy asked me. I told him I had.

"Well, pull it back. Stan [Kurland] has instituted a short term hiring freeze."

"But I already made him the offer; I shook his hand on the phone," I said.

"Sorry, call him back."

I called Sam back only to find out that the cat was out of the bag; he had already given notice at his old job, and as he described it, he couldn't go back now. Sam had to leave his old job with our offer rescinded. I was mortified. For my reputation, and for Countrywide's. Luckily within a few weeks I was able to finally offer Sam the position again, although he had been out of work during this awkward downtime. I always respected Sam for not using this incident in any negotiations thereafter; in fact, he never mentioned it again. Eventually he did so well that a few years later he replaced me to run Online Marketing. And I was proud to have been the one to have hired him. He was "very Countrywide."

The call center was operating at maximum capacity every day, training was seamless and strong, and per David Sambol's mantra that our firm would have *A Loan For Every Customer*, almost every prospect who called was offered some kind of solution; few would be turned away without first finishing an application to see if we could indeed fund him or her. Even those people with less-than-perfect credit, or Subprime credit, were quickly and seamlessly transferred and handed off to Full Spectrum Lending to get their loan options. And the call center was completely designed in the "Countrywide way."

All call transfers were done via the "warm transfer" method, unlike other firms where they just hit the transfer button and never realize you got cut off or hung up on. At Countrywide you might first get Agent 1, who realized you needed FSL for your loan needs. Agent 1 would put you on hold, get Agent 2 (FSL) on the line, then conference everyone in to make sure you and Agent 2 were talking, then politely get off with a simple "Okay, Mr. Smith, Agent 2 will help you now." This was a call center best practice, and consistent with our brand. Also consistent with our brand, yet hugely expensive, was your call first being picked up by a live operator. Unlike some other banks that first sent you perhaps into a mind-numbing computerized voice system ("press 1 for this, press 2 for that"), we had made the decision early on that those cold systems were not very "Countrywide."

We would provide the live, warm experience of immediately getting a human to talk to, who would then politely and quickly forward you to the right connection. Research showed that these personal call center "concierges" made a huge difference; they were living examples of our white-picket-fence warmth. With Bob's approval and over Emily's cost objections, we decided the expense was worth it to stay true to who we were.

So the systems and the team were solid, each specialists and superstars in their own areas. Brian, Julia, Sam, and I would execute the plan that Andy approved that spring of 2004. Jeff ran a great call center operation. By 2005, at the peak of our online, mail, and TV production within New Customer Acquisition, we were generating huge numbers of new Prime loan leads per month for Refis, HELOCs, everything. I had succeeded in helping to create a new lead generation engine like Countrywide had never seen before; we were competing strongly, closing in on the title of number one mortgage provider in the United States (competing neck and neck with Wells Fargo), eventually securing that position and providing one of five mortgages in the whole country. We were all over the web, showed up in millions of mailboxes every month, and were ubiquitous on national cable TV with the winning message of *Countrywide Can.*

We had overcome the slow rise in mortgage rates and the Prime rate, compensating with an ever more aggressive campaign of solicitation, to great success, and the analytics were meticulous and staggering. Every single product, at different loan amounts, had its own waterfall projections. Every one of the hundreds of different mail test packages had sliding response rate projections by product and state. Every Paid Search keyword had a different click rate and cost. The machine had hundreds of thousands of tiny moving parts, and each day we got it through the atmosphere of corporate profitability at peak efficiency. I felt that I had fulfilled my promise to Andy. With my smart, capable A-Team we had created the emotionally compelling messages that Bob directed us to do, elevating the Countrywide brand of advocacy, expertise, strength, and trust. We also had created an analytical marvel per Emily's direction, knowing each and every metric of profitability down to the penny, each week, per our duty to return value to shareholders.

In the mortgage market, in the housing market, and within New Customer Acquisition in Countrywide's Corporate Marketing department, it was the Roaring Twenties all over again. There was *a loan for every customer,* and I helped create new customers by the truckload. America, I, and Countrywide basked in the glow of success.

8

The Art of Not Lying

What if everything is an illusion and nothing exists?
In that case, I definitely overpaid for my carpet.
—Woody Allen

JUNE 2004

Prime rate: 4.00%

Foreclosure rate: 1.16%

CFC stock price: ~$35.00

BY JUNE 2004, my New Customer Acquisition group was already beginning to show signs that it could make real money. And in a Fortune 100, that draws attention like blood in a tank full of sharks. Countrywide fashioned itself a *meritocracy*, that is, whoever generated the most value, or profit, for the firm would be granted the greatest rewards, growth, and prestige. It also drew out the politics inherent in people, no matter how good they are, no matter how unintentionally.

In typical fashion, when Andy asked me to create this group he demonstrated either intentional brilliance or unintentional aloofness—I couldn't tell which—in having me report to two bosses: my longtime friend, and mentor to whom I was loyal, the right-brained Bob Griffin, who arguably was the heart of the Countrywide brand and guardian of the warm and fuzzy feelings that the brand evoked;

and Emily Simmons, the cool, calculating, hard-core finance jock who had grown into the quantitative mentor that I had been seeking for years to round out my business education.

I use the term *brilliance* when referring to Andy's requested reporting structure because if the New Customer marketing plan had been either all emotional or all quantitative, it would have failed either way. Bob would constantly recommend new elements to the language, scribbling comments to an early version of a letter or web copy, noting "make it more 'Countrywide,'" meaning more warm, approachable, neighborly. He had a keen eye and ear for the subtleties and awesome power of little things, from typefaces to colors to language. He was passionate and serious about keeping the Countrywide brand on the right path and, like a doctor, to first make sure that all communications "did no harm" to the personality and relationship we had built over the years with America through expertise, trust, and service. He could keep a meeting going for hours—and I mean hours—while debating some brand detail, but I appreciated his passion, and I was eager to learn from it. His stewardship of these ethereal elements was a critical role in a firm comprised mostly of finance people. I was glad he did it, and his patience, diplomatic skills, and sensibilities made him perfect for the role.

Emily was the exact opposite. She constantly challenged me to unlearn the tenets developed over years of warm and fuzzy advertising work and always to see the quantitative side of everything we did. One time we were in a meeting, with at least 10 people in it, to review some aspect of Countrywide's cultural experience—anything from the rules for the potato sack races at the annual picnic, to the number of sodas that would be in the vending machines—I can't recall exactly—but it was something trivial. Emily grumbled silently through the two-hour meeting and passed me a note. *Calculate how much this meeting is costing u*s, the note read. She smiled at me across the table, ending with an eye roll.

I loved quizzes like this. It was stuff that Bob never did. But as much as I knew that Bob was critical for the brand, I was also glad for our shareholders that much of the firm thought like Emily did, always focused on profit.

I zoned out as the meeting leader kept going through the agenda. *Okay, item six, the schedule for the Halloween party.* After a few minutes I sent the note scribbled back to Emily with a simple formula, completely ad-libbed: $V = R - O - LP$

She knew what it meant; we had done this before. It was a back-of-the-envelope equation that said that the value of the meeting (V) was equal to the revenue (R) generated by it, minus the overhead costs (O) and minus the lost productivity (LP). She slipped it back to me, scribbling, *Show me the numbers.*

Okay, first, revenue generated directly by this meeting was easy: zero. However, I am sure some enterprising young finance guru trapped in Human Resources could arguably show that picnics and parties enhanced morale, improved retention, and then saved us the costs of rehiring. But I did not have a supercomputer at my disposal to calculate such things, so in went the big, fat zero.

Overhead was a little trickier, so I used some assumptions. The attendees seemed to be half senior people and half junior people, so to be conservative I estimated everyone's salary at about $100,000. I backed into a projected hourly cost of each person, assuming 21 business days per month at 8 hours per day (although we usually worked 10 to 12 hours per day; *the boom didn't run itself, you know*), then multiplied by 12 months: 2,016 hours worked per year per person. If the average person made $100,000 per year, that equated to approximately $50 per hour per person for just salary. But overhead was much more than salary. It was benefits—health, 401(k), etc—electricity, pencils, air-conditioning, and so forth. I assumed a typical round up for overhead, about twice salary, which brought me to $100 per hour per person. The meeting was 2 hours, it had 10 people. The overhead for this meeting was $200 × 10 = $2,000.

Lost productivity was even stickier, and more arguable. We personally did not make loans or process paperwork; Corporate Marketing fueled the demand for the applications. So at the risk of having Emily cross it out with a red pen, I simply calculated the revenue we made every year and broke it into an hourly revenue stream, then multiplied by 2. I can't tell you those top-secret numbers here, but let's just say for this example that I plopped in $50,000 for lost productivity.

So, $R - O - LP$ became $0 - $2,000 - $50,000. The value of this meeting to Countrywide was probably a *loss* of about $52,000. I passed the paper back to Emily with the words *so this meeting is worse than worthless.*

She smiled when she saw it, basking in the glow of my finance jock training regimen. The meeting continued as she kept passing me more and more molecular questions, including directing me to calculate the loss per outstanding share to stockholders (which using my little Fisher-Price calculator came in at about a 0.00000001 cent loss per share) and a host of other orbital calculations dependent on the airspeed of a butterfly in Madrid. This training for me was important, fun, and helped me hold my own against the CFOs with whom I attended grad school at the time.

This was how finance jocks like Emily played in boring meetings, either with financial thought experiments, or by handing me a bound book of 3,000 Excel spreadsheets each showing grids of hundreds of numbers, with a note scribbled on the cover saying "Find an error within 15 minutes." I was not in advertising agency "Kansas" anymore; it wasn't just about picket fences and warm commercials and weepy messages about the American Dream. This was serious business with serious people handling serious money. So as childlike as these exercises sounded, each was in fact a set of a hundred analytical push-ups, an hour practicing on the firing range, a bayonet exercise that might be done by sentries guarding gold at Fort Knox.

So I had made an appraisal that the meeting had cost the firm

$52,000. Was I *lying*? No; I was *projecting*, and this is a key part of the story.

The media have chosen to vilify many of the players in the story, especially Countrywide early on. But I would argue this is simply because Countrywide was the leader of an industry that was now imploding, yet not due solely to its own activities or behavior. Back in my life in advertising, we used to have a saying that advertising was also the *Art of Not Lying*. That is, to state the benefits of a product or service as compellingly and as engagingly as possible, even perhaps to enhance and embellish them a bit, without actually *lying* about these benefits. Going back to the nineteenth century, advertising was maligned as the height of falsehood and embellishment. Back then much of it was actually made up of *real* snake oil salesmen, continuing into the early days of television when the public was told that Geritol "cured tired blood," whatever that meant, to even today, when every e-mailbox in America is inundated with male-enhancement drug spam. The only powers in our society that keep this type of lying at bay (as much as it can) are the ethics of the creators of such messages, the laws and regulation of our government, and consumers ignoring it. Perhaps Jefferson would rail against such regulation, claiming once that "Advertisements contain the only truths to be relied on in a newspaper," but history has shown again and again that left to their own devices, people will sometimes lie for profit.

But what constitutes a "lie" can be subjective. One person's truth may be another person's lie, depending on their point of view—just ask any religious zealot. And in our story, the definition of the truth can be argued from the macro to the micro.

On a macro scale, the values of bundled mortgage securities were priced at a level that the analysts and the marketplace felt was fair at the time. Loan rates were calculated using as much data as possible from the markets, also using credit scores to gauge, and predict, the risk factor in lending an individual a certain amount. Were they lying when they priced these financial instruments? No; they were predicting what the value should be, based on available risk, demand, and market data at the time.

Another critical macro element of this mess was housing values in general. As housing values rose fast, so, too, rose the hunger for speculators and buyers to jump in that much faster. It's an exponential effect. Bubbles create their own momentum, which in turn increases the size of the bubbles. Like physics, a price at rest will tend to stay at rest, a price in motion will tend to stay in motion. Housing prices were going up because people were making crazy bids trying to get in on the boom, which caused housing prices to keep going up. Now, in the downturn, housing prices are plummeting, suggesting prices will further plummet, causing many potential buyers to sit on the sidelines, which, in turn, causes housing prices to plummet. We saw this counterintuitive dynamic law of motion all the time with mortgage rates. When rates were *rising*, applications briefly *rose* as people rushed to get in before they got "too high." When rates were coming down, we actually tended to see applications slow down, as people sat out waiting for the bottom. Eventually they all jumped in, though.

But no one could get a Refi without a new appraisal on the home. If the *perceived* value—forget about actual value at the moment—was about 10 to 20 percent greater than the debt on the home, then you would probably qualify for some kind of Refi loan. *Congrats, we are going to "help" you; we're going to give you more money so you can spend more.*

An appraiser might see a home that he appraised two years earlier for $250,000, but now his new appraisal would value the property at $400,000. Why? Because the appraisal was primarily based on *how other similar homes were selling in the local neighborhood.* And this was the cancerous part of the problem. The appraiser had access to other similar homes on your street or otherwise near you, and his data were showing that other homes, due to the momentum of the bubble, were now selling for $400,000 to $500,000. Why *wouldn't* he appraise your home for the same range? The problem was, those much higher sales were based on the frothy price wars hard fought by speculators who hoped the value would increase still, by desperate homebuying prospects who just *had* to have that home they had fallen in love with, and by the new additions and improvements that some of the homes had built on using Home Equity money from these new, higher values.

Yes, as the media have reported, I am sure that some appraisers were unscrupulous and wrongly inflated the appraisals on homes. (I never personally saw any evidence of that at Countrywide.) But 99.9 percent of appraisers were diligent and honest, doing their jobs professionally and signing their name to a home that now, given the current state of the market and comparably, was really worth $400,000. Were they lying? No; they were *projecting* the perceived value of the home based on available and current data within the marketplace. That $400,000 price was now a fact, at that moment in the market. Welcome to the science of *Virtual Value*. (Part of the debacle has been made that much worse, as millions of homes then borrowed against that virtual value through so many Home Equity loans, now coming home to roost as well.)

The wildly fluctuating price tag on the only home I ever bought myself provides a good example.

For years I rented a small apartment in West Los Angeles with my girlfriend at the time. It was cozy, clean, and nice, but nothing to write home about. The building, along with many other buildings in the area, was owned by a small, elderly Chinese man, Mr. Chow. Mr. Chow worked in and lived out of a tiny, cramped, and hot dry-cleaning store in the seedy part of town, and was truly the "millionaire next door." He lived frugally, drove an old, beat-up car, and wore the same pants and gray sweater every time I saw him. Once his son hinted that they owned at least 25 buildings in the local area, which had to be worth a fortune. Yet, still, every day he toiled away at his little dry-cleaning store, working his butt off for the American Dream. And he was a sweet man, too. Maybe because I showed him great respect when I saw him, or maybe because we were good tenants, he would give me a month free every year for re-upping my yearlong agreement to stay. This would bring my monthly rent down to about $650, an amazing steal for our nice apartment in that area. With our two incomes, we were able to save money at a fast pace, preparing for the down payment on a house we had always talked about getting (although I would have been perfectly happy to pay $650 a month for the rest of my life in that apartment).

All throughout my life, I have never really needed *stuff*. Always more inclined to seek joy from experiences rather than *things*, I'm a saver, not a spender. I could live life quite happily with minimal living quarters and a huge savings just sitting in the bank. It just helps me sleep at night; I am naturally averse to debt. Just after college I went a little nutty and ran up what was then huge credit card bills, about $6,000 total, even though at the time I only made about $30,000 a year. In the five years it took me to pay off those cards with blood and toil and no spending, I vowed to myself that I would never again carry a credit card balance, and I never have. It is a nice feeling to be cash-positive, no matter what you own.

In the mid-1990s, after we got married, naturally we began thinking about buying a house. Well, frankly, *she* did. But I went along. It was something to do, looking at houses, and looking didn't cost anything. Also, many of our friends were buying their first homes, and well, it seemed like it was time. Eventually we came upon a Cape Cod–style town home in West Los Angeles that caught our eye. The gray clapboards and the white shutters seemed like a home out of *Architectural Digest*, and we fell in love with the place. It was three stories of heaven, on a quiet street corner with many large trees, which I loved. Suddenly I found myself caught up in the concept of the American Dream a decade before I would ever wind up at Countrywide, cranking out dreams by the millions.

We first approached our checking account bank for some loan rates (as most people do), but then a friend of a friend recommended a sales guy at Chase, who was the only one who had the patience to walk us first-timers through the mind-numbing, never-ending questions that we were asking. The array of choices in loans was staggering. Fixed, Adjustable, multiple types and terms of adjustables, it was dizzying. I told him I wanted the security of a stable monthly payment, which meant a fixed product, combined with as much of the benefits of an adjustable rate as possible. We settled on a 7/1 ARM; the rate and the monthly payment would be set for 7 years, which I considered an eternity when I was 30 years old, yet the adjustable-rate nature of the product would give us a slightly lower rate than a 30-year fixed. *Whew.*

The history of the value of the house, like the information stored in tree rings, told the story of the local economy in recent times. The town homes (there were 16 in the complex) were originally built in a boom time in Southern California, in 1988, and back then each had sold quickly for about $400,000. But in the early 1990s, recession had hit the United States, and Southern California especially hard. While the collapse of the Berlin Wall and the end of the Cold War were triumphs for America, they were disasters for the defense and aerospace industries, much of them centered in California. Unemployment soared in the mid-1990s, exacerbating the recession effects, and housing prices plummeted. That same town home that sold for $400,000 in 1988 was now about to be bought by us for only $250,000. Now, make no mistake: $250,000 was a frightening amount of money to me back then, so I was not basking in the glow of getting a home cheaply. But I really was; I had accidentally stumbled on the very best moment to buy a home in my market; it was near bottom.

During the loan and homebuying process, I educated myself. I kept a dog-eared copy of *Home Buying for Dummies* with me for weeks. I read it three times, and the hundreds of small yellow Post-its tagged all throughout told the story of a studious first-time homebuyer. It wasn't like the movies. It was complicated and required education. I learned quickly that our monthly payment would not be just the mortgage. It would also be the property taxes (about $300 per month), the Homeowners Association dues (HOA)—$250 per month—and miscellaneous extra costs. In our old apartment we didn't even have air-conditioning; this new magical convenience of comfort in our new castle would cost us another $400 per month in electric bills in the summer months. All this had to be figured into the monthly cost of the home, which I insisted stay below a third of our monthly take-home pay. I always wanted to leave some breathing room for trouble.

After the emotional rollercoaster of bid, counterbids, rebids, and final haggle, we did get into the place for $254,000. As I sat there on the floor of my new living room, surrounded by boxes on move-in day, I experienced a new feeling for the first time. In the English language there was not a word yet for the surreal mix of ecstasy and terror I felt as I looked upon my new home. This floor, this fireplace, this tree, this home, were mine. And so was my new debt, which I had promised to repay. For someone who lost sleep because of $6,000 in recent credit card debt that had finally been repaid, this was numbing. But tears welled up when I thought about the accomplishment I had achieved; the American Dream. Tears also welled up—and my hand shook—when I had to write that first check for my first mortgage payment. I learned fast that with great dreams came great responsibility.

At the height of the boom, that same property would be reappraised for my divorce paperwork. It was, at that moment, worth $850,000.

Or was it?

As I write this, the value of the properties in that area are dropping rapidly. My old unit now is hovering in the $500,000s. So on a macro level, it isn't so much about the *Art of Not Lying*; it is more about the *Art of Interpreting* the data we are told within the *context* of the time frame, history, and market dynamics of that moment.

Once again we stumble across a law of physics that has relevance to this dynamic. In physics there is something called the Heisenberg Principle, which basically says that you cannot tell both the exact location and the exact speed (momentum) of an object at the same time. If you can tell the exact location, it must be at that frozen moment in time, hence you have no context for how fast it is going. Conversely, if you can tell the speed, then at any moment you can't tell where exactly it is; if you are tracking speed, then by the time you check location it has moved. Similarly, if you want to assess a home's value, that is simply a static snapshot of that value's "location" (value) at one moment in history—only. It cannot speak to the speed or the trajectory of that value. Like cigarettes that tell you right on the package that they may kill you, every single investment vehicle in the United States—except home-buying—has attached to it a regulatory warning that says *past performance is no guarantee of future results.*

Within Countrywide, the *Art of Not Lying* was something we took very seriously. First it is critical to note that Countrywide had at its center a culture of ethics, which I appreciated. Every meeting, every report, every lunchroom poster really pounded it into our brains that we should always be doing the honest, right thing for our customers, for our shareholders, for our values.

Also, as this also was my time at UCLA Anderson working on my MBA, a core theme of the entire curriculum was ethics. Enron was still fresh in everyone's minds, and the Sarbanes-Oxley Act, relating to accounting, had just been signed into law. Forevermore, CEOs and CFOs would need to personally sign their names to the numbers they were presenting to the street, to attest to their accuracy, at risk of prosecution if they were misleading. Many of us in school felt this actually went too far. Yes, a captain should always be responsible for the actions of his ship and his crew, but to insist that a CEO in New York could personally attest to the accuracy of some inventory count by a junior flunky in a warehouse in Jakarta was problematic at best. Frankly, I think that this law, while still a good and necessary idea to weed out the crooks and deter unethical behavior, will also spook some great CEO candidates away from this kind of uncontrollable personal risk.

The UCLA faculty smartly had tweaked the education for this new generation of MBAs to focus much more on *doing the right thing* in business. Every class, from finance, to operations, to marketing, to business law, all focused firmly on the bedrock of ethical behavior. One visiting CEO even gave us a speech that focused on the need to make sure that each and every expense report was accurate down to the penny. "If you tip a cabbie $1, but put $2 down on your expense report, somehow, someday, they will find out. Then all of your numbers will be suspect," he said. His smart message of ethical leadership has stayed with me throughout my career.

Countrywide acted this way, too, on a micro level. Every advertisement, every direct mailer, every letter, every web banner, every TV ad, print ad, and windshield wiper flyer had to go through a rigorous meat grinder of both legal and regulatory approval. I separate them because Countrywide had intentionally set up a redundant system to check communications for any messages that were illegal or against regulations. And these rules could be different across all 50 states, in different media, and across different loan products, so I was glad to have this army of rule checkers on my side before anything went out.

Of course, that's not to say it was a completely altruistic enterprise. Like all financial firms, one of Countrywide's main goals was to *minimize risk*. And this meant weeding out any marketing messages that could even be confused with something that might be against regulations. Sometimes this Goody Two-shoes methodology of erring on the side of conservatism annoyed me, as my goals, my bonuses, were based on my numbers—the applications pulled into the system via my marketing efforts. While I also wanted to make sure we never lied or misled in marketing communications, any attempt to water down the messages would potentially lessen my bonus. Some cases clearly involved poor language and were changed quickly, but sometimes the meaning of a word or a phrase was arguable, and I would push for approval.

My contact in the Legal Department was a smart, no-nonsense

Southerner with a big swagger, cool boots, and a bigger smile. Billy Fields was a great lawyer with a handlebar mustache who understood the balance we were trying to achieve and who knew exactly how to talk to me. "Boy, don't argue with me on the law," he would say, "argue with me about what we're havin' for lunch." I trusted him, but I also knew from years in advertising that the role of marketing legal advisors was to find the "no's." My job was to find the "yeses." And sometimes we didn't agree. Final determinations would sometimes need to be brokered by a committee of leaders of the business units that the messages represented—and the risks would affect—and either Bob or Emily, representing the Corporate Marketing group.

One of Billy's favorite phrases was "Boy, just imagine this loan offer letter hea bein' blown up to about *yay* big, mounted on a giant board, and presented to a jury. Do you honestly think that *they* would find it misleading?" He was smart. Many times I would be forced to agree that we needed to tone down or clarify the language. Of course if I didn't, Billy would not let the letter off his desk. I respected him and his role immensely, and even now am convinced that Countrywide—at least in the area of Prime lending marketing that I managed—bent over backward to make sure that every communication was accurate, truthful, legal, and thoroughly vetted through the byzantine rules and regulations among the 50 states.

Sometimes the *Art of Not Lying* can be more political in nature, and is an acquired skill. As my New Customer Acquisition group grew and became more profitable within Corporate Marketing, tensions began to mount due to Andy's organizational directive that I report to both Bob and Emily. They were both professional, nice, smart people, but they simply saw the same marketing efforts through completely opposite points of view. This tension was arguably due to the reporting structure, but eventually it became intolerable, especially since I truly respected them both.

As mentioned, Bob was the warm and fuzzy expert in marketing; Emily was the analytical brain. In my responsible role as head of this Direct Marketing–based system, I knew that at the end of the day, the metrics would define success more than the brand feelings the marketing pieces conveyed. No one would think I did a great job if research showed that from my TV, mailings, or web banner that they "felt good" about Countrywide, and we made no loan applications; we had salespeople to feed. A lot.

For example, response data showed what I had known for years doing Direct Mail: the so-called "ugliest" mailers were usually the most responsive. Like some bizarre-world reality, Direct Mail is counterintuitive. Your classic plain, white, letter-size business envelope (also known as a "number ten" size) with a see-through front window was usually a winner. Yet Bob thought "they were ugly," and directed me to invest in testing some new, colorful, warm, "branded" Countrywide mailings. This meant expensive. This meant duds that would be unresponsive and I knew it going in. But sometimes I would get tripped up by his genius logic via my own axioms. One time he showed me a competitive mailer that was hugely expensive, large, and colorful. He directed me to test this type of mailing in our arsenal. I had to tell him that these "branded" mailings never did well, and weren't doing well in our own previous tests.

Smartly, he would say to me, "Well, have you tested this exact type of design approach?" I would have to answer "Um, no," of course; there were infinite numbers of sizes and shapes we could have tested.

"And you have never sent this *exact* type of design approach to *our* prospects, have you?"

"You know that answer is no," I would respond, smiling, realizing the direct-marketing logic trap I just stepped in.

"Then you cannot *prove* to me that this type of piece *will* bomb, because this exact type of design sent to our specific prospects hasn't *yet* bombed, true?"

Just like that, I was ordered to test this new, colorful, branded mailer I knew would do poorly. And if it did poorly, Emily would come looking for me. She used to spend hours and hours, locked in her office, poring through literally thousands of pages of microscopic marketing analysis reports, seeking out spots of waste, inefficiency, or poor performance. In fact, the numbers were so small, and the spreadsheets so big, that she needed a ruler to be able to see each of the rows distinctly. Micron by micron she would painstakingly lower the ruler one row at a time, adding tiny mechanical-penciled check marks to each row that met with her approval. Emily never used pen.

I had to tell Emily that I had just been ordered to invest in a mailing I thought would not make money for the firm. I felt bad about this necessary "tattling on Dad" to "Mom," but at the very least, I would need her to either second this approval, or go talk to Bob to agree to kill the idea.

I marched into her office, holding up the expensive piece, and blindly asked her, "Do you think we should do something like this in Direct Mail?"

"I dunno, what did 'Dad' say?" She said it with a smirk, totally hip to my conundrum.

"He wants me to test it."

"Well, *you* are responsible for the profitability of your group. What do *you* say?" she asked.

"I think it will be a waste of money."

"Then do what you think is best for the firm," she said, looking back down into her ocean of spreadsheets. She was tacitly agreeing with me; if she didn't, she would tell me.

Crap. Now I was caught between them.

With that mailer, like I wound up doing with many other ideas that came my way from everyone and their grandmother, I would quietly not proceed. I would never *tell* Bob I had disobeyed his directive, but I knew this was indeed best for Countrywide, and he rarely checked molecular results anyway, at least not mine; that was Emily's purview, and he had plenty of brand work on his plate.

Over time I drifted further toward Emily's daily oversight; I preferred the rigid analytics side of marketing. And although I still technically reported to Bob as well, I slowly began working only with Emily, and he didn't fight it. My metamorphosis from brand-focused agency man to hard-core financial metrics and marketing profiteer was now complete. At the end of the day, in a sales organization, the power of trackable profit would always win.

Yes, the *Art of Not Lying,* and the powerful effects of *Virtual Value,* were everywhere. From appraisals to marketing messages to hallway politics, what was "right," or correct, was an exercise in subjective balance within the context of the moment.

But by the summer of 2004 it seemed that this era when driveways were paved with gold would go on forever. Every day at Countrywide was exciting; every week seemed to mark a new milestone in loan volume, leadership, and surreal glee. Life went on, everyone made money, and the week-by-week tally of riches was becoming almost expected and mundane. Now more than ever, I *believed.* I believed in the magic, the profit, the career, the hopes and the dreams.

Then I received that fateful Meeting Invite, from Bibi in the Product Development group, asking me to attend a new product presentation.

The meeting would be held in the Vault.

———————

MARIA RUBIO WAS an ambitious speculator who wanted to get rich quick in the housing boom. Flexible and single, with no kids, she started with $30,000 in the bank, and carried about $60,000 in student loans, but she had a good job which paid in the high five figures. In 2004 she got approved for her first speculative loan by Full Spectrum Lending (the Countrywide Subprime division); they gave her $300,000 to buy her first investment property. She was only 20 years old.

With little money management experience and even less life experience, over the next three years, she would quit her corporate job as a marketer in a health care company, get her real estate license, get another job as a real estate agent, and borrow $100,000 more from her parents to buy two more investment properties, one in Arizona and the other in North Carolina. They were both nice properties within retirement golf course communities. When asked why she bought properties so far away from her Southern California neighborhood, she replied that she "had read that retirement communities were a great place to invest."

The three loans were all exotic, ranging from a 5/1 Adjustable Rate (rate is fixed for five years, then would reset to an adjustable amount), to an Interest Only loan with no money down, and lastly to a disastrous Negative Amortization loan, which actually increased her overall debt with every month's payment.

When prices started to go down, loans began to reset, and the economy began to falter, Maria began having trouble getting renters for her properties. She fell behind on the payments as this house of cards came down. And with each subsequent foreclosure, it was getting harder to renegotiate the next failing loan.

Now, at 24 years old in 2008, she has almost completed her spectacular flame-out in the world of high-risk speculation. She has left real estate and gone back to a corporate job. She has lost one house and the other two may follow shortly. She still owes about $60,000 in student loans, but also now has run up an additonal $30,000 in credit card debt, as well as the $100,000 she borrowed from her parents, which is now all gone and cannot be recouped. She has moved back in with her parents.

Asked if she expected this to happen, she giggled and replied, "No, it's just kinda that we are the microwave generation, ya know? We grew up simply pressing a magic button and then in one minute whatever you wanted was supposed to just happen."

9

The Doomsday Scenario

I am living so far beyond my income,
that we may almost be said to be living apart.

—e e cummings

JULY 2004

Prime rate: 4.25%

Foreclosure rate: 1.14%

CFC stock price: ~$36.00

I THINK I may have just witnessed the beginning of the end of Countrywide and maybe even the entire U.S. economy," I said, in deadly seriousness.

Emily sat in my office, fingers clasped together in her lap, and literally raised an eyebrow as I showed my concern over the meeting I had just attended in the Vault.

"I'm listening," she said with a slight smile. Her smile quickly faded, though, when she saw that all the color apparently had drained from my face.

"Wow, you ain't kiddin', are ya?" she asked.

"No."

One of the great things about Emily was that she could be a taskmaster and cut you in half in one minute for not generating enough revenue or profit for the firm, and the next minute she could switch into a nurturing, maternal, and inspiring Yoda of finance.

"Well, why don't you calmly walk me through what happened, and maybe then we can figure it out together."

"I just came from the PayOption products presentation with Bibi."

"Ah, the Vault," she said, nodding her head with a look of feigned awe on her face. "I love that place, it's very cool. But kinda creepy, right?"

"Yup. I thought that giant steel door was closing in on me there for a minute."

"Okay, so what did she say?" she asked, getting impatient with my stalling.

"It wasn't so much what she said, it's what she showed. Have you seen those projections on future housing values?"

"Of course. You know I always see those numbers before they go upstairs."

"Do you agree with them?"

She paused. "I agree that the momentum and potential for the growth in housing values is, at this moment, greater than the chance of a downturn in the near future, yes."

"But they had those tables showing home values going up in perpetuity," I said incredulously. "I even asked Bibi if she was nuts."

"You *didn't*."

"Yup."

"You DIDN'T!" she said, laughing as the words came out.

I nodded proudly.

"Ya got guts, kid. Atta boy, questioning authority—proud of ya!" she said as she slapped her legs.

"Well, that's what you taught me, isn't it, Yoda?"

"I suppose I did. So what's your concern?" she asked, almost knowing exactly what my concern was, but eager to see me show some smarts without her help.

That's when I rose to begin writing on my office whiteboard.

Countrywide's was definitely a "whiteboard culture." Like NASA engineers and MBA students alike, some folks like me just felt more comfortable standing up, staring at a huge blank writing space on the wall, and sketching their ideas or plans on this modern-day tablet of productivity. Some people used it simply to look busy—making lists of lists and massive messes of "to dos" that the boss could see. Enterprising project planners could draw enormous charts and circles and arrows if they really wanted to look smart.

Ed Leamer, my amazing economics professor at UCLA Anderson and also the director of the nationally respected UCLA Anderson Economic Forecast, once told our class something brilliant: Some people are *words* people, some are *numbers* people, and some are *pictures* (graphics) people, and you had better make sure that your presentation matches whichever style your audience is if you want to get your point across. (There is an old advertising urban legend that the Microsoft program PowerPoint was actually created internally first as a desperate way for the Microsoft technologists to somehow get their numbers ideas across to nontechie audiences via words and pictures. Another legend is that about 50,000 years ago one caveman did the first Power-Point, and all the millions of PowerPoint presentations and formats created since then have been "Saved As" from that first document...*Slide 1: This Fire. Slide 2: Fire Good. Slide 3: Questions?*)

As I began outlining some ideas on the board, I was asking Emily a series of "what if" questions.

"What if housing values stop rising? What if the credit markets dry up?"

She looked at me, nodding. "Go on." She knew where I was going with this.

"I think Countrywide could be at serious risk in the future," I said to her, looking her straight in the eye.

I continued, drawing as I spoke. "The entire industry business model five years from now is based on the assumption that housing values will rise, allowing customers—in fact, the whole country—to Refi again and again, right?"

"Yup, for the foreseeable future, yes. But only if they need to Refi."

"Yes, right," I said. "Yes, *but*, you've seen the numbers in our portfolio. You know just like I do how many of these people in our own portfolio—not even counting the other 35 million or so other mortgages out there with other competitors—are increasingly in Adjustable Rate Mortgages, scooped up during the Refi boom last year."

"Keep going," she said. "I will always expect due diligence from you on anything we do here. This is why we keep you around." She was half-kidding.

"Okay, hear me out." I began writing out columns of hypotheticals on the whiteboard, across different headers: ARMs...Pay-Options...Interest Onlys...HELOCs...and under each I created three subcolumns, labeled "Best, Likely, Worst," representing the future possible states of housing values; Higher, Moderate, Lower.

She watched intently as I grabbed the latest portfolio quarterly analysis document and used it to find the data I was looking for. Over the next few silent minutes I populated my board with the total numbers of ARMs in our portfolio, with total outstanding loan amounts, and labeled how many billions were due to reset when. I did the same thing for the Interest Only loans, and then pulled data from Bibi's document to plug in the projected sales of PayOption loans, and projected amounts, that I had just seen in the Vault an hour earlier. With my back to Emily, I had not seen that during my frantic whiteboard scribbling, she had grabbed a box of large paper clips off my desk and was meticulously bending them and stacking them into a lattice tower of twisted metal wires.

"Okay, let's assume Bibi is right, and housing values continue their current trajectory." I drew a thick arrow up. "Then we would all be rich and famous, because all of these massive ARMs here, which will reset beginning in 2007 [three years later] will be a piece of cake for those folks to refinance again." I pointed to that area of numbers, now circled vigorously with my trusty green erasable marker.

"Hopefully again with *us*—don't forget the fees revenue, too," she said.

"Right," I responded, jotting "Fees" on the board to remind myself to follow through on her guidance and calculate the projected fee revenue as well into my math.

"Same is true, kinda, if housing values keep their current value. Won't be as good, but at least those people who didn't use up all their equity with these HELOCs we are selling them might be able to Refi still." I circled those columns in yellow.

"Okay, I'm with ya," she nodded, focusing on her paper-clip sculpture. Her small architectural project grew higher and higher on my desk as I spoke. *Warren Buffett over here better get me a new box of paper-clips from the storage room when she's done*, I thought.

"But Emily, look." I pointed to the third row, showing what if housing values went *down* by 2007 and beyond. I pulled out my red marker from the drawer. I began circling number after number. The number of loans was in the millions. The monetary amount of loans was in the billions. "When all of these ARMs reset, and if these people can't Refi—"

Just then Emily poked a pen into her paper-clip superstructure. They collapsed in a heap onto my desk and onto the floor. She looked up at me.

"Then they're screwed," she said.

"Yeah, screwed. And not just them, but us, too, and the whole system. We are only about 15 percent of all mortgages. The other guys who hold the other 85 percent would be in the same boat."

"Good work, brand boy."

"Can you see now what made me nauseous in Bibi's meeting? Now we're going to offer loans that may give people the option to not even pay the minimum amount needed to keep from going deeper underwater?" I asked incredulously.

"Well, Adam, everyone is offering them. Are you suggesting that the number one mortgage provider in the United States not offer what is sure to be a hot product this year, and let our competition scoop up those loans? Do you want your bonus? I know I do."

"Yes, of course," I said, slumping back into my chair.

"Whaddya want to do, kiddo, walk over to Angelo's office and recommend we stop selling what we are supposed to sell? I wouldn't be able to protect you from that move."

"No, but what if?"

"Well, c'mon, Finance has vetted these scenarios and the organization has decided that the opportunity outweighs the risk for now. Don't forget why we're here…"

I nodded as we both said simultaneously as we had chanted many times before, *"To return value to shareholders…"*

"Yes, Adam. To return value to shareholders. That…is what we do."

"Bob would say that we help people achieve the American Dream," I added.

"Yes he would, and he's right. Kinda." She smiled.

"But the whole country could wind up being underwater, Emily."

"Yes and an asteroid could hit the Earth, too. Do you want to worry about that? You can't control rates, the markets, or housing values—focus on what you *can* control, and focus on your job. Now—right now—housing values are UP. Drive in those loan leads."

"I know, I know. But interesting you should use the asteroid metaphor."

"Why?" she asked.

"Because this doomsday scenario—I feel like I was the only one to spot the asteroid in the assumptions I saw today."

"Nobody truly knows what will happen," she said. "All we can do is continue to give the market what it wants so that we achieve our mission."

"But are we being *responsible*?" I asked like a silly idealist.

"It is legal, these people make their own choices, and it is what we do—we lend people money. It would be more irresponsible to our shareholders to suddenly stop taking in revenue that we could be."

I nodded, thinking, taking a sip of a stale Diet Coke on my desk from the day before.

"You gonna clean up those paper-clips for me?"

She quietly began pushing them toward me, smiling, and pushed them under my desk with her foot.

"Also, these housing values—Emily, we now live in a terrorist world. Even if housing values don't come down on their own, what if there is another attack? Another shock to the system?"

Growing weary of my negativity, she said, "You know what? You worry too much." She stood up, turning toward the door.

"Emily, shouldn't we say something, do something, *anything*?"

Now she was getting annoyed. "Sure," she said sarcastically, beginning to count on her thin, manicured fingers. "Let's tell Angelo that we need to stop competing, lending money, being number one. Let's tell the American public to stop borrowing, buying stuff, and spending money, which, by the way, is like *70 percent of the entire* economy. Let's begin restricting access to the American Dream. Let's fire thousands of employees. Let's…" She paused, seeing I was struggling with my own helplessness, a corporate drone powerless to change anything.

"What would happen to us? We'd be no longer solvent," I said.

She thought for a moment. "I don't think the U.S. government would let the largest mortgage provider in the U.S. fail, do you? They bailed out Chrysler, and we are at least ten times that size."

"Or maybe more likely that somebody would buy us?" I asked, getting up to begin writing on the whiteboard again.

"Only a handful of banks would be large enough to absorb us," she said as I began writing the short list of potential buyers on the board. "Besides, if we go under, the whole country would also be in trouble. Something significant would need to happen for us to get into that bad position."

On the board my list was growing: *JPMorgan Chase, Citibank, Bank of America, Wells Fargo, US Bank, Wachovia, Washington Mutual....*

Emily looked at the list. "Okay," she said. "Now you're the CEO of Countrywide, something terrible has happened and you need a buyer. Who is it going to be?" she quizzed me.

"Well, could be anybody," I speculated. "I don't have enough information about the future, do I?"

"Most CEOs make many critical decisions without all the information; sometimes you gotta trust your gut. Who would buy us?"

"Well, let's see...I would guess that it would make the most sense for a buyer to get what they wouldn't have in the first place...so I think it would be an East Coast bank, or maybe someone who needs or wants a bigger mortgage portfolio."

"Go on," she said, pleased with my thought process.

"I think WAMU and Wells are out; they already have large West Coast ops....I would have to bet on Bank of America, JPMorgan, or Citi."

"Interesting."

Then I looked at these finalists from a brand perspective. "Citi, I think would have a tougher time repositioning themselves as a consumer mortgage provider; I think their brand skews toward a "Corporate New York" type of bank. If JPMorgan bought us, that would be really interesting. Not sure how many people outside your Finance Department remember that JP personally tried to stop the Great Crash before it finally happened."

"Probably," she mumbled.

As I speculated, I crossed out each of the firms I mentioned until there was one left.

"B of A. It's perfect," I said.

"Why?"

"Well, ever since they moved to Charlotte they've kinda become an East Coast player—they would love our West Coast presence, like a mortgage market share Louisiana Purchase. They would be able to shore up their mortgage business, scooping up a huge market share with one shot. It's always cheaper to buy it instead of building it yourself. But also, they're the only brand that is as apple pie as Countrywide..."

"If this did happen—and believe me, it won't—brand will have nothing to do with it at that point," she said.

"I think Angelo would care," I reacted. "You forget I worked on Bank of America in a previous life. They own the checkbook side of America's white picket fence; we own the mortgage side. I would hope they get us; it would be perfect, our brand would get a good new home."

"Won't happen," she scoffed. "Especially if Angelo is still here; he would never sell his baby."

"Oh, yeah?" I asked, pulling out a piece of paper and an envelope from my desk drawer. "Let's...make...a...little...time capsule...prediction..." I said each word as I was writing on a piece of paper. When I was done, I held it up to her.

"*Bank of America buys Countrywide in autumn, 2007 for $60 a share, after just the first wave of ARMs readjust—Adam Michaelson, July 2004.*"

Emily rolled her eyes as I solemnly licked the envelope, sealed it, and stuffed it into my bottom desk drawer, under hundreds of folders.

"Perhaps some bank archaeologist will find this like a thousand years from now," I quipped.

"Don't *worry* about it," she said, smiling again. "Now get back to work...enough silliness. We all have mortgages to pay."

I SAT THERE staring at the several different futures of America I had written on my whiteboard. Of course, no one could have, at that time, accurately predicted the future. Who knows? Maybe home values would have really continued their stratospheric rise, as Finance was comfortable predicting. Maybe they had to assume that to support the growth and the risk of such exotic products as PayOptions. Maybe I was overreacting.

But Emily was right. Even if my most dire predictions were correct, what was I to do? Personally change our entire system of economics? Somehow alter consumers' decades-long, never-ending hunger for more and more spending money? Figure out a way for Countrywide to make money by doing something else? Get everyone to agree to cut the size of the company in half and finance only "old-fashioned" loans? Change all the laws and regulations that allowed us to sell these products perfectly legally?

Who was I kidding?

But looking back, that day in the Vault with Bibi, then walking through the worst-case doomsday scenario with Emily, was for me the day I stopped believing in the good we were doing. It was the day that the potential damage of the risks outweighed the dreams of doing good.

I felt like I was inside a bubble that had taken on its own momentum. Like a wildfire or a black hole, fueling itself with its own fury. Only an equal and opposite force would be able to stop it from growing; only a downturn equal to the upswing. And only an opposite force greater than this could reverse it altogether.

I had children. I had a mortgage to pay as well. I had responsibilities to my career, my family, my shareholders.

I thought about that as my eyes covered the board, eventually settling in on the area of greatest red: the time period that, given worst-case predictions, could spell the beginning of the end I was so worried about. I remembered my history, how the Great Crash of 1929 did not occur suddenly, as some stories watered down by time forgot to mention, that in fact the economy and the markets struggled for weeks and weeks, being precariously and courageously propped up with infusions of cash from J.P. Morgan himself. It too was like a train wreck in slow motion before it finally derailed. I knew the term lengths, the amounts, and the number of Adjustable Rate products that were out there, so I also knew when they would begin resetting, at what scales.

Inside the furiously scribbled red circle were the words, *autumn, 2007.*

10

Taking My Concerns All the Way to the Bank

I am opposed to millionaires, but it would be
dangerous to offer me the position.
—Mark Twain

NOVEMBER 2005

Prime rate: 7.00%

Foreclosure rate: 0.99%

CFC stock price: ~$34.00

So, LIKE ANY frightened corporate animal unable to affect its envi-ronment, I instead sought shelter from it.

What began as an exciting year of growth within Prime New Cus-tomer Acquisitions eventually became a slowing part of the business and, I felt, it was risky to "double down" on it in the long term.

Concurrently, the rush of excitement I felt as I helped build Prime New Customer Acquisitions had devolved into the monotony of bore-dom as the business matured. Our operation had become even larger and more comprehensive, now generating trackable and sustainable new profits for the firm. Where new mailing innovations or TV concepts created exciting levels of risk, we were getting into the maturity phase of our marketing.

The risk that this could fail was now gone—or so it seemed. Now, endless meetings would be held to argue about how to squeeze one more tenth of a point from response rates of our winning mail package; whether a subtle changing of sentence tone would affect response; how to further enhance the efficiency of our TV media buys; how to eke out a few more applications from the call centers every day. Maintenance of existing marketing campaigns was not my cup of tea, and we had been asked by Andy to now coordinate our efforts more with our counterparts at our Subprime unit, Full Spectrum Lending (FSL), which made me cringe.

The Pasadena offices of FSL were known internally as the "Death Star." Unlike our offices at Countrywide, which were lively and energetic, bustling with optimism and growth, the offices at FSL felt to me like a dreary, ominous place, and, with their much more intense sales culture, a strained atmosphere. Unlike the nurturing and positive reinforcement style of Bob and Emily, the FSL folks I knew and spoke to always seemed to me to be tense and afraid. I hated going there and couldn't wait to leave.

Also, as I've said, their style of marketing was much different from Countrywide's branding guidelines. By using the different name, they could engage in every cheesy, tacky direct-mail packaging there was, because to Subprime audiences, for whatever reason, those mailings worked. The tone was more saleslike, using lots of exclamation points. At Countrywide, my team had standing orders never to use exclamation points; we were Countrywide—we *didn't have to yell.* FSL messaging was more like a carnival barker screaming at a hungry credit crowd to "Stttttep right up, get yer money here!" I knew that every single mailer had gone through intensive legal and regulatory review, just as our pieces did, so they were all deemed legal. But unfortunately, tackiness was not against those rules.

Perhaps I was being snooty, like someone used to the Ritz having to stay at a Motel 6. But they were our cousins and we would assist them whenever possible, join their printing runs as much as possible to save costs, and combine our data resources for the same reasons. Spanky had run the marketing for FSL but had been replaced by a Countrywide lifer who would change my working life.

Mark Katz was a bold and confident "old-time" direct marketer who had been the real reason why FSL marketing had flourished over recent years. Outspoken, smart, and strong, he was a no-nonsense, hard-core number cruncher and a good leader, with a loyal team. He had been the perfect foil for the FSL style, letting their occasional yelling and chair-throwing antics roll off his back. All he cared about was the numbers, and how they would benefit FSL, and Countrywide, and that made him a genuine star. Numbers always did better under his experienced eye, and up until that point he had quietly built the success immensely while Spanky acted like he did everything.

Eventually the leadership at FSL caught on to who was bringing the real marketing value to them, and Spanky was moved to handle some other research area. Earlier in 2005, Mark took over all FSL marketing within Corporate. He was older and more experienced than I, and at the same level that Bob and Emily were. And he was becoming an even stronger dynamo just when my interest levels were starting to wane. Perhaps that's why Andy decided in early 2005 to have me now report to Mark in an attempt to merge all New Customer Acquisition (Prime and Subprime) under Corporate Marketing.

Until that point, even though I struggled to report to both Bob and Emily, I appreciated the fact that both of their leadership styles were essentially hands-off—that is, they assigned me goals, resources, and then got out of my way. Even at the most intense periods of startup or growth, my interaction with these two mentors never exceeded one or two status meetings per week. Perhaps they knew me well enough to know that this style (to delegate responsibility to me) was the best way to motivate me. Micromanaging was a fast way to completely shut me down, and they knew this. Not so with Mark.

Within weeks Mark began exerting his authority over the Prime area, too. I really couldn't blame him, as this was what he was now assigned to do. But he did not prefer the delegation style of Bob and Emily. He was hands-on with his entire team.

And worse, he was what I called a "woo!" person. Although I had managed to channel my energies into a winning series of select relationships, I always had managed to avoid the "woo!" part of the Countrywide culture, until now. Status meetings would not be complete thereafter without a series of "high fives" and motivational speeches from Mark. Some people responded well to this cheerleading tone. I didn't.

Later that year at his Christmas party, which I did not attend, there were reports that he had cordially commanded everyone to sit in a circle and share with the team "what they were grateful for that year." Several attendees noted the awkwardness gauge going off the charts as one by one each employee began with stating how grateful they were for Mark's leadership, Countrywide, and other sycophantic soliloquies.

But I understood his passion. One of the reasons why Mark had done so well at Countrywide over the years was that he fit well with this part of our sales culture. To those who responded to it, it engendered loyalty, passion, and purpose. In fact, one cultural motto that was posted on hundreds of lunchroom posters across all our buildings was our credo of "People, Passion, Principles." Mark was totally a people person; I was not. He was intensely passionate about small and large successes; I was more reserved. But we did both share a deep belief in the principles of Countrywide, including hard work, ethics, and sharing our deep belief in our *mission* of homeownership. So, at once, I appreciated Mark's talents and value to Countrywide, but his style was not for me, especially during this new period of my own moral quandary.

I also resented, perhaps immaturely so, that the group that I had worked so long and hard to build, ramp up, and execute, was essentially and slowly being turned over to someone else. But I had mixed feelings. I really was getting bored; I had built it, now I wanted to go build something else. Also, Mark was perfectly suited to take the growth of this to the next level; it would be in good hands. Over time, an unspoken understanding would emerge between us, one that projected my desire to move onto something else, yet offered him the support and respect he deserved while I searched for the next big thing.

But times were getting tougher already in early 2005.

As mortgage and home equity rates continued to rise, the growth of our numbers began to slow further. Eventually the rates for our Home Equity products were getting so high, we had to pull rates off the TV spots altogether. Since the beginning of the Refi through the HELOC boom, we knew that showing a compellingly low rate was the most powerful motivator for a prospect to respond. *Duh.* The HELOC rates were changing so often, however, that when we would ship a completed TV spot to all the networks on which it would air, we would generate as many different rate versions as possible. A HELOC TV ad may have begun airing with a stated rate of only 2.75%, but the rate was gradually yet steadily changing as the Fed upped the Prime Rate. TV stations would need to begin airing the revised rates the next day, so we would preship them versions of the same spot with different rates; 3.00%, 3.25%, and so on. Our instructions to the stations would tell them which rate version to air, consistent with the direction we would be given from the finance and product groups.

When the rate started to creep up into the 4s and even higher, we saw call volume precipitously drop. Eventually we had to resort to pulling the rate off the spot altogether, and just motivating viewers to call "for their great rate." Being vague about these "great rates" would usually produce more call volume than showing a terrible rate that we may have been charging, but when they called, they would hear this higher rate, so then applications rate began to dip as well. In 2005, all the numbers were beginning to show some ominous trending changes.

Calls were down. Applications were down. And nothing creates more tension in a sales culture than numbers going down. Meetings became edgier. Blame became more pronounced. It was the very early stages of tiny leaks in our hull that would eventually lead to the sinking I had feared. But selfishly I also wanted to leave this group *before* the numbers collapsed.

As rates would rise further, and as fewer and fewer people would qualify for Refis or HELOCs in the year ahead, I sought out other growth areas within Countrywide. I wanted to stay on at the firm, but shrewdly wanted to find a growth spot that would enrich me, and maybe even allow me to build something anew, yet again. But options were dwindling in the Home Loans area.

As I started to gently put the word out that I was open to new opportunities, I was shocked to have been approached by none other than Spanky himself, offering me a "choice spot" on his new research team. At first I balked, but, as New Customer Acquisition slowed, I wanted to leave any options open. Especially since I wanted to keep my stock options and stay with Countrywide. Who knew? Maybe I could ride out the storm in the warm recesses of research and hang on until we got bought? But the thought of toiling away in this function offered no excitement, no risk, just numbness. More disturbingly, I would have to report to Spanky; a nightmare in the making. I mentioned this potential opportunity to Emily. She just laughed out loud and walked away.

This momentary insanity ended within weeks. I think Spanky knew what a boring area he was now in, even as he tried to sell me. The final act of this surreal play occurred at a surreal place in surreal surroundings. Spanky asked me to join him at a local restaurant for lunch to "discuss terms" even though I had already told him I probably wasn't interested. It was one of those new restaurants that tried waaaay too hard to be hip, cool, funky, and weird. All the dining tables looked like leftover props from a 1970s cheesy "futuristic" sci-fi movie. We grabbed a booth. On the walls there were big screens playing a movie; it was an odd choice for lunchtime. Sitting there with Spanky droning on about the wonders of research, and hearing him tell me what a great leader he was, I couldn't believe what I was seeing on the screens as I ate my Astroburger or whatever the hell it was. Over his head I was watching *Barbarella*. The TV was on mute, so all I could hear was Spanky talking as what looked like half-naked spacemen with feathered wings walked around the screen. I had never seen *Barbarella*, but after that day, I wouldn't need to. This almost comical juxtaposition of a Fortune 100 executive touting his job offer while half-naked guys danced around his head behind him had me gritting my teeth to prevent me from laughing, and it sealed the deal for me. The total weirdness of the omen, although having nothing to do with the potential of the role, was like some career angel telling me, "*If you join his group it'll be THIS weird.*" The next day I sent him a "thank you but no thank you" e-mail.

Soon after, the Chief Marketing Officer of Countrywide Bank, Peter Blume, suddenly resigned. Peter had been there for a few years, and rumors had swirled months before that the new leadership they were bringing on wanted to make some changes.

Countrywide Bank had been added only a couple of years earlier, when Countrywide bought what was then Treasury Bank out of Virginia and made it their own. During the boom times, Countrywide made the smart and seemingly strengthening move to invest in diversified financial services functions. They bought the Bank, and invested in insurance products as well. On paper at least, by lessening their total revenue dependence on mortgages, they could hedge their bets against a downturn. It was the right thing for them to do when they had oodles of cash to invest. It would protect them, or so they thought.

The Bank also had been growing tremendously, and its interesting business model was part of the reason. Countrywide Bank did not have giant branches like other banks. Instead they had a nationwide network of small banking "kiosks"—booths, really—that were usually manned by only one or two employees, and accepted deposits and account openings only. No cash withdrawals were done there; all cash business was done via mail to their main customer service center. This streamlined business model comprised of "branchettes," or simply "twigs," allowed for serious cost savings. Those savings were then passed on to customers in the form of higher rates—the highest rates, in fact. Just flip through an *AARP Magazine* from back then and check their "National CD Rates" listing; Countrywide Bank was always number one or two, with some of the highest CD rates in the nation. Hence we strongly attracted the seniors audience. Countrywide Bank was the place where American seniors placed their money to grow in Certificates of Deposit. And the "Countrywidification" of the Bank made it the perfect environment where Grandma enjoyed chatting with that lovely young girl Molly at the local kiosk every time she would dutifully deposit her Social Security check. It was really a miniaturized version of the local town bank feeling from long ago.

But that's where it had stayed for years, stodgy and cobwebbed, yet continuously growing to serve an ever-increasing seniors population. Then a new investment in energetic young leaders pushed it to a new level. There was talk that the Bank "was the next big thing" from Countrywide. Angelo bragged about their growth on analyst conference calls and in CNBC interviews. The growth in deposits was outpacing that of many other banks, and there were even rumblings that Angelo and others were considering the possibility of making Countrywide Bank the front-and-center name for consumers in the future, with Home Loans simply becoming a part of this larger, more diversified portfolio of financial services for customers.

Countrywide Bank needed a new person with a title I craved:

Chief Marketing Officer. *Say it with me...Adam...Michaelson... Chief...Marketing...Officer...of Countrywide Bank...* had a nice ring to it. The moment I heard Peter was leaving I marched directly over to Emily's office. I knew she knew people at the Bank.

"I want that CMO slot at the Bank," I said, barging in.

She didn't even look up from the numbers she had been analyzing on her gazillionth results report. "Can't you see I am busy reviewing last week's seriously crappy results from your group?"

"Emily—I'm ready for that CMO slot."

"*Are you* now?" she asked coyly.

"I can do it. They need me. And I need them. Mark's got New Customer Acquisition covered. You know I need this, and it's perfect."

She knew I wasn't happy ever since Mark took over the group. And perhaps she also knew that the Bank could use more entrepreneurial energy; maybe she knew the long-term plans for the Bank. Or maybe she just felt sorry for me. Either way, she thought for a moment, finally saying, "No promises. Let me sniff it out."

I thanked her with my big smile alone as she barked, "Now get the hell back to work—this meeting just cost Countrywide fifty bucks."

Within two days I got a call from the head of the Bank's Retail Division—they wanted to see me. Apparently, Emily had put her reputation on the line for me, recommending me directly to the Bank's leadership for the CMO slot. I never forgot that.

The Bank building was even farther away from my house, which meant that if I got the job, my commute would be more than an hour each way, but I didn't care. This was a huge opportunity, and I studied intensely for days before I met with Donna Butler, one of the Bank's top people. A few days before my interview, Donna e-mailed me and suggested that before our meeting, I read Jim Collins's *Good to Great: Why Some Companies Make the Leap...And Some Don't*. My meeting with Donna was that coming Monday; that weekend I read it dutifully. Twice.

Now, normally, I hate reading trendy business books. Every few weeks there is some "must read" book from a professor or an ex-CEO or whatever, and most of the time the motivator to read those books is simply the boss mentioned that they read it. *Better read it; quick! Better yet, be sure to reference it in a few meetings with the boss over the next few weeks [wink].* But occasionally there are some that use disciplined scientific analysis to try to unlock the mysteries of human behavior and, in turn, the companies they run. I think a good example of this is *The Millionaire Next Door*, by Thomas Stanley and William Danko, which proved through data analysis to be an eye-popping reality check on what makes the wealthy truly wealthy in this country; it debunked myths and taught me something new.

Good to Great was another solid book. In it, Collins does more than five years of research into 11 firms that transformed themselves from "good" companies to "great" ones. And quickly after I began reading it I discovered why Donna loved it. Donna had previously been with one of the companies Collins argued was a transformational company story. *Okay, I got it.* But eventually it would be other, more surprising aspects of the book's conclusions that would complicate my career soon after this meeting.

The Bank's executive suite was less ostentatious than Countrywide's main headquarters, but still clearly a bank's executive floor. Dark, rich wood walls holding up majestic images of Washington D.C., landmarks, and paintings of American ideals. Dark green carpets lined the immaculately clean, almost sterile corridors. Basically it looked like Countrywide Executive Suite *Junior*. Donna greeted me warmly, with a bouncy enthusiasm that was classic Countrywide.

Although it's always nice to be referred to a role via internal channels, it can also create a subtle, uncomfortable atmosphere of entitlement in an interview. Emily had called Donna's boss and recommended me. It could have been that Donna was the type of manager who would be cordial but never hire me, simply because I wasn't truly her discovery. It's a good thing that Donna wasn't like that at all. She was classic Countrywide, passionate and almost giddy as she described the vision she had for the Bank; how it was going to be the leader of all the divisions someday; how she wanted to invest in a new, pristine brand specific to the Bank; how she wanted to do great things and foster the Bank's version of Angelo's vision—and this is where she hooked me.

Ever since the Vault meeting, and the subsequent doomsday scenario I shared with Emily, I had lost my faith in the true good that we might be doing for America by cranking out these exotic loans that were potential madness for the future of the American economy. Conversely, the Bank's role in helping Americans achieve their dreams was the other end of the financial spectrum. With a focus on growing the hard-earned deposits that customers—frequently seniors—would trust us to keep safe for them, there was no moral ambiguity in this element of the mission. If I came on board, my only focus would be to maximize people's savings, and literally give them the greatest return on those assets. The mission was clearer and purer than lending, and I would get to stay within the Countrywide family, which I still admired. I really wanted the job now.

A few days later I got a call that included good news and not so good news. The good news was, they wanted me. The bad news was, not for CMO. Instead, they wanted to build a triangular senior structure within Bank marketing. Their chosen CMO would turn out to be a lifetime bank marketing guy named Todd Yates, who got the CMO job because he was also a certified public accountant. "Would you be okay with reporting to him?" Donna asked me.

"As long as he gives me the resources I need, and doesn't micromanage me, things should be fine," I replied.

There was more. I would come aboard still as a Senior Vice President of Marketing, but not the only one. *What?* They also wanted to hire another SVP to be "my partner." Toni Flores was a talented woman who had a great laugh that just added to her charm. While my background was in advertising and direct marketing, Toni's experience had been solely in bank marketing and other specialized roles within that industry. She was an expert in checking, savings, and other fun, fun, fun financial services products.

During my interview, Donna had described the new, powerful, and distinctive brand that would become Countrywide Bank; how it would assume leadership in American banking over time; and how she wanted to build a gutsy, entrepreneurial team based on some of the teachings of the business book *Good to Great*, which used her former company as one of their case histories. But it was Donna's potential misunderstanding of one of the teachings of the book that may have caused the initial disaster when all of us were brought together.

One of the chapters discusses an organizational concept that you should first go out and secure top-level stars with strong skills, and only then worry about who will have what exact role. But as is often the case with popular business books, senior executives sometimes read only part of the teachings and totally screw up the rest.

Somehow in Donna's interpretation of her business bible, she forgot that research studies about successful businesses may be educational, but in the real world sometimes it may not always work exactly as planned. There is a potential downside to putting many smart, leader-like talents in one playpen; sometimes they all try to jockey to be the one leader. Once Todd, Toni, and I were all hired, Donna encouraged us to assign the roles and responsibilities *ourselves*. She might as well have thrown a juicy steak into a pit of starving tigers and asked us to use our little paws to pull it apart in three equally divided pieces.

To make matters worse, as part of his agreement, our new CMO Todd Yates was going to be going on a long-planned, monthlong vacation. It would be up to Toni and me to build our own roles with no direction from Donna or Todd. For a month.

Now, Toni and I were both professionals, but we were both alpha-type leaders, used to being totally in charge of our teams. And from the outset, in building this new marketing team for what could be Countrywide's newest shining star brand, it was clear that the functions would be split into two distinct yet equally critical areas.

The first half would be mine, or so I was told. This would be the team that would be in charge of building and promoting the new Countrywide Bank brand, including imagery, messaging, creative, and media budget oversight. This would include creative materials for online as well as any advertising, newspaper, and in-branch designs and materials. Also, as Countrywide Bank had a robust commercial business banking arm, we would be responsible for the brochures and engaging materials that salespeople would lug all over their territories. It was exactly where I wanted to be, and where my strength was; my team would *engage, inform, and motivate* customers to open an account—today.

The other half of the marketing department would be those areas in which I had little expertise, but Toni did, including pricing (setting rates), as well as the critically necessary talent of developing compelling banking products (checking, savings, money markets, etc.) that people wanted from their bank. Ideally, together, our combined experience would make for a powerful team as long as everybody stayed within their area of the sandbox.

Within our first week of being hired, we met for lunch in scorching Thousand Oaks, California. Todd had already left on vacation, and it was our task to present to Donna within two weeks our plans for the organization, and how we would define our roles nicely by ourselves. In an odd way, Donna had, inadvertently I believe, devised a Machiavellian little game of "who could play nicer?" As both of us were eager to win, it was in both our best interests to play the nicest, smile the widest, and demonstrate our organizational planning value as fast as possible.

It turns out, Toni was great. She was smart, savvy, warm, approachable, and mature. Within moments we were laughing about the tension that had already been created by Donna's assignment, and the strange course of events.

Now at ease, she went on to describe her long and interesting career in banking, eventually working her way up to senior marketing management. I was genuinely impressed with her and her style.

Then I proceeded to recap my Countrywide experience, first building their Online Marketing group then moving on to build the now-successful Prime New Customer Acquisitions group. I stressed my expertise in Branding, Direct Marketing, and customer acquisition, finishing with the simple phrase, "I guess that's why Donna thought I would be perfect to handle those responsibilities for the Bank."

As I uttered those words, her fork stopped midway between her Cobb salad and her mouth, and she froze in place, as if I had just told her that the salad was poisoned.

"What do you mean Donna told you that you would handle that?" she asked.

Confused, I asked, "What do you mean, 'what do you mean'?"

In an instant, we both knew what had happened.

"Donna told me that *I was going to handle* Branding, Advertising, etc.... That's why I took this job, to get away from years of product work!" Toni said.

"Donna told me that you would be the product expert!" I replied.

Well, every first date has an awkward pause *somewhere*. And this was a doozy. In stunned silence, we both sipped our respective iced teas in unison, contemplating the conundrum we were both faced with. I had already told Andy I was going to the Bank; there would be no going back to Corporate Marketing. Toni had just left a long and distinguished career at her previous employer, including the financial and political gains that came with such seniority, and she could not go back either. Yet Donna had promised us both the same role in the organization, and we were both alphas.

And that's where the story gets even muddier. For on top of this political nightmare, I had promised Emily and Andy that I would stay on with Corporate Marketing for a few more weeks, where for about a month, my job would be a hybrid of both ensuring a smooth handoff to Mark in Corporate Marketing, as well as beginning work for the Bank. [I was keenly aware that in professional life, how well (or not) you handle your job in the remaining few weeks, is often how they will always remember you, and I was eager to end my tenure within Corporate Marketing with precision and polished professionalism.] Yet this gave Toni a chance to move in at the Bank and be the only senior person on site who was overseeing the team of middle and junior managers. And, of course, Donna never informed any of the teams that any of us were coming on board, what our roles would be, and who would report to whom.

It devolved into pandemonium.

As I would come over to the Bank a few times a week, I had to introduce myself to all of the players, explain what my (maybe) role would be; then, per Donna's orders, "get in there and straighten those guys out," which I took as a directive to establish order, processes and procedures, planning, and new organizational reporting structures. Of course, I had to work with Toni on this, who, for all her smiles and nice lunches, was naturally eager to establish control over the Branding and Advertising areas that Donna had promised her as well. She also had a monthlong head start on me in setting up camp, building alliances, nurturing relationships and new loyalties with the staff, and generally letting them imprint on her like a mama bear. I didn't blame her for this; she was acting just like Countrywide was, just like the markets were, and just like consumers were during this time—naturally pursuing their own self-interests.

So, of course, the crew resisted my requests, resented my invasion, and more importantly, took out their frustrations at not knowing what the hell was going on or who was in charge of what, on me.

By the time Todd got back from vacation, I was beginning to hate my new job. As a way to survive the clash that Donna had created, Toni and I decided that the only way to play nice while Todd was away was to maturely share the responsibility in all functions, then let Todd decide when he returned. But a few days before Todd's return, I got a strange e-mail from him that said something like:

"Need to speak with you the day I get back."

My spidey senses told me that this was not good.

"What about? Sounds bad," I replied.

"We'll talk when I get back. Can't discuss it yet."

Well, needless to say, those were a tense few days. Was I being let go before I even got a chance to really begin? Something was up, and the meeting I had with him upon his return confirmed it. As I walked into the conference room to meet him, in also walked a woman from Human Resources. *Uh-oh.* She was a burly woman with a cherubic face, and I could immediately tell that there was tension in the room as she began to speak.

"Adam, I'm not sure how to say this, so I'm just going to say it."

She paused, and I gave her a look like, "Out with it already."

"Well, they *hate* you."

"Who hates me?"

"They do—the team, the staff—they hate you."

It was like someone had just thrown scalding lava in my face. I paused, silently processing what I had just heard. I looked at Todd. He looked at me but quickly darted his eyes away, obviously uncomfortable with this meeting. Who wouldn't be? I responded in the only way I knew how.

"So?" I asked.

Incredulous at my reaction, the ruddy HR director struggled, nervously flipping through notes in a tattered little spiral notebook. I refused to react in the way I felt they wanted me to react; saddened, cowering, whatever. I was determined not to let them see me in the shock that I was.

"They find you too aggressive," she continued. Then she spouted off a list of names they were calling me, not at all pleasant.

"Donna asked me to 'straighten those guys out,' to provide them some direction, guidance..."

"It's not working," she said seriously.

It felt like they were firing me but didn't have the guts to simply say so. Todd sat there silently. I understood how no one should have to come back from his vacation to such a situation. And he was not even the one who hired me; Donna had. As the HR director continued bashing my apparently Hitleresque job performance, her face became redder and redder, as did mine. The weeks of amateur-hour that this organization proved to be, the stress that it had unnecessarily caused, made me boil with rage. *Fire me? Fire ME?* I cut her off in midsentence.

"This is...total bullshit."

I let it all out. *Good to Great* had suddenly become *Good to Sucks*. I had had it with the promises of a utopian corporate society, with no structure, no organization, no support.

"This has been the most embarrassingly amateurish on-boarding process I have ever seen in my entire career. There was no welcome, no definition of role or of responsibility. The team was not informed of who I was or what I was responsible for, so I don't blame them for rejecting me. They're confused. Even Toni and I were told we'd have the SAME JOB!" My hand hit the table. With Todd and the HR lady taken aback, I continued. I didn't fucking care.

"No one knew who was in charge. You got a totally fucked org chart where no one knows who is doing what. I wasn't even told where to SIT!"

And in a final piercing statement I said simply, "You guys...you're not very *Countrywide*, are you?" I could see that that made them think.

They sat there in stunned silence. Maybe they were not used to a New York mouth.

I considered myself a fair but demanding boss, depending on the culture, the circumstances, whether I was happy and/or motivated, and depending on the quality of the team talent. But this organizational chaos was getting ridiculous at the Bank.

I looked from Todd to the HR lady. "If you want to fire me, let's do it, right now, right here. But I will make sure that Corporate Marketing knows how messed up this place is before I leave. Or you can offer to solve this with me, if you prefer," I subtly remarked.

I pointed to Todd, and said, "I need *your* help here."

Just then, Todd decided to respond.

"Okay, everyone let's just settle down. You're right, Adam. I will get with Donna, finalize the roles, and make sure the team knows who reports to whom. Then let's see where we stand in a few weeks, okay?"

I nodded, responding, "And I will try to be much nicer until this settles."

And it did. Within a day, Todd had e-mailed the entire group outlining the new organization, the reporting structure, the responsibilities. A "separate but together" strategy was built. I would handle the things I was promised I would do, and what I was good at: branding, advertising, direct marketing. Toni would be part of that process, but not responsible. She would oversee product marketing and pricing, with my input. We would all work together on everything but would be accountable to our specialties and to Todd. After that HR enema, order was restored, and we all held hands at candlelight vigils; peace was at hand. We got busy generating tons of new deposits.

WITH BROAD AND deep expertise in marketing to seniors—our "sweet spot"—I was eager to begin building the new superbrand that was to be Countrywide Bank. Similar success stories within the category abounded, where either securities or other types of financial services began pushing their bank brand out front and center to varying levels of success. Examples include Charles Schwab Bank, E-Trade Bank, and others. I was enthralled by the idea of being part of the story that would one day make Countrywide *Bank* a leading brand in the U.S. But I quickly learned that the magical opportunity that was the Bank was not to be.

The upside of being part of a megaconglomerate is the enormous clout, resources, and opportunities it provides a hungry marketer—I would never get bored with the myriad of different divisions, products, services, and audiences to market to. But the equal downside is that you are part of a megaconglomerate, with a larger brand than any of your little products or smaller divisions. I quickly learned that the Bank would face an uphill battle to use television to market any of our products or services. From my experience marketing to seniors, I knew that television, especially direct-response television, would have been a perfect tool to target our senior audience. But the Bank was told "no" by Corporate Marketing, and I understood their reasons.

Home Equity and Refi television—the campaign I had also worked on the previous year—was still running all over the country with tenuous levels of success. Corporate Marketing did not want anything to confuse the audience, or the brand, via this hugely powerful medium. It could be consumer chaos if one spot for Countrywide Home Equity loans showed up on CNN and offered a rate of 4.75% (at the time a fairly good, low loan rate), and then moments later, another spot, and this time for Countrywide *Bank*, offered a deposit CD or a money market account for a rate of 5.25% (a very great, high money market rate). I saw their point. Either banking customers would think our rates were too low, or mortgage customers would think our rates were too high, if they got the messages mixed up.

For the Bank, direct mail would also be a struggle. The previous Bank CMO had limited experience with direct mail, and apparently it didn't do well under his reign. Lots of glossy, glitzy mail was tried and none of it seemed to impress senior management, except maybe for the occasional branch opening picnic postcard announcement.

In fact my first not-so-pleasant meeting with the CEO of the Bank, Carlos Garcia, involved direct mail. I began talking about the plans we had to bring it back to life via a methodical testing strategy, just as I had successfully done at Corporate Marketing for loans, when Carlos abruptly cut me off.

"I heard mail didn't work for us," he said plainly.

"Well, that's just because in my opinion the previous team didn't know how to do it properly," I said smugly. I don't think he was used to that level of effrontery.

"I heard it can be very expensive," he continued.

"Maybe because they didn't know how to print it efficiently. I do," I pushed.

"No direct mail," he said.

And that was that. I had heard this from countless other CEOs in countless other board rooms—throwing out the baby with the bathwater. When a CEO would say "TV doesn't work," or "Direct Mail doesn't work," I always pushed back. I would say, "No, that *particular* mail (or TV) with that offer to that audience with that creative didn't work. But it can."

In agency life, I would usually create some small test mailings anyway, only then to show up with positive test results to a meeting months later with a surprised CEO. It's easier to beg forgiveness (vs. asking permission) after you have some great results to show. (You had better know what you are doing, though—I only recommend thoughtful risk-taking in very small amounts first, to test marketing theories. If successful, then exactly replicate it. If replication is successful, only then is it worthy of a larger "roll out" discussion with your colleagues.)

In banking, if you have a superior rate, it is the marketer's job to get out of the way of a great rate as fast as possible. If your rate is so-so, then you become an average commodity that requires increased brand messages of service, trust, or locality, such as "your neighborhood bank." Countrywide Bank's CD rates were among the best in the nation, and although they also offered checking accounts, that's not where the giant opportunity of 2005 would be. It would be in the ever-exploding subcategory of online savings accounts.

Countrywide's new online savings account, eventually called "SavingsLink," would be the crown jewel in the marketing efforts for the entire year, and touted by Donna as a key reason why they were investing in a new, stronger marketing organization. Recent competitive activity had demonstrated the untapped market opportunity of online savings accounts, with the successful introductions of the ING Orange Savings Account, as well as online savings products from HSBC, Emigrant Savings, and many others. And yes, Countrywide, the giant of financial services, would come out with their own online savings account that would have one of the highest rates in the country.

Opened, funded, and managed primarily via the web, the online savings account was essentially a money market account online, and offered rates greater than so-called traditional savings accounts. For example, at its height, SavingsLink offered an interest rate of about 5.25% for deposits over $50,000, while a traditional savings account at a savings bank might have offered a rate of about 1% or less. Companies were able to offer these higher rates online because most of the labor was done by the customer themselves, and there were no overhead costs for branches or other things; it was all done online. So a savvy and trusting customer comfortable with the online banking experience could quickly and easily open an account, set it up to link to all of their other accounts at other banks, and be able to seamlessly move monies around from account to account, keeping the bulk of it sitting in their online savings account, earning serious interest. A $50,000 account could earn over $200 per month in interest.

It was exactly what I needed. A new product launch—an entrepreneurial enterprise that could fail if we didn't have our act together. A chance to make news within the Countrywide hallways, across divisions, a chance to once again build something from nothing, and this time something that would help Americans grow their hard-earned money safely, smartly, and easily. This is why I loved Countrywide.

I set to work with the team by January 2006 to build the marketing plan for this launch, which was to be in spring or summer. A budget was carved out for this effort, agencies would need to be hired to do the creative work, and rigid timelines were established. Like in the old days building the New Customer Acquisition engine for Prime loans, my wall looked like a war room of D-Day proportions.

But by early 2006 there were disturbing rumblings from my old friends in Corporate Marketing about what was going on with the loan volumes. Applications were slowing, rates were going up further, tension was mounting. Nothing gets a sales organization more freaked out than sales slowing, or going down, even slightly, and marketing is usually the first group to get put to the thumb screws.

I could tell that things were getting scarier in the loan groups by how many people started asking me to have "catch-up" lunches and those who wanted to "hear more about the great things that were going on at the Bank." I understood. The Bank at that time was a new frontier, and deposits were growing rapidly. Many wanted to see if there were any slots open there. And I certainly wanted to help my friends if indeed there were any opportunities at the Bank. I felt at that time that I had completely perfected the timing of my move. Like a monkey in a video game, I kept jumping from rising pillar to rising pillar, and however accidentally, getting the timing just right. Or so it seemed.

I got the true sense of the mood over in Corporate Marketing when I invited my old colleagues to come to the Bank one day for a briefing on the launch of SavingsLink. With a limited budget, and constrictions on television and mail, the marketing would be confined primarily to newspaper, online, and a little radio testing. We proudly unveiled the new name, the new concept boards, some print and showed meticulously through research and message how our campaign would not only be "very Countrywide" but also would complement all of the other loan marketing that was already ubiquitous on American TV screens and elsewhere. Emily did not attend the meeting, as all she would be interested in were the deposit figures once the product launched, but Bob was there. Bob especially seemed pleased with the campaign we had developed, and also seemed proud that I was making strides at the Bank. Always supportive, he left the meeting with a characteristic comment. "I knew you would do great things here, Adam. Let me know how it goes." Bob was great.

In the crowd gathered around the conference table at Bank headquarters was my old pal Tim Shay, who had been my counterpart in Corporate Marketing, focused on the Subprime work for Full Spectrum Lending. He now reported to Mark, which he said he enjoyed, and I was happy for him. During the presentation, while someone else was talking, I gave him a look like "You okay?" He looked stressed. He gave me a somber, slow head shake. On his way out, I stopped him.

"What's up?" I asked.

"Not here; let's do lunch next week."

The following week I met Tim at the same café where I had first met Bob almost two years before. Oddly enough, they sat us at the same table.

"Great stuff on SavingsLink," he commented right away.

"Thanks. It could be a winner."

"Good, then there might be extra room for me?" he asked half-kiddingly.

"Why? What's up? Things okay over there in loan land?"

He looked pale. He put down his fork.

"It's bad, bud."

"What's going on?" I asked him.

"It's like one of those, what do you call them?" He made a motion putting his two index fingers together. "A Chinese finger thingy."

"Yeah, a Chinese thingy." We laughed.

"Seriously, it seems like the harder we try, the worse the numbers get."

I nodded. He continued, "It's almost like we are running out of prospects out there."

That was a frightening thought for the loans group, either Prime or Subprime. He went on to say that the data was beginning to show some disturbing trends. Calls trending down. Applications down. Nothing cataclysmic, but any signs of trouble were a concern.

"Did Emily ever tell you about the conversation she and I had about a year ago, about the doomsday scenario?" I asked.

"No. What scenario?"

"About how all the ARMs were due to readjust next year, and if home values didn't sustain, it could be a bloodbath. I had just seen the PayOption presentation, and I got spooked, ya know? I mean, actually allowing people to go further underwater? Are we and all the other lenders out there crazy?"

"Well, the market demands growth, right?" he said with resignation. He looked weary.

"I just hope those Subprimes hold up, especially the exotics."

He nodded slowly. "There is some talk of maybe some lay-offs...I...could be in trouble."

I understood, and told him I would keep an eye out for anything at the Bank, but also told him, frankly, that the Bank ran a little lean, conservatively, on purpose. He understood, but said he appreciated anything I could do. We were both similar ages, we both had kids, and we both believed in Countrywide. I would try to help him.

Well, turns out I didn't even need to, because in the coming weeks there were minor layoffs, but Tim was safe. Apparently, as long as he stuck with Mark, he would protect him, just as Bob and Emily used to do for me, and still did, however now more subtly. Tim got back to work and got quiet for a while.

That spring, SavingsLink launched with muted fanfare, appearing in national newspapers around the country, and through e-mails to all of our millions of customers across the Countrywide product line, as this was our most fertile, accessible audience.

Within days, the data began coming in, as would millions in new deposits. SavingsLink was a success.

The downside of any major launch like that was that with finite budgets, the remaining months of 2006 would be an exercise in simple maintenance, customer communications, and other mundane chores while we stretched our remaining budget dollars through the end of our fiscal year. And as usual, getting bored, I poked my nose into things I probably shouldn't have.

Like all of Countrywide, the Bank also had an intense, sales-driven "woo!" culture. Everything was about sales, about gaining more deposits, about growth, in a take-no-prisoners style, which sometimes bordered on cultish. And as summer approached, something happened that made me speak up.

Someone had the bright idea to be the only bank that would remain open on Memorial Day and Independence Day. The concept started around weekend "sales events," where on some Saturdays (and Sundays potentially), customers might be able to secure a slightly higher rate on a certain CD if they came in that day. As the frenzy of those new deposit numbers began to please the executive boardroom, and as holidays approached, the idea was naturally floated to hold the sales on those holiday weekends as well, "to better serve our customers."

Now, I totally understood the idea of a weekend sale. Retail brands across all categories have used this tried-and-true technique to bring in waves of store traffic, who frequently buy way more than just the advertised specials. Also, I could see the interesting angle to staying open on a Sunday, which most banks did not do, to support such a sale.

But federal holidays, especially patriotic ones, posed a special problem.

As I've noted, because our CD rates were among the highest in the nation, we attracted a larger than normal share of the seniors audience, many of whom were old enough to have served in either World War II or Korea. We knew this. Also from personal experience researching and marketing healthcare to seniors, I knew that they were much more likely to be intensely patriotic and conservative, generally. And even though my own history of service was only a couple of years in the Air Force Reserve, I, too, had a patriotic streak in me. Also my two brothers were military officers, serving and sacrificing for many years.

So in the final analysis, I felt strongly that Countrywide Bank branches should not be open on Memorial Day or Independence Day. This decision was not simply a selfish one based on my own beliefs. No, it was a strategic marketing decision based on my concerns that this older generation may see it as a slap in the face to those faithful service people who sacrificed and perhaps even died in our conflicts. It could be a public relations disaster. So I fired off an e-mail to senior management. In it, I articulated my concerns, adding an obnoxious comment, wondering out loud if I was the only one in the company who had served in any way. I stressed that what mattered most was what our customers felt, not what senior management felt about the issue. And, of course, just to make this e-mail the most feather-ruffling it could be, I cc'd the world.

Within hours I got a terse response from Donna, stating that we would be open on those two federal holidays. The tone of the e-mail was such that it appeared that once again I had gone against the cultish grain of our "woo!" culture. It wasn't a smart career move, but I was beginning not to care.

Starting in mid-2006, from the point of the "great patriotic debate" debacle, as the market began to show signs of softening, my enthusiasm for Countrywide overall began to wane as well. The Bank especially had a uniquely conservative tone that just accentuated the cultish regime. And marketing deposits—unlike the romantic notions associated with homeownership—was an exercise in tedium.

Maybe I was just getting sick of working within such rigid corporate cultures. Perhaps it was the culture that was giving me a bad attitude; perhaps it was my bad attitude that began to shift the culture against my grain.

Gone were the earlier days of Bob's electric chat at that first lunch, the brilliant mentoring and financial teachings of Emily, and shared glory in helping Angelo's dream become a reality. Now it was becoming just a grind. And I had no real mentors at the Bank to teach me things I didn't know, to motivate me to be better, whom I could admire. Unlike ever before, the hour-plus drive to work each morning had become an increasing chorus of nausea and dread. In past jobs, I was careful to monitor my own internal nausea meter; when it got too high, maybe it was time to move on.

Everything began to annoy me: The giant jar of green money-colored M&Ms on the conference table, each etched with a cute little Countrywide Bank logo on it; a senior manager's strong suggestion that I "look into" sponsoring a local school that his child happened to attend; the days-long meetings, with yawns, to discuss yields and rates; Donna's admonitions that I need to "generate more Savings-Link deposits!" yet cutting my budgets drastically each week to pay for knucklehead projects that yielded no revenue; the petty political infighting; the never-ending, scorching heat of Thousand Oaks; the sales guy who was always "containing a crisis"—he would constantly run into meetings late, out of breath, with literally 40 stuffed binders.

And, of course, the office classic: the *Offsite*. Some companies call them "Retreats," or "Strategic Encounters" or whatever, but no matter what you called them, I called them wastes of time and money.

In my career I had attended at least a hundred of these boondoggles; some included golf, spas, and assorted cold cuts. Maybe only one out of those hundred actually yielded any actionable strategies, revenue, or breakthroughs; but they were a ubiquitous element in all sales cultures. More likely, they accomplished less than a good, solid half day locked in a conference room could achieve, and usually wound up becoming much more about having everyone trip over themselves in the conferences to appear valuable, brilliant, and awake.

Countrywide Bank's official corporate Offsite would be one of my last experiences with this great company, and would be a sad ending to what had been a fun ride at Countrywide, if I didn't find parts of it so funny.

Held at a hotel on the campus of Universal City (next to Universal Studios), it was a standard mix of presentations, "teamwork" exercises ("Okay, everyone, you and your group of six colleagues need to take this string, this salad dressing, and this roll of quarters and figure out how to build a car—you have five minutes—GO!"), and "trust" exercises (insert the ubiquitous Outward Bound montage of business people falling backward into each other's arms, walking on hot coals, or jumping off cliffs).

But looking back on it now, two events at that Offsite encapsulated for me the ironic absurdity of where Countrywide was heading, and the beautiful dream it had once been.

In one particularly odd exercise, the group was assigned the task of reading and analyzing the famous poem by Robert Frost titled "The Road Not Taken." It was first published in 1916, and I had studied it intently in high school, under the careful eye of my brilliant English teacher Mr. Glass. For context, this is the text of the poem:

> *Two roads diverged in a yellow wood,*
> *And sorry I could not travel both*
> *And be one traveler, long I stood*

And looked down one as far as I could
To where it bent in the undergrowth;

Then took the other, as just as fair,
And having perhaps the better claim,
Because it was grassy and wanted wear;
Though as for that the passing there
Had worn them really about the same,

And both that morning equally lay
In leaves no step had trodden black.
Oh, I kept the first for another day!
Yet knowing how way leads on to way,
I doubted if I should ever come back.

I shall be telling this with a sigh
Somewhere ages and ages hence:
Two roads diverged in a wood, and I—
I took the one less traveled by,
And that has made all the difference.

For weeks before the Offsite, it was curious to see pinstriped bankers walking the halls with bound reams of mind-numbing financial data, and this small yet powerful poem. Like a balance sheet, they studied every line, looking for smart things to say in the group meeting.

I watched and winced as my boss Todd got up in front of the group to moderate the discussion. How exactly would this bright group of Countrywide superstars correlate the meanings, both obvious, hidden, elegant, and sublime, of this masterpiece into knowledge that would generate an additional billion dollars in banking deposits from seniors? With Todd positioning his marker atop the giant flipboard of pages for noting all the comments, he asked the group, "Who can tell me what this poem means?"

Toni shot me a look; I shot her an eye-roll as the first shouts began.

"It's about the woods!" said one overeager idiot in the crowd.

"It's about choices!" shouted another master of the obvious from the back.

"It's about being...the BEST!"

The room broke out in thunderous applause. ("Woo!" culture.)

As the sycophantic shouts flooded the room with forced ebullience, Todd dutifully wrote down all of these genius insights. In group meetings like this, "no idea is a bad idea," they used to say.

I quickly scribbled a tiny note to Toni, passing it to her under the table.

She opened it, reading what I had written: "It's about blowing $100k on a worthless Offsite." She quietly chuckled to herself.

Always appreciative of her sense of humor and the friendship we had forged over the previous months, I scribbled another little ditty for her amusement. She opened the second note, which read "It's about only posting a competitively high rate from a trusted brand and not worrying about anything else." She nodded and smiled, as she was already familiar with my bank marketing mantra.

As the lowest-common-denominator comments slowly ran dry, there was a lull in the room. Either no one in the room could see anything more in this poem, or they were afraid to say. The cultish fear of making waves, of using obvious answers to justify intellectual value, was palpable in the room, and maddening. So, deciding to continue my recent streak of bad attitude, I threw a verbal hand grenade into the crowd, just for fun.

"It's about *death*," I said.

The entire room fell silent, then slowly turned in their chairs toward my words. I loved beginning conversations with shocking words.

"Let's try to stay positive, shall we?" Todd asked, with that *I know what you're trying to do, Adam, please don't* look.

"No, seriously," I continued, channeling the cantankerous and brilliant Mr. Glass from twelfth-grade English class.

"It's also about life, and death, maybe even heaven and hell. He says the wood is yellow, like the autumn or winter—death seasons. It could just as easily be about justifying the *poor* choices we make, the hubris of confidence, or the stupidity of that same confidence, right?—or regrets."

Mumbles began forming at the other tables.

"He says 'that has made all the difference'—but he doesn't say that was a *good thing*. In fact, he sighs, wistfully. Maybe he went on a road to some kind of *ruin?*"

The words hung in the air for a moment as the room fell silent except for the squeaking of Todd's furiously scribbling marker. Toni shook her head at me, shaking her finger to tell me to behave. I knew that the loan numbers were faltering in the other divisions of Countrywide. I recalled the look of dread in Tim's face at lunch a few months before. I felt the magic fading. In my head I saw my whiteboard from that doomsday talk with Emily almost a year earlier. And I saw this portentous poem differently from everyone else.

The sharply negative bubble I had so perfectly created was popped simply by the next anonymous shout from the back.

"It's about . . . *Leadership!*"

The room exploded once again into applause and cheers as my commentary was wiped away with one giant wave of hootin' 'n' hollerin'. *Perhaps I shall be telling this story with a sigh somewhere ages and ages hence . . .*

After two full days of this cacophony of corporate conformity, I was at the height of my cynicism. But like life itself, something happened unexpectedly that, like a ray of sunlight through a cloudy sky, rekindled my belief in the good parts of Countrywide, and what it had once meant to me.

As a final group exercise, the entire corporate organization was broken into 20 groups of about 10 people each. Each of us stood together in our respective groups in the massive conference hall, fit for a wedding reception of at least two hundred people, I assumed. With the chairs removed, the high ceilings and the new carpet of the convention room made the room feel larger than it was. The moderators then rolled into the room a large box for each group to open. In each was an assembly kit for a supercool new kid's bicycle. Our assignment was to assemble our kits as quickly as possible as a team, and to continue the "challenges" Offsite theme, we were also then to present our finished, assembled product to the entire room via some sort of skit or play that we would act out. We would only have 10 minutes to assemble the bikes, and, of course, one piece would be missing from each kit. We would need to forage among the other groups for our missing piece, quickly assembling alliances and bartering deals for missing pieces we had that they may have needed. In a frenzy of madcap antics, we each assembled our bike projects, complete with streamers and pink seats and cool bells and whistles, and, one by one, acted out our cute little skits. There were moments of fun, but with each passing performance, I counted down the time that afternoon when the Offsite would be done and we would be allowed to leave.

Just then the head moderator stood up to presumably make his closing remarks, as empty cardboard boxes and piles of wrapping plastic from all of the kits made for a cleanup nightmare. I remember thinking as he began talking, *Oh, good, only a few minutes left until this is over.*

"I wanted to thank all of you for your hard teamwork over these last two days," he began. Blah, blah, blah.

"As you know, Countrywide is a special company, a company dedicated to the powerful and meaningful concept that everyone has a right to achieve the American Dream." He looked around at all of us as he spoke.

Twenty assembled bikes gleamed among the groups, under the spotlights of the carpeted convention room. As he raised the idea that was once close to my heart, of helping to achieve the American Dream, I began to listen in earnest, almost ashamed for having become so cynical.

"And we wanted to help all of you remember why you are part of Countrywide..."

As he said this sentence, another moderator opened the outer doors of the large hall, welcoming into the room a group of 20 children, and what appeared to be their teachers. The children were about 10 years old, and as they entered, their eyes were at first confused, as if they didn't know why they were there.

"Please welcome some of our guests here today..." He extended his arms to welcome the kids into the hall, going on to mention that they were from a local home for underprivileged or orphaned children—I don't recall exactly—but the meaning of the event was suddenly clear to all as he continued.

"And on behalf of our family at Countrywide, we would like to give each of you a brand-new bike for the holidays!"

The children's eyes suddenly glowed with joy and giggles as each of them ran to one of the bikes. In an instant, as they began hugging us, my feeling toward this seemingly purposeless exercise had morphed into one of the most memorable moments I had ever experienced in any corporate setting, let alone the firm that I had once most believed in. Countrywide would make these children's holiday dreams come true, and we were a part of that fulfillment. As a parent of little ones myself, I struggled to hold back tears among my colleagues as I shared what was pure joy with these elated children, who never imagined anything like this.

Each of those bikes glimmered just as Bob's shining house key glimmered during my first interview lunch more than three years earlier. And the same magic that came to me at that first meeting, from what Countrywide provided to America, from Angelo's story and passionate mission, from the feeling I got by doing good for the country, enveloped me. For one last moment, I *believed*, again.

And that, once, had made all the difference.

11

No More Options

To be admitted to Nature's hearth, costs nothing.
—Henry David Thoreau

OCTOBER 2006
Prime rate: 8.25%
Foreclosure rate: 1.19%
CFC stock price: ~$36.00

MY BRIEF VISIT back to romantic notions of my perfectly altruistic company doing perfectly noble things for a perfectly grateful public soon faded back into the realities of working for a profit-hungry corporate beast.

That fall of 2006 began the yearly ritual of strategic planning, which was comprised of assembling a list of objectives for the next year, and then developing necessary strategies, tactics, and plans to accomplish them. Oh, and this all had to align with the assigned budgets that came down from the mountain each year.

For marketing, the year 2006 had revolved around the now-successful launch of our online savings product, SavingsLink. Donna had hired an all-new group of marketing talent in the form of Todd, me, and Toni, as well as investing in several other great team members with a budget never before seen at the Bank. Times were good then;

hopes were high and dreams of making the Bank a formidable, stand-alone brand among the financial landscape were on everyone's mind.

But 2007 would be different, and in this planning process, we would get our first glimpse into just how different.

Countrywide Bank was indeed large; in fact, it was proud of distributing press releases that cited that we were "the eleventh-largest bank in America." Well, that was *partly* true. Like all statistics, however, that boast could be considered suspect depending on how you defined "large." Statistics also can represent the "Art of Not Lying." Yes, Countrywide Bank could be viewed as the eleventh-largest bank in the U.S. *if* you judged it at that time solely by *assets*. Most people generally think of a bank being large or small based on its *deposits*, or number of customers. But part of Countrywide Bank's assets included the *monumentally enormous* number of mortgages that flowed through the Bank, courtesy of our sibling, Countrywide Home Loans.

As stated concisely in Countrywide's 2006 Annual Report, "Our goal since the acquisition [of the bank] in 2001 has been to leverage the Company's existing residential mortgage capabilities to create additional earnings by holding a portfolio of loans at the Bank." It goes on to explain the fundamental structure of the arrangement in laymen's terms: "Countrywide Bank has helped strengthen the Company by lessening the earnings volatility inherent in our mortgage lending business. Primarily, this has been accomplished by supplementing the gain-on-sale income from mortgage loans sold into the secondary market with generally more stable net interest income from the mortgage loans we retain on the Bank's balance sheet."

SavingsLink was indeed a hit, and deposits were growing. But investing in marketing to encourage the growth of deposits was still arguably a secondary exercise for the Bank, whose primary purpose was to house Countrywide loans to generate interest income. Well, as loan volume continued its precarious slow-motion spiral, so, too, then the Bank would be squeezed. Note the ominous language in the following paragraph of that same Annual Report, which struggled to downplay what could happen in the future: "In the current environment, asset growth at the bank has proven to be challenging. A shrinking mortgage market and increasing concerns over credit quality have reduced the availability of high-quality assets..."

Of course, Bank management probably knew about these brewing troubles at some time before that Annual Report would be published, so the mood around the place became increasingly dark. More meetings were held behind closed doors. Whispers about layoffs began to waft through the lunchrooms. An eerie quiet layered onto the offices, like when birds go silent before an earthquake. But I had learned over the years to just relax, focus on my work and on things I could control, and not worry about things that I can't control.

That first strategic planning meeting would set the tone. Used to big budgets and focused marketing efforts from the year before, I had hoped that we were gathering to discuss what would be our next SavingsLink—our next big push for 2007. Instead what we got was a rude awakening.

Donna began the meeting. "Thank you all for coming today. What I am passing around the table now are the budgets for 2007...."

As Todd and Toni and the rest of the assembled senior staff and I passed around the document, quiet gasps could be heard. When I took my copy, I saw it immediately.

All budgets were being slashed across the board. It was worse than I thought.

As Donna went through the numbers one by one, she asked us to "try to stay positive for your teams, and please come back to me with plans for what we *can* accomplish within these budgets."

I looked at Donna across the table, incredulous. These numbers I stared at were much lower than they were the year I came on board at the Bank. In an instant it looked like the lofty dreams of major Bank brand were either being vaporized, or at the very least, tabled until the squeeze had passed. There would be no major marketing initiatives in 2007; in fact, the Bank would truncate, huddling together for safety and taking as few risks as possible. A full ten months before the mortgage market would begin its rapid collapse, from my view there were already serious hints that something bad might be coming. It was looking like it had already subtly and quietly become about survival, not growth. I wondered if some finance jock high within Countrywide Financial had taken a second look at those PayOption projections that I saw in the Vault two years earlier, and got scared.

I looked around at Todd and Toni, who looked as stunned as I was. I looked at Donna and said, "With these numbers, we may not even be able to support or justify having a marketing department *at all*...?" Donna grimaced and slowly nodded, then silently and solemnly assembled her papers, got up, and left the room. That was it; she had answered me in the affirmative, projecting the anguish of her responsibilities first to the firm via her facial expressions and body language. I felt more for her than I did for me. But clearly, there would be layoffs coming.

As every economist knows, nothing brings out the true character of people faster than a threat to their existence in a competitive environment among scarce resources. As soon as it was clear that layoffs would be coming, the gloves came off. Many people immediately jockeyed for position in the pecking order in obvious ways, taking the Countrywide cultural concept of "velocity" to silly heights.

Suddenly there were more meeting Invites than usual, when a senior manager would try to demonstrate his or her critical value quickly by calling for larger meetings, "Summits," to discuss the work of their recently formed "Task Force." Oddly enough, I didn't care. Whereas my nausea level during my morning commute should have spiked during this time, it didn't. More like a terminally ill patient who becomes resigned to whatever will happen will happen, I was serene and much calmer than I had been before. I had been through layoffs before—in the advertising business they happen almost every month—so this time, wiser, more mature, I was confident in my abilities and equally comfortable that my work at Countrywide was coming to an end.

Indeed, I secretly hoped that I would not be kept on. On a grander scale, I sensed that this might be the completion of what was to be my first career—in marketing—and the bright opportunities to begin the hard work of developing a second career would so be upon me. I loved risk, I loved building new things with entrepreneurial passion; I also loved writing. Perhaps this event would finally force me to get on with building my second career.

The mood in the hallways was tense, naturally. Todd, Toni, and I all had offices next to each other, so much of our time was spent huddling together sharing any whispers, rumors, or tidbits we had heard. Frankly, not much got done during this time. In fact, just as Countrywide Bank had completely bungled my coming on board, so too would they break the first rule of orderly layoffs: do it quickly. Weeks and weeks went by, prolonging the agony of the unknown that everyone felt. No answers were forthcoming; Donna would change the subject. An occasional team panic attack would occur when the executive floor would ask all of us to submit brief descriptions of our role and responsibilities. *Are you kidding me?* They actually forced the staff to all write out their value to the firm, and many folks felt they were writing their epitaph, or digging their own graves. It was truly an exercise in cruelty and humiliation for many. Everyone would submit their paragraph in terror, only to have the executive floor go silent again for even more days.

Sleepless and scared, my team, many of whom were obviously miserable, would come to me, asking me what was going to happen. I didn't know, and I told them so. I was angry that I was not being allowed to inform them of any timetables or anything else.

Finally, in mid-October 2006, the word came down. There would be layoffs in the third week of October. We all held our breath. Whatever would happen, at least it would be over soon.

Tuesday, October 17, 2006, was a crisp and cool fall day. The day before, on Monday, I had received what would be my last meeting Invite e-mail, asking me to be in Donna's office at 10:00 A.M. I knew what that meant.

When I arrived that morning, Todd was already packing. He had been let go only 30 minutes before I arrived. There was seasoned integrity in his face as he stoically packed up his books and personal items into a single cardboard box. For the first time, the emotional realities of this day were becoming all too real. Not knowing what to say, I simply uttered, "I'm sorry, Todd." He replied, "It is what it is." He kept on packing.

Toni was not packing. She had not received an e-mail to attend an HR execution. I stopped in to her office, asking her if she was okay. I could see her eyes were getting watery as she continued staring into her computer screen, not looking up. "Yeah," she replied. Already I had become a ghost.

As 10 o'clock approached, I sat in my office, staring out the window. I peered out onto the majestic canyons, desert hills, large mansions, and distant horse ranches that marked Thousand Oaks's topography. I decided then and there that it had been a fun ride.

My "involuntary termination" meeting (read: layoff) lasted only about 10 minutes. There were papers to be signed and checks to be accepted. Countrywide, perhaps because they felt for us going through this just before the holiday, was generous in its severance policies, so I would not starve for a while, at least. And the following month, in November 2006, I would finally dump my stock options, now vested, near the peak of the stock's price, $42. I was not rich, but it would give me time to build my next adventure. (In the spirit of full disclosure, I also would lose a fortune in Countrywide stock late the following year, when my romantic feelings toward the firm would have me stupidly hold on to my own private shares of CFC even as it plummeted to $5. I, too, believed that it would recover, especially when Angelo said publicly in the fall of 2007 that "Countrywide is a strong, viable financial company," and "we continue to be bullish on the long-term prospects of both Countrywide and our industry.")

The termination meeting was part business, part therapy session, as the pretty and empathetic Human Resources lady asked me if I wanted to share any feelings about the day. I appreciated her offer, and was sure that many of the other folks who would be let go that day would begin blubbering and let it all out: anger, frustration, sadness, fear, everything. That wasn't for me, though. I smiled, signed the papers, and thanked them for the sensitive way they were handling this day. Then, as I got up to leave the room, I turned back briefly and said to them, "I just hope Countrywide is around a year from now." They looked at me as if this were some kind of parting shot, a comment from anger or resentment. No, it was my real hope, as I believed that what was happening slowly to the company and the industry would surely continue. I actually felt worse for them; those who perhaps had spent their entire careers in mortgage banking, or housing, or real estate, and might struggle to get into other industries if this one should collapse on itself. With marketing experience in hundreds of different categories, at least I would have more career options, I thought.

In silence I brought the few boxes of personal effects out to my car, needing to make three embarrassing trips as people watched me, saying, "I'm sorry," as if I had been sentenced to death. It was more annoying than anything else. I just wanted to get out of there as fast as possible. I said good-bye to Toni at her doorway, where she seemed busily immersed in some nonsense. "Yeah, I'll call you," she said, getting up to give me a hug. It was understandably awkward. We have rarely spoken since that day.

Like a million other corporate executives from a million other firms on a million other crisp autumn days, I drove off, my car full of boxes of memories, into an unknown future of adventure.

My days at Countrywide were at an end.

THE FOLLOWING DAYS were spent doing the customary professional things, sending out thank-you notes to all my colleagues for the fun we had, asking them to keep in touch and send me any job leads they might come upon. I called Bob and Emily directly to tell them what had happened, although they already knew. They, of course, offered the most sincere support and encouragement to me, as I knew they would. Even Andy responded to me with a kind note, thanking me for "accomplishing a great deal often under difficult circumstances." That was nice.

What was I to do now? Personally, it was a chance to get back to my passions, running, tennis, writing, and finally to spend some well-earned time with my two little boys. Trips to Disneyland and other adventures with the boys filled our days together that first week I had left Countrywide, and it was wonderful. By November 1, I would set about building plans for what would become my second career. Also, I knew that most likely I might still do marketing consulting—I still loved marketing, and I was good at generating profitable new customers for clients.

But for that week, at least, all I knew was that I was sick of profit, sick of capitalism, sick of conference rooms and e-mails and politics; sick of mail and television and casting and typefaces and financial analysis. I needed the guidance of an invisible hand—fate, perhaps—or some brilliant visions of the other worlds out there, some courageous commentary on what else could be. So one morning I went to my bookshelf and pulled out just one book. Tucked tightly under my arm, it accompanied me to the local park near my home, a grand lawn of perfectly pedicured grass, circled by joggers and laughing children on playdates. That warm November day in Santa Monica, I opened that book to page one.

It was Henry David Thoreau's existential masterwork *Walden; or Life in the Woods*. Arguably one of the world's most powerful treatises on how and why we should live simpler lives, seeking simple pleasures, and avoiding the pitfalls and corruption of a life seeking goods, things, and material wealth. The words spoke to me as I turned the pages.

When the farmer has got his house, he may not be the richer but the poorer for it, and it be the house that has got him. I smiled to myself as this wisdom, written way back in 1854, seemed still so powerfully true today. *Most men...are needlessly poor all their lives because they think that they must have such a [home] as their neighbors have.*

And so, in that grassy field, among the birds and the trees and the wind, with my book in hand and warm sunshine on my face, I set about deprogramming myself from the corporate life I had just led, finding myself again in the pages of its profound philosophy as the sun rose higher in the sky.

ALMOST A YEAR later, on one bright Sunday morning in the summer of 2007, as I had done so many Sundays before, I awoke and staggered my way through the unseasonably chilly air to the kitchen, where the familiar aroma of burned coffee filled the room. Sipping a precious few sips to help wake me up, I continued to walk over through the foyer to the front door to assume the weekly ritual of picking up my Sunday newspaper. As usual, I planted myself on the outside deck of the condo I was staying in, which, on the fourth floor, gave me a panoramic view of one of the wealthiest neighborhoods and real estate in Los Angeles, and in America: Brentwood, California. The vista of the city below gleamed with office towers, topped with the well-known logos of familiar financial titans: Citi, Wachovia, Bank of America.

I glanced at the stories on the front page before I sought out my trivial little word puzzle. As I meandered my way through the different columns of the main section, a headline and iconic image on the front page stopped me cold.

There, embedded in the copy, was the story of a family that was losing their home to foreclosure, standing in front of what used to be their home, with a *white picket fence.* The white picket fence had, years earlier, become an unofficial image of the Countrywide brand, a symbol of the dream I worked so hard to market. As I scanned the story, the magnitude of what it meant began to hit me.

It had been almost a year since I had left Countrywide, and now my own consultancy business was thriving. But in that one year, the downturn began to generate an ever-increasing chorus of victims.

Oh, no, I thought, as I continued reading furiously, *please let the loan be from Wells Fargo or Bank of America or something…*

"…and when the value of her home dropped, she was unable to get refinancing, as her loan need was larger than the new value of her home. After falling behind on her payments, the lender, Country-wide, began foreclosure proceedings."

I was part of the team that built the massive marketing engine for Countrywide, partly due to the housing frenzy of the early 2000s, partly creating it. I built programs that targeted loan prospects with fairly good and excellent credit, driving tens of thousands of sales leads per month, which then entered the sales "conversion" process. I was at the center of the team that created dozens of television commercials of various lengths, messages, and offers, sent out millions of direct-mail pieces, managed hundreds of thousands of paid search keywords, online banner ads, and many more efforts that motivated potential home buyers and refinancers to act, to call Countrywide, to get a new loan.

For a moment I wondered what it was like in that family's house that dreadful day when they realized they could not refinance the house, when they could not make the payments, when the foreclosure mail began to arrive. I imagined what it must have been like over that kitchen table, the realization when they knew they would lose their home. The moment they lost the dream.

For so long I used all my marketing talents and experience at Countrywide to engage loan prospects to understand the "wonderful options" at their disposal. I had felt that I was doing *good* for people. But now I wondered if I had done nothing more than made a mess I was powerless to clean up. How far would it go? What did I really contribute to? Who was really responsible? *Was I?*

I remembered back, when I truly believed in what I was doing. I can remember feeling bad for other marketing professionals working at other firms, in other categories, who toiled away each day on selling items that didn't *really* make people's lives better. Like those poor bored marketing folks who sold paper plates, or who were forced to find ways to sell intensely sugary cereals to kids who shouldn't even eat it. I had hit the marketing jackpot, I felt, truly helping people change their lives. Yet in the end, I may have been just as delusional as the tens of thousands of homeowners who signed for loans they could never afford.

Not to worry, the internal analysts always said, *home values are projected to increase for the foreseeable future. The values will still be there.* Uh-huh. Tell that to the thousands of other families who were quickly falling into this nightmare.

And then, having been out of Countrywide for over a year, all I could do was continue to read the stories in the coming months and watch the drama unfold.

SUSAN EVANS IS a proud, hardworking, divorced, African-American mother of four children in Columbia, Maryland, a working-class suburb of Baltimore. She bought a four-bedroom, 2½-bath home for $545,000, after her apartment complex was sold. As she signed the papers on her new home, she was technically homeless, caught between being a renter and homeownership; this provided some extra pressure for her to get something as her loan paperwork accelerated.

Her credit score was a marginal 649, which put her into the Sub-prime category, which made her secure an 8.25% interest rate, a standard higher Subprime rate. She got an Adjustable-Rate Loan, which started out with a monthly payment of about $4,500. Working multiple jobs as a day-care provider, and in retail part-time, with some additional child support income each month, her entire monthly take-home pay was about $6,500. With a yearly take-home income of only about $72,000 (grossing about $100,000 per year), she was granted a loan for $545,000 by her lender (a major bank), with not one dollar down.

When asked how she could sign a mortgage that required a $4,500-per-month payment when she was making only $6,500 a month, she claimed she was told by her loan officer that she would "be able to Refi in six months." Once the first payment coupon arrived after her 45-day "no payment" period that came with this loan, she realized that actually she had signed for two loans; it was an "80/20" loan to cover the cost of the house. While still a total of about $4,500 a month in payments, she was struck by the fact that she was now getting two different loan bills.

Then several hardships occurred at the same time. The State of Maryland had shifted their child-care budget. In the transfer, a massive state computer glitch prevented thousands of state workers from getting paychecks. Susan received no paychecks for weeks, with many other state workers. Then her ex-husband lost his job, and the child support payments stopped. It seemed like the whole world was closing in on her. She was able to pay four months of the "20" loan, but only one month of the "80" loan. Eventually both loans went into default.

She called her lender, to seek assistance with her situation, and asked for a modification. She filled out the "hardship" paperwork, but when she saw the offer, it included new penalties and fees related to the defaults, and would not be able to be supported by her income.

I asked her about the moment the crisis came home to her. It was when her property tax bill arrived, for a whopping $5,000; money that she did not have. On the brink of falling into a depression, she stayed strong for her kids. She found resources to help; she got help from the county tax board, and reached out to ACORN. According to its website, ACORN (Association of Community Organizers for Reform Now) is "the nation's largest grassroots community organization of low- and moderate-income people." (I guess grossing $100,000 per year, like Susan did, is considered "middle-income" in Baltimore.) During the burgeoning mortgage and housing crisis, ACORN has emerged as a powerful advocate for low-income and minority families affected by the crisis. ACORN did research on Susan's behalf, investigating her loan papers through the State of Maryland, and alleged that her income had been inflated on the documents by someone in the loan process.

Her four children also were struggling. Ranging in age from three to seventeen, the little ones have difficulty understanding why they can no longer get certain things, or live the life they once lived, but her oldest, a girl, has stepped up to help watch the children while Susan took a job at night to try to survive. She expressed the pride that only a mother could have when she described how much closer this has brought her to her daughter.

She was forced to declare bankruptcy as the home continued going toward foreclosure. The lender took ownership of the property as a Refi became out of the question; it was now valued at only $430,000. The lender has begun the paperwork necessary to force an eviction, as Susan and her four children continue to live in the home even as the ownership has changed. ACORN has filed an appeal on her behalf to try to allow her to stay in the house, and the law allows her to stay in the house while the appeal is being processed.

I asked her who she blames for all these troubles. Courageously, she initially responded that at first she "blamed herself" for signing those papers. But once ACORN began her investigation and claimed to have found incorrect loan documents, she got angry. She also began to see how many more in her community were falling down this hole, and began blaming the government, lenders, and those "golfing CEOs."

I asked her outright if she felt racism was a factor in her nightmare.

"No, I believe it was not about racism; it was about greed. We can't even get justice."

When asked what she will do if the eviction comes through, she paused.

"I don't know what I'll do."

12

A Kingdom Conquered

I see in the near future a crisis approaching that unnerves me and causes me to tremble for the safety of my country... corporations have been enthroned and an era of corruption in high places will follow, and the money power of the country will endeavor to prolong its reign by working upon the prejudices of the people until all wealth is aggregated in a few hands and the Republic is destroyed.

—Abraham Lincoln, November 1864
(letter to Colonel William F. Elkins, after passage
of the National Bank Act)

JANUARY 2008
Prime rate: 7.25%
Foreclosure rate: 2.47%
CFC stock price: ~$6.00

COUNTRYWIDE WAS ANGELO Mozilo's life's work. He had built it with vision, hard work, salesmanship, and a dash of luck. In almost 40 years he had created an empire making billions of dollars in revenue per year, with more than 60,000 employees all across the nation in many different businesses. He was proud of his baby, this colossus that he had built with his own hands.

Then in the summer of 2007, Countrywide would be the first giant to begin the journey in earnest toward the end that was both fast and slow in its cruel evolution. The forecloser would become the foreclosed.

Like for so many families going into default and then falling into the frightening abyss of foreclosure, events leading to Countrywide's demise were a combination of mistakes within their control and many forces out of their control. Not the fault of any one person, or cause, or effect, it was a uniquely destructive combination of factors that swirled into a vortex to create the perfect financial storm from Wall Street to Main Street that year and beyond.

As 2007 hummed along, I got word that things were getting really bad inside Countrywide. Occasionally I would reconnect with old colleagues there, seeing if they were still employed, offering to help them secure new contacts or potential job leads. Sometimes I would e-mail a few folks there just to find out by default who had been let go; by e-mailing Countrywide addresses, I could see whose address would be returned by the servers with a "user not found" or "no such address" error message. This meant they were gone.

Then, in August 2007, almost to the month when I had predicted the worst on my office whiteboard with Emily almost three years before, like a house of cards, all hell seemed to break loose from every direction at the same time.

Loan volume was plummeting. Mortgage rates were not coming down. Foreclosures were skyrocketing, especially in Subprime loans. The firm had accelerated their layoffs. And most ominously, the market's appetite for buying bundled, securitized mortgages seemed to suddenly dry up.

While rising foreclosures were bad unto themselves, much of the media coverage of the events did not adequately give weight to the much greater danger on Wall Street, and to financial firms, that few seemed to want to buy mortgage securities anymore, which rippled quickly through all of the credit markets as the perceived value of these financial instruments dropped.

Countrywide Home Loans made most of its money through a few key channels; it would get one-time fees from processing the loans themselves; it would charge interest for the loans it granted directly; it would take in an ongoing steady stream of small loan servicing fees after the customer got his Countrywide loan; and, it would "securitize" chunks of mortgages together into bundled "mortgage-backed securities," that then would be resold to investors on Wall Street. These bundled investment vehicles were priced based on complicated, *theoretical* mathematical formulas that were designed to ascertain the true levels of risk, high or low, dependent on what kind of loans they were (loan types, and Prime vs. Subprime, etc.), interest rates, and chances of prepayment of the loans.

But markets are like animals, and when spooked, they can rear up and run.

By the summer of 2007, when defaults and foreclosures began escalating faster than anyone expected, especially in the Subprime area, the theoretical price values that had been assigned by the marketplace to certain types of mortgage securities no longer seemed reasonable to potential buyers. That's when *confidence* in their value collapsed, and the credit markets went haywire in August 2007. Suddenly no investors wanted to go anywhere near them. It was like trying to sell barrels of apples, when the buyers can clearly see that many of the apples on top of the pile are rotten.

I had heard that the tone internally at Countrywide during this time was "don't worry, they'll be back." Although just an anecdote I had heard, however, it was consistent with the cultish hubris that had developed over the years since 2003. From Angelo on down, the message was "let the chips fall, this will be good for us in the end when we are one of the few firms left standing." Everyone still believed, until they slowly realized that the securities buyers would not be coming back anytime soon. And the wildfire wasn't affecting just Countrywide; it also was hitting all lenders, quickly.

As I began reading more and more stories of foreclosures, I was dismayed that the dramatic realities of this fast-spreading scourge were bringing so much pain to thousands of neighborhoods all across the country. I began questioning my role in it, how I may have contributed to it. I wanted to get the perspective from the inside about what was happening, so I began checking in with more Countrywide folks. Everywhere I looked, the story was the same. Shock. Fear. Incredulousness. Disbelief. And in some cases, denial.

Eventually the staggering impact of what was happening hit the numbers for real. Newspapers reported in August that Countrywide was drawing on its total credit line, about $11.5 billion, just to keep operations running. Bank of America, one of the potential suitors I had noted years earlier as well, took a $2 billion stake in Countrywide, with the option to buy it if it were ever put up for sale. The unthinkable had already begun.

Sudden, severe stresses can make people do crazy things—panic, show poor judgment, or rise to the occasion with inner strength, calm, and leadership. Those are the moments within which character is forged and legacies are defined. But for Countrywide foot soldiers and generals still trapped inside the bubble of surrealism as the world began to collapse, "doing the right thing" may have been difficult to define objectively.

With markets panicking, shares plummeting, confidence buckling, and foreclosures soaring in the late summer of 2007, the media feeding frenzy reached the point where it made Countrywide do some stupid things. Looking back on it now, even if the inevitable downfall of the firm was out of their control, that period of August through December 2007 may have been the last opportunity for Countrywide, and Angelo, to at least try to turn the ship around, carry out courageous initiatives under bold leadership, and create a legacy. But in my view, they blew it.

That October, word got out that Countrywide was embarking on a new public relations initiative that in my opinion has to rank up there with one of the embarrassingly dumbest of all time. Headed by a senior executive in the Home Loans division, it was probably spearheaded by a team of Countrywide PR folks and their agency (a large and well-respected public relations firm). The "PR blitz" would be called "Protect Our House."

Instead of being empathetic to the national disaster hitting millions of homes all across the country, and seizing upon this tragedy to build what could have been a sympathetic and effective campaign of assistance and help for its customers and for America, "Protect Our House" had instead somehow managed to be created as an angry reaction to media scrutiny of Countrywide itself. "Protect Our House" would be focused on defending the virtues of Countrywide, lashing out at any detractors, and making it *personal*.

When I heard it, I could not believe my ears.

Years of marginally cultish behavior within Countrywide, combined with the unprecedented wave of sudden and even some undeserved criticism, recent stock collapse, layoffs, and the like had morphed into a spastic fit of rage, outward, in all the wrong directions toward all the wrong people for all the wrong reasons. Some of the criticism Countrywide faced was not unwarranted, of course, and ironically was focused on what seemed to be a disturbing lack of empathy for what was happening at kitchen tables all across America. So what did they do? They created a public relations debacle that focused on their own defense, not on the aid and support of their customers.

Countrywide had decided at this terrible time to play *the victim*. The fact that Angelo was so silent about it, thereby providing his tacit approval, made me incredulous.

I could easily imagine what it must have been like in that conference room when "Protect Our House" was devised. These employees' lives and the company around them, like so many of the loans they had sold, were also now unexpectedly "readjusting" into untenable positions. You had a once-proud culture of leadership and doing the right thing, and then the very market on which it was based was crumbling and turning on them. You had a demoralized staff; there had been a huge number of layoffs in the months leading up to August, while Angelo was, reasons aside, indeed selling great chunks of his stock and making millions. I could see how those who were left after the layoffs were probably shopping their résumés and trying to jump ship as fast as possible. Maybe they were frightened out of their wits trying to figure out how to pay *their own* soon-to-be readjusting mortgages. Human Resources might have a flood of departures on their hands, making the staffing and operations around customer service solutions even worse. They must have felt the need for some sort of internal "woo!" PR campaign—a new rallying cry to inspire those who were left to stay, to continue to believe, to try harder, to make a hostile press eat its words... *to fight.* I could see how that idea would be floated during such stressful times. But that is where the better judgments and cooler heads of senior management are supposed to come in, to advise, to at least try to push back, provide objective assessments of the risks vs. the reward of such a campaign, and not be afraid to throw cold water on the room by asking, "Are you *nuts*?" Apparently this did not happen. Everyone in that conference room that day, raised on a never ending rush of "Woo!" culture at Countrywide, advised by an agency that perhaps did not want to see their hefty fees end, apparently fell into *groupthink.*

Humans tend to huddle together in times of emergency and stress; they seek leadership, and migrate to conformity. Everyone who was part of that new PR program was probably afraid that the mortgage debacle might cost them their jobs; people must have been scared, and eager for a warm huddle. These are the times when that one person who might respond with a negative comment or a cautious appraisal might be the first to be ostracized. There is great risk in nonconformity in any feverishly frothy environment like that, and that is how—

in extreme examples—wars have not been stopped before they have begun, how McCarthyism flourished, and how armbands and goose-stepping came into vogue. And speaking of armbands, it did not help matters any when the nuttiness of the program came into full view.

Employees were asked to sign something tantamount to a "loyalty oath" to Countrywide, promising to "tell Countrywide's story to all." Signers would earn the right to wear a green wristband with the words "Countrywide" and "Protect Our House" imprinted on it. Most disturbingly, the document that would be signed by a senior executive included the phrase "join me in this *crusade,*" giving it creepy overtones of destiny and divine religious purpose. And then he refers to it as a "crusade" *again. Dude, relax—it's a mortgage company.* Apparently he had not been advised and reminded that this exact language caused an uproar in the international community when George W. Bush used it to describe the U.S. War on Terror just a few years before; or maybe he was and chose to ignore it.

Also, the pledge stated that "detractors" were "attacking" the firm's "business policies." Remember, Countrywide was a public company that had seen fortunes vanish and value plummet. So, frankly, investors, shareholders, etc., aka "detractors" would have a right to question—in fact they might feel that they had the *obligation* to question—or "attack," as Countrywide perceived this scrutiny, their "business policies" if they are related to how value in this public company is returned to shareholders. In that context, their criticism certainly would not be "unwarranted," as the pledge claimed.

Then the pledge shifted the nature of the debate, saying, "It's now become personal." Well, maybe they never saw or learned from *The Godfather,* which taught us, *"It's not personal...it's just business."* It *is* just business, and a serious one at that, with serious monies at risk. And the business was failing, fast. I don't recall seeing any reporters slamming anyone at Countrywide personally; in fact, it was their actions they were questioning, such as some of Angelo's stock sales, the Subprime business, the decisions the firm had made, and ironically this PR blitz itself.

I had heard that the internal peer and cultural pressure to sign this pledge was enormous, however subtle and unofficial, and bordering on what some might call fanatical coercion. Those who dared to show up to any meetings not wearing their arm—er, wristbands—might be in danger of subtle forms of prejudice.

I would argue that this cultish leap into the outer fringes of coocooville was counterproductive via the stress it added to the firm. When an employee and an employer agree to a mutually beneficial partnership or contractual obligation—either via document or handshake— the fundamentals of the agreement are an exchange of services for compensation. I agree to come to work, work hard, dedicate myself to fulfilling the role I promised to provide, and go home. The company pays me on time, provides a fair and legal work environment, and the support structures and resources required for me to provide that service to the firm. But there is a line. Who the hell ever said anything about oaths, pledges, or cultural commitments? That's called *the military or the police,* where you are willing to literally give up your life for a greater good. That's not just a job; it's a philosophy, a commitment that penetrates every aspect of a life, where the lines between work and family blur from the sacrifice of it all. Those who do not choose that life are called civilians and perhaps work in corporations, and they should be allowed to work at a civilian company unburdened by such additional stresses and pressures that they themselves chose not to pursue within a militaristic career. The pledge, oath, whatever it was, that Countrywide pushed its employees to sign their names to, in my view, teetered dangerously close to one possible interpretation of what Lincoln had warned about almost 150 years ago: That a corporation, if left to its own vices, might *"endeavor to prolong its reign by working upon the prejudices of the people..."*

The public backlash was swift and severe. Someone had leaked the text of a conference call that was held regarding the new "campaign," and it got picked up by the media, to the shocked delight of reporters, apparently. It fed right into their arguments and proved charges of hubris. Worse, one enterprising and ballsy Countrywide employee dared to put his green wristband on eBay for sale, and this quickly circulated among the blogosphere. It was arguably a disaster.

Not only did it alienate an already adversarial press and cause consternation within an already panicked employee base, but it actually diverted critically needed attention *away from* those programs that Countrywide and other firms had initiated to help people save their homes. There was another great program called "Protect *Your* House" that was one of the early incarnations of a mortgage relief process for troubled customers, but that got totally trampled by this gargantuan clusterf*ck of a PR blitz.

I can recall staring at the story on the web, and saying out loud to myself in my office, *What the hell are they thinking?* I felt sick as I saw this company, this brand that I still admired and that Angelo had built, being run into the ground. As an outside consultant to clients that year, having been on my own since November 2006, I frequently heard clients' appreciation that as an outsider, I sometimes would be the one to give them honest, objective feedback and insights when everyone inside those firms was simply telling the CEO what he or she wanted to hear. I wondered if Angelo was getting *any* objective advice at this time, and, in "outside consultant" mode, wondered if my objectivity, such as it was, might help now. I had nothing to lose. Maybe it would achieve nothing, I thought, but I e-mailed Angelo directly.

I was determined to forcefully tell him what I thought he needed to hear, and I had no fear. What were they going to do, *fire me?* I assumed he would not respond, but perhaps I did it anyway for my own sanity, not to mention I was still a shareholder of Countrywide and I was concerned by its behavior. I reminded him of who I was, articulated my reasons for writing, and then set out to rationally tell him what to do right now and how to do it. I told him that the crisis had created a unique *opportunity* for a leader to emerge who could lead the country through this crisis to a resolution, as no one in the federal government was stepping up and providing this critically needed leadership. Although I generally preferred to see free markets self-correct, I told him that this crisis was different, that it was too large and widespread, and that the current vacuum of leadership required and demanded a bold titan willing to set bold initiatives and lead with strength. I told him he should be that person.

Apart from the company he had created, the millions he had made, and the loyalty he had engendered from his staff that had the honor of working with the founder of the firm (and arguably the father of the entire business), I argued that this was a chance to create something transcendent for generations—to create a *legacy*. Like Lee Iacocca's "saving" Chrysler, like Tylenol forever securing loyalty from a trusting public when it pulled every single bottle off the shelves—overnight— in response to the tampering of their bottles, Angelo could act quickly and grab the reins. Perhaps it was over the top, but I likened that fourth quarter of 2007 to the first weeks of FDR's presidency, when his fast, bold, confident steps to shore up the United States with his New Deal enshrined him in the carved marble of history. I urged him to at least try to assume this role.

I made the following stark and clear recommendations:

1. *Kill "Protect Our House," and personally apologize for it, immediately.* In my view one of the stupidest PR campaigns of all time, it was, I believed, doing serious damage to the firm, and to the trust in it, showed callous disregard for those homeowners who were genuinely in trouble, and pulled attention away from other good programs designed to help homeowners. I told him that it was "turning what used to be a warm, white-picket-fence, neighborhood-friendly, customercentric personality into a selfish, belligerent, and spiteful

firm." I recommended a swift turnaround to this program, making it "Protect *Your* House"—only—as fast as possible, and erasing any traces of the other misguided approach.

2. *Turn Countrywide, and himself (Angelo), into heroes.* Quickly reposition Countrywide as the only player that was stepping up to solve the crisis with some tangible tactical programs immediately, namely, institute something like a "loan recall." The idea was that the problems were so pervasive, so complex, that from my car days I knew that just the word "recall" would immediately be understood and appreciated. A Pavlovian response forged via years of baby toy and car battery recalls would let the customer choose whether they wished to continue driving that Adjustable Rate Mortgage even if the wheels might fly off. I knew that it could not be a *literal* recall, as many of the loans had already been packaged into securities and resold, but it would encourage customers to reengage with Countrywide and hopefully at least be able to explore their options to Refi into a more fixed, stable, affordable loan product. At the very least, it would be a *call to action.*

3. *Angelo should get out front and personally take command of the situation.* It was his baby. He had created it, and it had run off the tracks. Like Steve Jobs, Michael Dell, and other titans who reengaged when their babies ran into severe trouble, that's when a founder steps in and reasserts the passion for helping people that made it great in the first place. I told him he needed to talk directly to America, right away, and tell them how Countrywide was willing to help them during what was becoming a national emergency. He should have bought TV time to express his regret over the recent events, and step up and at least try to solve it. America appreciates, and tends to forgive, anyone who makes a mistake but takes responsibility for it and tries to actively make it right (even if it really wasn't Countrywide's fault—everyone *believed* it was). This could have been his "The Buck Stops Here" moment.

4. *Donate some or all of his recent stock proceeds to a foundation dedicated to preventing this from happening again (through education, grants, assistance, etc.), and take only $1 in salary until the crisis passes.* He could symbolically share financial "pain" with suffering homeowners by forgoing some of his own personal wealth. The size and timing of some of his later stock sales were already being publicly questioned. He was already wealthy. Did he really need more? (This is a major philosophical question that our society has been struggling with since the beginning.)

I WANTED—NO, I needed—Angelo to step up and be the hero I thought he was. I needed him to demonstrate some act of deep sacrifice at that moment; some act that would tell me that it wasn't all about the money for him, that he remembered what Countrywide meant, that he was willing to take personal responsibility for whatever *perceptions*—however unfair they may have been—the public had about the loans we provided (even if he believed it was the borrowers' fault). This is what a leader does. This is what a hero does. This is what a founder does, what a legend does. And I needed him to show me that there are still some heroes left.

He didn't. And to me it felt like Mickey Mantle walking away from a six-year-old autograph-seeker.

To my amazement, he did respond though, quickly, agreeing to consider my suggestions and that he would get back to me. When he did, he focused not on the strategic opportunity for leadership and legacy I suggested, but rather one technical challenge inherent in actually creating a "loan recall" program. He reminded me that unlike cars, where they had total control over manufacturing and distribution, Countrywide had to function within the rules and regulations of the overall mortgage market, including the government, Freddie Mac, and Fannie Mae, and the secondary mortgage securities markets.

He was right about that tactical point, of course, but he had completely missed the strategic "big picture" opportunity. I obviously knew the realities of the current system; what I was recommending was a bold new call for a "moon shot" program meant to challenge America to *change* the system. By being the first to have issued a national loan recall program, he could have then told customers that it was the *system that would not let him now do it*. Then he could extend his leadership as an *agent of change* and call for a "Mortgage Summit" (perhaps to be held at Countrywide headquarters), with all of the key players required to make such changes—lawmakers, financial CEOs, the Treasury Department, the Fed, and regular homeowners too—to convene such a congress and create solutions. Such a call to arms to solve this crisis could have solidified him and Countrywide as having set the tone for reform and leadership, as he might have shaken hands with the president in the Rose Garden as the bill was signed. Or not. But Countrywide, as the industry leader, could—and should—have tried.

I thought it was possible that his response to me was crafted by his legal team, or even Dave Sambol (whom he had cc'd on all his communications to me), but then I thought not. I genuinely believed that Angelo cared—about people, about the company, and about my sincere advice, but I could almost feel through those brief e-mails a man who was under siege, who was surrounded by people afraid to question the momentum that the firm was caught up in, unintentional sycophants who, like me years before, were in no position to change the system that clearly needed changing. Perhaps I was projecting, but I could almost feel a sense of overwhelmed helplessness in his e-mails. And I felt for him, especially when the last e-mail came.

Still slightly stunned that I was now engaged with the CEO of the largest mortgage company in America in an e-mail dialogue about the future of the company, the system, and maybe even the country, I briefly was encouraged that maybe he would take me up on my offer to drive to see him. I had every intention of meeting with him, and perhaps in a bit of silly romanticism, I imagined that he and I would lock ourselves in a conference room and map out the new solutions for the crisis. I cleared my client calendar for that week and next, and waited to hear from him again as our e-mails began going back and forth every hour or so that day. Then, the last e-mail came, that stopped me dead in my tracks.

Perhaps exasperated, perhaps told by his advisors to stop this dialogue, perhaps overwhelmed by it all, or just annoyed by it all, he replied one last time.

He basically told me—and I am paraphrasing now—that public relations issues probably won't matter anyway if there winds up being no company left to run.

I was floored.

I stared at the e-mail in my Inbox, confused, concerned, crushed. Maybe it was worse than I knew. Maybe I didn't know how bad it really was. Maybe I was the last straw of advice that broke that camel's back. Maybe he wasn't who I believed he was.

Once upon a time I related to Angelo and his vision. I even related to some of the personality traits I had heard about him. Not a product of priviledged Ivy League education and polish, he would sometimes say that Harvard types would look down on him when he was a young man in New York trying to make his way. I had the same experience. He was my height, had the same chip on his shoulder that I had, and he had made it. Never underestimate what an aggressive, short, ballsy, street-smart New Yorker can do. And his vision, all histrionics aside, was powerful. Once.

To add salt to the e-mail encounter, shortly thereafter I got an e-mail from Andy Bielanski, the Chief Marketing Officer of Countrywide with whom I worked while I was there and admired. As I would hear later, he had been kept in the loop on all of my e-mails back and forth with Angelo, and he was *pissed off*.

Out of my intense anger of that day I erased the actual text of the e-mail, but the gist was that Angelo had been copying him on the e-mail dialogue. He subtly questioned my motives but then said he wanted to assure me that all issues were being handled internally. Maybe that was his way of saying, *Stay out of this, Adam, mind your own business; you're getting in the way.*

As still a shareholder in the firm, I had every right to e-mail the CEO of the company to offer suggestions within my expertise of mass communications. *Sorry, Andy, but I don't work for you anymore,* was my first thought. That was the last time I had contact with Andy or Angelo, and the last time I even wanted to help. Now, whatever would happen to them would happen to them. I would sit back in my office with a giant bucket of popcorn and watch the show get even more weird and sad through the rest of that year.

Then, like a cheesy montage in a generic Nora Ephron romantic comedy (insert cliché Cole Porter tune here in background), I could not help but think back on all the hype that accompanied—indeed, helped—the incredible growth of the mortgage industry, the housing boom, and the meteoric rise of Countrywide and of Angelo. While waiting in the lobby of one of their smaller buildings for yet another in an endless series of interviews before I joined the company, I can remember the walls being lined with huge, blown-up versions of magazine covers and assorted stories of financial fame. *Fortune. Mortgage Banking. BusinessWeek.* Headlines such as "Fire in the Belly," "Meet the 23,000% Stock," and similar themes, all with the classic shot of Angelo in his bold yellow power tie, pinstripes, and crisp standard-issue white shirt with cuff links suitable for a maverick of his rank. Oh, and his cuff links were tiny Countrywide logos.

Then I looked at the small, silver Countrywide lapel pin that was in my paper clip box that helped clutter my desk. I stared at it. It seemed to stare back at me, lost, a symbol without a lapel, the representation of a once-great American business empire in a dusty mix of clips, lint, and one rogue yellow pushpin. Awarded to me (I think) on my third anniversary of "service to the firm," at one time I wore it with pride, in that I believed in what we were doing, and it easily dethroned the regular multicolored pin I had earned after only one year of service. I plucked the little silver badge from the pile of mangled clips and looked at it in my palm for a moment. Then I tossed it in the trash.

"Never put too much faith in people, in heroes," my father would say, "they may eventually disappoint you." On that day, he turned out to be right.

THAT AUTUMN WAS the final fall. Reporting horrible third-quarter numbers, Angelo seemed indignant or delusional, I couldn't decide which. Slightly adversarial with the analysts on the earnings call, he continued to be intensely optimistic, with the charismatic flair of the lifelong polished salesman he was. It had served him well for years; he would need all of his skills now. He firmly declared that the ship would right itself, even as rumors on the street remained to the contrary. I am not sure why I did it, but perhaps I still wanted to believe, so I took Angelo at his word; I held on to the large chunk of private stock shares I had bought on my own (not through options), even as the stock was coming down. Maybe he was right, I thought; the concept was if Countrywide was indeed left standing after many other firms failed it could lead to Countrywide becoming a larger owner of the market than ever before.

That December and January, every contact I would have with anyone inside Countrywide would be filled with dread, worry, and uncertainty. Phrases such as "waiting to hear," "pins and needles," and "fingers crossed" became part of the everyday vernacular within the venerable halls of this once-great company. An eerie quiet had overcome the cubicles and offices of the groups for Marketing, Home Loans, and the Bank, like the way animals go quiet just before an intense storm.

Then the storm finally came.

As the numbers entered a screaming nosedive, with Countrywide's own "credit cards" maxed out (in the form of a $11.5 billion credit line already tapped out), they ran out of options. All the hubris and cuff links and magazine covers and flashy trade show booths and TV ads and mailers and bellicose bravado in the world would not allow them to keep the lights on. It was time for Countrywide to itself be foreclosed. Like the default and foreclosure letters that were appearing in hundreds of thousands of mailboxes, like the feelings evoked when the sheriffs came to evict those who had lost their homes, so too would Countrywide and all of its employees feel that sting (of course, some senior folks would ease the sting with millions as they left).

Hat in hand, Countrywide agreed to be bought by Bank of America in early January for $4 billion. Countrywide Financial as an independent, publicly traded firm would be no more.

When Ken Lewis, CEO of Bank of America, was asked by the press if Angelo was going to stay on, it was widely reported that he replied, "I would want him to stay until the deal gets done, then probably I would guess that he would then want to *go have some fun.*"

Perhaps I was not the only one who found this particular choice of words to be grating, especially since the pain the country was suffering seemed to be increasing each and every day. Perhaps Mr. Lewis was not aware of just how much of a negative lightning rod Angelo had become, however fair or unfair it really was. (Heck, even I had once idolized the man, and now, after having a huge chunk of my savings vaporize as the stock plummeted to under $5, even I did not want him to necessarily "have fun.") In marketing and branding, perception is reality. And make no mistake, there were intense and very real branding forces swirling around what the blogs had deemed to be a corporate "takeunder," in addition to the financial aspects.

And this merits some commentary. Besides being one of the only financial firms large enough to absorb the absolutely huge mortgage portfolio, legal woes, and liabilities that Countrywide brought with it, Bank of America was one of the few truly powerful brands in America capable of potentially undoing the marketing damage that had been done. Having had Bank of America as a client during 2000–2002 while I was at Grey Direct (Advertising) to relaunch their online BillPay product, I had had a clear view of their internal culture, brand power, and intensive focus on brand stewardship, customer service, and quality. Bank of America was still the *other* white-picket-fence brand in financial services, and it projected pristine, powerful Americana.

One wonderful brand campaign in the 1990s (now abandoned, sadly) was the brilliant "Banking on America" campaign. Reminiscent of Reagan's "Morning in America" campaign from the 1980s, it juxtaposed Bank of America with salt-of-the-earth farm and homestead imagery, and broad-sweeping vistas replete with purple mountains' majesty. Only such marketing power could overshadow and reverse the tarnish that Countrywide had attracted. If any brand was to gobble up Countrywide, I was glad it was Bank of America.

That winter and spring of 2008, the story continued to grow in so many directions that it could fill an entire other book (and I am sure it will). There were lawsuits, many directed at Countrywide and at Angelo, from state pension funds and investigations by the Securities and Exchange Commission. I can even remember watching fireworks with my son at Disneyland, with music about pursuing your dreams blaring throughout the park, when my BlackBerry buzzed with news that the FBI was investigating Countrywide. There were congressional hearings about CEO pay where ironically, my own congressman, democrat Henry Waxman of California, berated Angelo and some other financial services CEOs, accusing them of getting rich while Americans were suffering. As usual, committee opinion cut along party lines, with the Democrats vilifying the executives, and Republicans noting that the committee seemed to just be looking for crooks when none were present. Angelo was poised and polished as usual, his deep orange tan providing a striking contrast to the paler New York executives. Angelo's statement talked about Countrywide being an "only in America story." On many different levels, I felt he was right about that part.

The press hemmed and hawed that the Bank of America buyout was going to be canceled, then it wasn't, then it was. Then they were reporting that indeed the sheriffs from Bank of America would be banging their flashlights on the front door of Countrywide for final eviction within the third quarter of 2008.

As the third quarter approached, and as Countrywide and Angelo were most likely living the impotent nightmare of any lame-duck administration and the cold, administrative, sadistic reality involved in transferring power from a conquered kingdom, nerves were increasingly frayed within Countrywide and across the country.

The debate raged over whether government should intervene and develop bailout programs for homeowners. One side blamed the evil corporations for duping innocent citizens. The other side blamed reckless overspending by nutty borrowers and overreaching by speculating homeowners, and argued against rewarding personal irresponsibility. The polarization of this issue had begun.

Numerous blogs and websites had sprung up as centralized venues for troubled homeowners to seek assistance and spew their anger. Some of the more organized sites encouraged homeowners to deluge lenders with the carpet bombing of form letters, the templates for which the sites gleefully provided. Eventually the proliferation of pleading combined with corporate persecution complexes led to some explosive incidents. One instance in particular became a key indicator of how volatile the debate had become.

In May 2008, a beleaguered homeowner wrote a letter to Angelo, asking for a modification to his loan. The communication was partially a form letter provided by the website loanworkout.org. It described his previous and current troubles, admitted that he had "misunderstood" his loan agreement, and asked for a modification so he could keep his home.

Then Angelo did something accidentally that has, at one time or another, made us all cringe at another's embarrassment, or made us vomit from our own accidental yet monumental mortification the moment we had hit the Send button and realized what we had done: As reported in the press, he hit Reply instead of Forward and typed the following words from his own e-mail address:

This is unbelievable. Most of these letters now have the same wording. Obviously they are being counseled by some other person or by the internet. Disgusting.

Yikes. However, Angelo was partly right. Parts of the letter were indeed preformed from a template provided by the loan assistance website. There were also reports that the inundation to Countrywide's e-mail system from the deluge of incoming requests for loan resets, many of which were clearly form letters, wreaked havoc on Countrywide's ability to keep their engine running smoothly, just when they needed that work flow to work at peak efficiency. The torrent of form letters may have actually prevented Countrywide from helping homeowners in a timely fashion.

Yet it was one little word used by Angelo that set off the furor: *disgusting.*

This was exactly the kind of spark that this powder keg within and outside of Countrywide did *not* need at that time, when the Bank of America merger was being questioned, and when many more adjustable loans were to reset soon in the summer of 2008.

The homeowner replied in a respectable and restrained fashion, given the shock of what he must have felt.

Interesting to find that you think my letter is disgusting. I will send this on...

And send it on he did. The e-mail response sped back through the blog of the website loanworkout.org, then through the entire Internet, literally at the speed of light. Within hours, the story, and the e-mail, had been picked up by the press. *Whammo*. Instant public relations nightmare, again.

But what exactly did Mr. Mozilo find "disgusting"? The request itself? Probably not. The homeowner's circumstances and clear history of some poor choices and behaviors? Doesn't seem so. The fact that people who are not very good at writing letters utilize a recommended template for such a request? Lobbyists and policy peddlers recommend many such form letters each and every day when they ask constituents to "write your congressman" about a specific issue.

Most likely, it would appear that Angelo was reacting to the existence of sites that provide consumers the tools to attempt to renege on their promissory notes. Also, I believe his reaction speaks to the many levels of frustration and outrage and, yes, disgust that Angelo must have been feeling during that period, and when he saw this e-mail among all the others he must have been receiving every day by the bushel.

I imagined it must have felt like some twisted version of *Miracle on 34th Street*, whereas instead of the mailroom delivering bags and bags of letters to Santa from delighted children, Angelo was getting the electronic (as well as paper, I am sure) equivalent of such bags by the ton, brought in each day by burly guards who proceed to dump them all on his desk, many addressed to "the guy who wants to take my house."

This accidental exchange in cyberspace cut to and clearly demonstrated the heart of the debate in a visceral, emotional, polarizing fashion. Bloggers from every part of the nation chimed into this story on that website, yet, notably, it seemed to become a 50-50 split.

Half of the contributors to the site's forum slammed Countrywide and Angelo, as profiteers and mongers feeding off the bad times of Americans. They would write messages like *How could they? How could Countrywide knowingly set me up to lose everything? How could those 'evildoers' give me a loan that eventually I would not be able to pay back? Damn them all!*

Regular folks love to hate monolithic companies. Moreover, some even relish the vilification of the leaders of those companies, if, somehow, the firm is connected to or responsible for their personal hardship, even if there is no proof of formal wrongdoing.

But, almost surprisingly, the e-mail exchange also awakened another formidable giant in this debate: those who perhaps, yes, have struggled, but who are working their fingers to the bone to sustain their mortgages and pay their monthly bill. Why should some troubled homeowners get redesigned deals on their loan while others should not? Why must we depend on the charity of a corporation—whose sole reason for existence is to return value to shareholders as quickly and as profitably as possible—to be willing to accept a loss on a promise not kept by the lendee? What is the corporation's motivation to do this? The threat of mob rule and vilification? The fear of being blogged negatively? Yes, there are multiple levels of "disgusting" in this story, depending on who you ask.

If you buy something via someone lending you money—a house, a car, an education—and you sign a document that says you will pay back that loan using such terms and such rates, then you are obligated in our society to meet that promise. If you stop paying your car loan, your vehicle is repossessed, period. If you stop paying your mortgage, you are officially defaulting on your loan, your promise, your word, and your home should be taken away.

And yet, is this agreement—this promise—still valid if the terms of the agreement (the loan) change, midterm? I believe it is one thing for a homeowner to agree to the initial terms, but even if they know and agree that the Adjustable Rate Mortgage terms will change in X years, is it fair to assume that they are agreeing to the new payment level that this readjustment will create, even though both the lender and the owner have no idea what that actual payment will be in X years? This question is at the core of the debate.

The trust that comes from such deals and handshakes is a most powerful glue in our society. Yes, there are lawyers, lots of lawyers, but many daily transactions occur on people's word, on handshakes and verbal agreements.

But where should the lendees' obligation end and the lenders' compassion begin?

This calls for an unemotional, methodical, quantitative, structured approach to this ethereal moral dilemma, which I propose in the last chapter of this book.

13

A Train Wreck in Slow Motion

In dreams begins responsibility.
—William Butler Yeats

JUNE 2008

Prime rate: 5.00%

Foreclosure rate: 2.75%

CFC stock price: ~$6.00

IN THE FIRST half of 2008, the public relations hits to Countrywide just kept on coming.

With the power of throwing chum into shark-infested waters, the press continued slamming the Countrywide cage when word got out about the "Friends of Angelo" program. I had never directly interacted with this program while I was at Countrywide—I was way too busy generating hundreds of thousands of smaller, new "non-FOA" customers—but I had heard the term in the halls. Generally, "FOAs" was the colloquial reference to VIPs who somehow knew Angelo, played golf with him, or whatever. But then the reports began surfacing about special friends of Angelo allegedly getting special deals on large loans, especially people in Congress and in other private industries. To be fair and clear, from what I have read it seems that no one got free loans or free money; they simply may have received special waivers on the sizes of the loans, or discounts on fees.

Keeping with a consistent theme of this entire saga, there are two ways to look at the FOA story, depending on your point of view. On the one hand, let's get real: if you have a pal or a cousin or a brother-in-law or a golf buddy who owns a Cadillac dealership, you are probably going to get a special deal on a sparkling new Caddy. It has long been an unspoken reality in our economy, I would argue, and not shocking unto itself and, in many cases, not even illegal. Countrywide employees "enjoyed" discounts on loan costs as well; nothing wrong with that. That being said, almost every professional training I have had—in the Air Force, in corporate life, in business school—pounded into me the concept that one should never do anything that could even *hint* at a perception of impropriety, conflicts of interest, or unethical behavior, especially if you are a *public figure* beholden to stockholders or a higher code of conduct. Expense reports should always be accurate. Never meet with a subordinate of the opposite sex with the door closed. Don't drink and drive. Be a role model.

Of course, I am sure some readers would argue that my entire career spent selling things to people that they don't need or could not afford was wholly, grossly unethical. And maybe they would be right. But in this case, if Angelo did indeed provide special waivers and discounts to key influencers who had specific power to positively affect his business, well, *it just might look bad* to a public already in scrutinization mode, even if it was not illegal per se. It could be seen as a conflict of interest, and inherently difficult to justify; the press used language and tone that implied some conspiracy.

But I wonder what the volume of the backlash would have been—indeed, I wonder if anyone would have even cared—if it was "discovered" when the housing and mortgage boom was at its height, and millions of homeowners and stockholders were getting paper-rich and gleefully satiated with riches, enjoying never-ending spending options by using their homes as ATMs, and watching shows like *Flip This House*, which exploited the madness for entertainment value. I don't think it was a sinister and calculated program of formal influence-peddling. I believe it may have been just a polished Caddy salesman getting a deal for some pals when things were good, if at all. But when things get bad, everything starts to look worse than it perhaps was.

BY LATE SPRING 2008, newspapers all around the country were reporting an ominous milestone in the path of this collapse. Based on new data released from the Mortgage Bankers Association, the number of American homes in foreclosure had, for the first time since the tracking of such data, eclipsed the 1 million mark. Of the 45 million or so mortgages in the United States, about 2.5 percent were in some part of the foreclosure process.

However, the larger implication of these data, which the media often glosses over in favor of a more compelling headline, is that the number was continuing to grow. With any curve, one looks for the crest—the point at which the growth begins to slow, then evens out, then finally begins to come down. No such luck with the foreclosure numbers, which continued to rise, the pace accelerating, with no slowing in sight. This meant at least another several months, if not years, until the crisis crested.

With a second wave of Adjustable Rate Mortgages readjusting in the summer of 2008, many of which were now no longer just in the realm of Subprime, but now drifting into the affluent, wealthier, Prime credit neighborhoods where people felt invulnerable to such a collapse, the true size of the storm was finally beginning to show its panoramic scale.

The final weeks of June 2008 represented the end of a love affair between Countrywide employees and the firm they built and adored. Like the survivors of a plague, they had watched many of their friends and colleagues pass away into unemployment, leaving or being pushed out of Countrywide slowly over time as the end came closer and the firm was absorbed by Bank of America. Many privately called it "watching a train wreck in slow motion." Survivors' guilt impacted those who remained. Even as the buyout close date of July 1 approached, many still did not know what their fate would be—would they be kept on to continue the transitional work, or would they be let go with a potentially huge payday in exchange for their rank and years of service? Like many emotional traumas, it was the loss of control, the "not knowing" that was the worst part.

The poignancy of Countrywide's rapid metamorphosis from only-in-America success story to corporate ash heap was apparent everywhere. Empty cubicles now filled football-field-size office spaces where, once, armies of busy bees tried to process all of the loan applications fast enough for a ravenous marketplace. Some archaeological evidence of a once-thriving corporate culture remained in the random artifacts left behind in various dusty cubicles; an old calendar, dog-eared voicemail instructions pinned to the felt wall, an old birthday card signed by the entire team stuffed into a half-open desk drawer.

However, all across America at the same moment, entire communities, neighborhoods, also were in ruins. But these weren't cubicles. These were homes. Homes in disrepair. Homes with weeds on the lawn up to your knees, walls covered in graffiti, windows broken, and memories gone. Homes where once birthday parties sang songs, doorway jambs showed marks where kids measured their new height, and families watched on their televisions as nobodies became "idols," were now shelter for squatters and carpeted coffins for dead pets left behind amid broken glass. Entire communities of both offices and homes were wiped out by the same blight, the same plague that took the dreams of corporate do-gooders and aspirational homeowners and ended them precipitously, yet, arguably, *with* warning.

As that June drew to a close, the Countrywide career of the Chief Marketing Officer and one of my role models, Andy Bielanski, would end. There would be a gathering of marketing folks at the local Mexican place, a dusty yet charming watering hole called the Sagebrush Cantina in Thousand Oaks, California, and the site of many a marketing strategy session and other dalliances. Andy's illustrious career at the marketing helm of one of the greatest rises and falls in American business history would be honored at a little hole-in-the-wall with plastic chairs and cheap booze—a far cry from the silver-spooned and white-gloved aura of the third-floor executive suite at headquarters where I once lunched with him. It would be bittersweet.

I didn't feel bad for Andy; in fact, I thought that maybe after his margarita, he might buy the restaurant. I can remember when every few months the hallways would be abuzz with the news of the latest Mercedes or BMW parked in Andy's reserved spot. His proud flaunting of achieved success and obvious wealth drove many of us young Turks to work harder for Countrywide. We wanted to be like him when we grew up.

ON JULY 1, 2008, Bank of America completed its buyout of the company that Angelo had started from humble beginnings almost 40 years before. At the final stockholders' meeting, Angelo was said to have been visibly shaken, and not quite the brash, confident optimist of countless CNBC interviews in previous years. Words were stuttered. Poignantly, he accidentally knocked over the microphone as he spoke of Countrywide still being "a great American success story."

I can only try to imagine how it must have felt for him. His baby, his child that he made with his own two hands, which at its height was fulfilling the dreams of millions of Americans, was now, it seemed, in shambles. Gone were the dreams of projecting the need for hiring 50,000 new employees and expanding the empire further by 2010 and beyond. Angelo was the founder who had lived to see this tragedy unfold. How much he was personally responsible for the collapse is arguable; yet, as the captain of this ship, he is, of course, formally responsible.

His millions should keep him comfortable in his retirement, for sure. But that day in the convention center in San Diego when I met him for the first time, and we chatted alone about his beloved Countrywide, I believed. And I could see in his eyes his passion for the mission, the dream, the leadership. I wondered what his eyes must have looked like on the day it ended, and I could not help but feel for him. I wondered if he walked out of his grand executive suite for the last time, a lonely walk all the way to his privately parked Bentley convertible, grasping in his arms the last mementos of his career in an old Bekins moving box.

Vilified in the press, he had become a lightning rod of anger, outrage, and blame. His expensive clothes and trademark tan were now salt on the wounds suffered by so many Americans; a reminder of his wealth and privilege while they were losing their homes. But many homeowners caught up in this mess can put their lives back together once the storm clears; people do emerge from bankruptcy, from foreclosure, and especially Americans with notable grit and determination can rebuild their lives and see better days ahead. How can losing a home, as horrible as it is, be compared to *losing your life's work*?

Perhaps it is an unfair comparison. But for maverick entrepreneurs like Angelo, it can't be all about the money—I mean, really, how many millions does someone really need? No, it's about what Countrywide culture used to refer to as *velocity*—it's about the "rush" of building something from nothing, about raising cities of business, about leading all the competition; the drive to succeed in a noble mission. He really did build a better mousetrap, and it made him the father of the modern mortgage business—until the trap snapped, catching America and Countrywide in it together.

For men such as Angelo, and all of us who believed in our mission with him, it was indeed like a *crusade*. It was truly an "only-in-America success story," forged through smarts, charm, grit, luck, and rates. Yes, the mortgage meltdown is a terrible blight on our nation, and will continue to be for some time, but it will recover. But during the heyday of the mortgage business, Angelo inspired a whole generation of business people to *believe in something* and to do it well, and I thank him for that experience.

EVEN THOUGH COUNTRYWIDE formally ended on July 1, 2008, the larger story continued, swirling into fits and starts, much like the monetary crisis itself; a mix of fear, tragedy, and an increasing unknown about how far the fall will go, and when it will end.

As America often does, it sometimes fought back with humor, and the story started to permeate prime-time and late-night television shows. At about this time I saw a Jay Leno monologue on the *Tonight Show.* He was commenting on a large fire in northern California that had engulfed many homes near Big Sur, and went on to say that "of course, this was not anywhere near the number of homes that *Countrywide has taken.*" [Roaring laughter.] On David Letterman, newly presumptive Republican presidential nominee John McCain commented that something had to be done "about that Countrywide outfit." The vilification of the once-venerable brand of Countrywide was complete; it had officially made its way into the public consciousness when sleepy Americans watched the Enron-like bashing while they ate their late-night snack.

Even a home from the popular ABC show *Extreme Makeover: Home Edition* fell into foreclosure when the lucky family took out a $450,000 loan on the house for a construction business that failed. Echoing an increasingly loud chorus across America, the mayor of the town who helped erect their new home expressed disgust and disappointment at the family in the press. I don't believe it was a Countrywide loan, but heck, it might as well have been at that point.

Within days after Countrywide was absorbed into Bank of America, unbelievably, the news continued getting worse as the scourge spread across the market. And the stories crossed the vast spectrum between the potential for a total financial system collapse and a reminder of the deeply human, emotional toll that this crisis was taking on American families, way beyond just the icy statistics.

Especially notable and concerning to those who may be aware of economic history were the eerie parallels in rhetoric from senior officials regarding the crisis, with quotes from 1929. Contrary to what most people believe, in 1920s America it was not a case of everyone doing the Charleston dance while sipping champagne from women's shoes one day, and breadlines the next. The Great Depression actually happened slowly, over a period of months and weeks before the final, eventual implosion of the stock markets, and the causes of it have filled many books. Like today, government and financial firms hobbled, borrowed, and injected cash before the bottom finally fell out, and, like today, officials made pronouncements alluding to the "worst being over" and "the crisis will pass."

Of course, no one knows the future for certain. And in all fairness, what were our financial leaders today supposed to do, run through the streets naked screaming that the world is coming to an end? I believe they were doing the best that they could, but I also believe they really did not know how bad it could get; and that they were petrified to actually say that. The echoes of 1929 rang in my ears every time I heard a press conference as the news kept coming.

The sad ironies kept popping up everywhere. The week that the press reported the arrest of a former Countrywide employee, charged for allegedly stealing customers' personal data and selling it for identity theft was the same week when the *Countrywide Classic* tennis tournament descended on the campus of UCLA. Is no one aware that the name is negative now? It brought back memories for me of previous summers, when I was at Countrywide and would help man the Countrywide booth at the tournament. As the affluent and the socially respectable wandered around the grounds of the tennis center, they would mosey over to our little tent and sometimes fill out a

Home Equity or other loan application right then and there, with ice cream dripping down their wrists from the melting cones. In the heyday of the housing and mortgage boom, the circus atmosphere could appear anywhere, and I helped sell the cotton candy. Yet seeing these signs all over the campus today, touting the sponsorship of a now dethroned brand (which surely must have been booked and planned long before the company's image collapsed), I wondered what other previously booked sponsorships had also peppered America's past after the brands had faded: *the Enron Open; the Worldcom Classic.*

With rumors flying fast that Lehman might go under (which it eventually would), and many other banks such as IndyMac and others on the ropes, shares of Fannie Mae and Freddie Mac, the giant "government-sponsored" mortgage entities that were the foundation for much of the entire system, went into frightening free fall. Bear Stearns had just collapsed a few months earlier, so it all seemed very real and fathomable. Then, in a surreal spectacle, there was an actual "run on a bank," and a subsequent collapse.

IndyMac bank, which claimed to be the seventh largest mortgage originator in the United States, and the largest savings and loan firm in Los Angeles, with many billions in assets, went under and was seized by federal regulators. It was the largest bank failure America had seen in decades (although the much larger Washington Mutual would also collapse weeks later). Reminiscent of 1929, lines formed around the block of IndyMac branches and at its headquarters in Pasadena, California (and just a few feet from the offices of Full Spectrum Lending, Countrywide's once-massive Subprime lending arm) as the feds closed it down, with hundreds of anxious depositors eager to take all of their money out quickly. Fistfights ensued, and police had to be called in. Ironically—or ominously, depending on your point of view—IndyMac had in fact been created by Angelo Mozilo at Countrywide in 1985, first being called "Countrywide Mortgage Investment." In the late 1990s it was spun off and became a separate company, and many times when I was at

Countrywide, an unspoken yet intense and bitter competition between Countrywide and IndyMac was mentioned in the halls. No sooner had the federal takeover of IndyMac begun, the market panic increased over the solvency of Fannie Mae and Freddie Mac.

It's been said that failed banks are like roaches; if you see one, that means there could be many more lurking behind the walls, and the system and the markets become very nervous. What was once unthinkable was now being discussed all over the news. Those two venerable firms, ironically, were started by FDR's administration during the Great Depression to provide a government-backed channel for homeownership to still become possible. Seventy-five years later, Fannie and Freddie held or guaranteed more than $5.3 trillion in home loan debt, almost half of the entire mortgage debt in the United States, and for a few days it appeared as if they might now become the causes of the *second* Great Depression. The Federal Reserve and the Treasury Department worked with Congress at lightning speed to build programs and a "rescue bill." The Housing and Economic Recovery Act of 2008 would try to shore up these critically important entities, among other things. Congress would soon pass it and Bush would sign it, reluctantly, after threatening a veto over a provision that provided funds for local communities to buy up distressed properties. Yes, the government would be potentially getting deeper and deeper into assuming huge amounts of private debt, a ridiculously dangerous development, and yet, incredibly, the alternative seemed much worse.

(By September 2008, the federal government would indeed take over these two giants when it was determined that their cash cushion would not be large enough to counter the downturn of the debt they carried on their books. Freddie Mac and Fannie Mae, just like the insurance giant AIG, which weeks later the government would also essentially take over, had clearly underestimated the downturn, and the risk they took on. In my view, I would also argue for what has been called our "Great Moral Hazard"—that, in fact, it was the federal government's tacit backing of Fannie and Freddie, providing them with the misguided comfort of this safety net, that actually *encouraged* them to take on unreasonable risks, thereby contributing to their collapse, and may motivate future firms to do the same. This hypothesis will be another great debate that historians and economists will need to decipher in future years.

But either way you look at it, within weeks, the beacon of capitalism in the world suddenly seemed to become, arguably, quasisocialist; the United States itself, incredibly, had no choice but to get knee-deep into the insurance, mortgage, and banking business, including all the risk that implies. I now cannot even begin to speculate on the potential financial dangers in our future. But we had no choice; doing nothing could have meant world financial collapse.)

In typical government fashion, the Housing and Economic Recovery Act of 2008 was actually three "acts" wrapped under one title. While I won't bore you with all seven hundred pages or so of the text (does anyone actually read these bills in their entirety?), some elements of it are worth noting.

In it was first the "Federal Housing Finance Regulatory Reform Act of 2008," which established new regulatory oversight of the mortgage industry. Okay, that's good; it seemed like everyone was in agreement that some sort of watchdog group should keep an eye on the mortgage business in the future, lest it get all nutty again like a Labrador spinning in circles with the leash in its frothy mouth. *Down boy*.

Second was the HOPE for Homeowners Act of 2008. My first thought when I saw this was curiosity about what kind of acronym the government had shoehorned into the word *hope*. Governments, like marketing clients, love goofy acronyms. Perhaps it stood for "Help Only People Elected," "Have Old People Evicted," or maybe even "Have Only Partial Expectations." Either way, this portion of the law provided a "new, temporary, voluntary program" to help "qualified" homeowners secure Federal Housing Authority–backed loans so they could try to keep their homes. But the banks would need to agree to their participation in each case. Buried deep within the text was the note that the program would start on October 1, 2008, a full two months after the president would sign it. When payments are missed, lives are crumbling, and the world is collapsing, two months can be a lifetime of delay; I wondered how many homeowners and firms might get sucked down the drain long before this new process of assistance took effect.

The third and last "act" of this bureaucratic play was comprised of the Foreclosure Prevention Act of 2008. It did include some smart changes to the system, offering counseling services, community assistance, and mortgage disclosure improvements (which almost every one of my foreclosure cases interviewed for this book requested be enacted).

Some would argue the bill was too much too soon and interfered with the natural market correction; others would say it was too little assistance, delivered too late. Projections were that it could wind up assisting over 400,000 families at risk of foreclosure, out of the several million that were in trouble. Critics argued that markets should self-correct and should not be regulated. But it could be equally argued that doing something was better than doing nothing.

During the final debates over this new legislation—as if to viscerally and violently remind us all of the true impact of this crisis and the apparently delayed futility of the bill—Carlene Balderrama used a high-powered rifle to kill herself.

Ms. Balderrama was a 53-year-old wife and mother in Taunton, Massachusetts. She ran the family's household finances herself, for her grown son and for her husband, who worked as a plumber. As the value of the home plummeted and the loan reset, she could no longer afford the payments on the house, but internalized her anguish, sharing this news with no one. She defaulted, and then went into foreclosure. The auction of the house was to occur at 5:00 P.M. At 2:30 she faxed a letter to her mortgage company saying that by the time they read the note, she would already be dead. She was right. As lawmakers hundreds of miles away in Washington worked to save the system, potential bottom-feeder buyers circled Carlene's home waiting for the auction to begin. But when they arrived, instead they found it surrounded by police, with Carlene's body inside. Her note to her family had asked them to use her life insurance money to pay for the house. The shocking news of her death was compounded when her family discovered only then about the upcoming foreclosure; she had not been able to bring herself to tell her own family or her friends; she bore this burden alone until the end.

When I heard this report, I felt numb. I wondered if her original loan had been financed through Countrywide, if perhaps she had seen the TV ads I had helped create, if she had received a mailing I had done; I wondered truly, what had I done. I thought about the people I had interviewed for this book; people from all walks of life who had for one reason or another collapsed under the weight of financial burden. I thought particularly about Sally Ridgeway of Colorado, who told me that she had taken a handful of pills in a failed attempt at suicide, also to try to secure life insurance money so that her disabled husband could pay off the house.

At that point I realized just how real this crisis was; how deeply it was affecting lives, how it would be with us for a very long time, and how many more suicides there would be before the crisis had subsided. I thought about the legends (which are still being argued) that during the final stock market crash of 1929, people were jumping out of windows. I prayed there would not be copycats if the story got too much coverage.

I considered the possibility that Carlene's last, desperate act of depression could be foreshadowing a financially broken, equally depressed and desperate nation which, too, may run out of options someday if our value plummets further and our debt continues to soar. Perhaps, like Countrywide, we, too, might someday be foreclosed by a stronger entity if we don't confront our overconfidence.

For me, the death of Carlene Balderrama was a turning point in this story. It was as if a higher power had timed this powerful and telling death to coincide with my nearing completion of this manuscript; to reinforce the true perspective of the crisis. Suddenly I did not care about Countrywide, or Angelo, or marketing. Suddenly I felt slightly guilty and foolish for infusing the story with humor to aid its readability (although I would snap out of this feeling quickly; this mortgage topic would rapidly get dull if I didn't infuse it with *something*; please forgive me, Carlene). Yet moving forward, this would no longer be just a curious and historic tale of corporate, economic, and consumptive hubris, of the fall of Countrywide, the mortgage crisis and my role in it.

Now, like other historical periods of massive, impending crisis and struggle in America, this forevermore would be a story that included blood, on a wall in Massachusetts.

14

The Great Debate:
What Do We Do Now?

We have it in our power to begin the world anew.
—Thomas Paine

AUGUST 2008

Prime rate: 5.00%

Foreclosure rate: around 3.00%

CFC stock price: $4.25 (as of July 1, 2008, last day of trading for CFC stock)

WE ARE EMBROILED in a great national debate that is raging across America. We are experiencing what is arguably the worst financial crisis since the Great Depression, and there is more anger, confusion, resentment, and fear than we have seen in 75 years. There is less hope, optimism, clarity, and vision as well. It is what I now call our "Great National Worry"—a profound shift in our perspective in recent times, about everything, big and small. Food. Drugs. Health. Money. Security. The future. Not since the malaise of the 1970s have we entered this state of mind. And when historians look back at the triggers, I believe that the symbiotic madness of the mortgage and housing booms, which arguably began with rock-bottom interest rates after 9/11, combined with the destructive waltz of greed and consumerism that had been building since the 1980s, will be seen as the causes of what could be a possible Second Great Depression, in 2010.

Who would have thought that the great scourge of our time would be financial, not biological? And that it would be our own doing? And with our debt soaring to unthinkable levels, and rising, it now seems conceivable that this illness may finally kill the patient if we don't change our ways. Our enemies must be laughing their asses off.

At the time of this writing, there are more than one million foreclosures completed or under way in America, and the number is rising fast. Every foreclosure, every lost home, every ended dream, every ruined life is a small financial nuclear blast, causing a shock wave through the local neighborhood and economy, both physical and financial. A foreclosed home does not pay critically needed property taxes. A foreclosed family does not spend money at local restaurants or buy items at the local home improvement store. The physical blight caused by a run-down property with broken glass, dead pets left behind, and overflowing weeds attracts squatters, vermin, and vandals, and mercilessly drags further down the property values of those homes near it, whose owners may be trying to sell to escape their own adjustable mortgage that may have unexpectedly reset to an unmanageable payment. Now, imagine more than one million local blasts across the nation, and you get a visceral understanding of what is happening out there.

There are questions, so many questions. How did this crisis happen? What were they (lenders, borrowers, the Fed) thinking? Who is to blame? What do we do now? Who should be helped, and how? Who should be punished, and how? How do we prevent it from happening again?

If I have done my job correctly, the "What were they thinking?" question should at least have become partially illustrated through my own story from within Countrywide during the bubble.

As far as the other questions are concerned, I must admit, I am not an economist, although I have been a student of it. Nor am I a professional "finance jock," although I learned much from my time in the corporate trenches with some of the smartest finance minds in America. But based on my view from having been inside the mortgage business during the bubble, my interviews with so many foreclosed homeowners, my immersion in this larger story during my research for this book, my knowledge of history and business, and having spent a lifetime redirecting the perceptions and behaviors of millions of people through developing and disseminating marketing messages—here I will do my best to fairly illustrate and review the now polarized views of the debate, make some humble suggestions for what else we should do now, and offer up what I feel are some commonsense ideas for how to prevent this from happening again.

I have to try. And from a career in advertising, I learned never to underestimate the power of at least throwing some ideas on the table to get the debate started. At the very least, I hope these proposed solutions and mechanisms for change will spur some thoughtful dialogue by policymakers that could help lead to a financially safer America in the future.

The Polarized Positions of Blame

As our favorite national pastime—assigning blame—bubbled up over the past year around this crisis, I ran into one of a writer's most difficult challenges: there was simply too much material. Every day there were literally hundreds of new stories and analyses from every angle and viewpoint about the crisis. But after these hundreds of reports, thousands of blogs, and millions of comments from every pundit, talking head, radio talk show host, comedian, lobbyist, legislator, and even after some knucklehead celebrities weighed in, I saw that the great debate was clearly boiling down to two main opposing viewpoints, so I needed to find a way to make it interesting: Let's make *you* the judge in the courtroom of this debate. *(Okay, I'm not a lawyer either, so this might sound like a case on* Murder, She Wrote. *But we wouldn't want these points to get boring, now would we?)*

You don your regal black robe and feel the weight of the gavel in the hand as our imaginary bailiff in our moot court says "All riiiiise. The honorable Judge [Your Name Here], presiding."

On one side of the debate, the lawyer for the People; on the other side, the lawyer for the System. As the winner of the coin toss, the lawyer for the People has opted to go first.

"Your Honor, the System about which I will speak is so vast, with so many tentacles, that I will not be able to articulate every wisp of its web in these proceedings. If it pleases the Court, I will confine my elocution of the System in question to the basic elements of corporations, governments, and markets, if I may."

You nod, rolling your eyes a bit at his highbrow speaking style.

"Thank you. Your Honor, ladies and gentlemen, all corporations are corrupt, horrible, mindless creatures who feast upon the fears and the resources of the People. Their lust for profit blinds their sense of right and wrong, their thirst for revenues and market share obscures their moral vision, if they ever had any. They exist only to sell things people don't need, or can't afford, and titillate and tantalize them with glossy brochures and funny and warm and sexy television ads. They inundate their mailboxes and e-mail with thousands of pieces of mail and spam, essentially harassing them—coercing them, really—to buy and buy and buy."

"Objection!" shouts the lawyer for the System as he stands up. The screeching of the feet of his wooden chair rubbing against the floor echoes in the chamber.

"Overruled," you say sternly, because you believe his objection is out of order (and, let's face it, you always wanted to say that). "Continue, counselor."

"Thank you, Your Honor. Corporations are stalkers, lying in wait.

Not only do corporations encourage innocent consumers to buy too much, but also much of American business—in fact, America itself—is actually focused on selling money, credit, debt, and risk," he says, as muffled gasps come from the courtroom audience.

"Yes it's true!" the lawyer for the People continues, spinning toward the huddled masses in the audience. "Corporations that sell products and services are inherently evil if not regulated and watched over by a strict government. They are beasts that feed on suspicions, ego, and vice. They market potentially unnecessary medications to seniors by heightening their fear of previously unheard-of ailments. They market sugary cereals to children and cigarettes to teens using animated characters. They encourage even more consumption to those people afflicted with 'spending issues.' They use sex as a selling tool!" A slight shriek sounds from the audience as an elderly woman faints; the lawyer for the People pauses, then continues as the woman is carried out.

"Financial services corporations, especially, send never-ending offers, inundating mailboxes and airwaves all over the country for new credit cards, exotic home loans, and even home *equity* loans—so people use up all of their home's equity on spending that they otherwise may not have done had they not received those offers. Companies use readily accessible legal and public data on a household's finances, credit history, and current life stage to *specifically* target them with offers that tests have shown will reap the greatest responses, the greatest rewards and profits, based on their past *propensity* to respond. And yes, the CEOs of these giants continue to make millions, even as their companies' values may plummet and their customers—the People—enter ruin."

There is a dramatic pause. Everyone in the courtroom is riveted; motionless and silent.

"Another culpable cohort in this corrupt System is the government, Your Honor, in two ways. First, after the terrible events of 9/11, our government naturally lowered the Prime interest rate to spur economic recovery. We grant that that was a good thing for America. However, as the trauma of the impact began to fade, rates were kept so low as to encourage Americans to spend more and borrow more, and our president even encouraged unsuspecting, financially strapped Americans to 'go shopping.' I submit to the Court that interest rates could have been raised to slow credit-card and home-equity spending, but they were not.

"Our government, the entity entrusted with keeping the greedy corporations at bay, protecting its citizens, and ensuring proper regulation, let these corporations continue to feed on the public, letting this bubble get out of hand. Companies offered ever-riskier, yet legal, 'exotic loans' with slick names like 'PayOptions' and 'Pick-A-Payment', which allowed the borrower to wind up owing *more* each month, and 'Ninja' loans, which shockingly allowed loans with 'no income, no job.' They even had 'Alt-A' loans where they would give people money even if they could not verify their income—'no doc loans' or 'Liar Loans' they called them, meaning 'no documentation.' Even now the true terrible effects of these loans have yet to be known; many are due to reset in 2009 and 2010, and no one knows how bad those defaults will get. Your Honor, this was madness, perpetrated by companies and allowed by government. It has been a scam of historic proportions perpetrated on our citizens, and the government, like any good customer service department, should see to it that every foreclosed family gets its money back."

More murmurs from the transfixed courtroom.

"Your Honor, last but not least in this sinister unholy trinity of consumer exploitation, were the markets themselves. Even more mindless, more soulless than corporations, in our society we have designed these wild beasts to be 'free'—yes, free markets—free to roam and seek out unsuspecting prey at their whimsy, from Wall Street to Main Street. They feed on naïve investors, inexperienced speculators, and control how much we pay for everything from bread to money. Oil prices soar as supply is constricted, and even more demand is encouraged by the big automakers, big industry, as well as emerging industrial nations. Markets are the pinnacle of the system feeding on its constituents, like tigers turning on their handlers. And when a tiger turns on its handlers, we need to shoot it. But truth is, the handlers never really controlled their tigers. They just fool themselves into thinking they did.

"This is our case, Your Honor. The System, through its pillars of never-ending profit-seeking, immoral persuasion, lack of government regulation, and random and unpredictable fluctuation, have brought upon us this housing and mortgage crisis. Our own system now threatens our very way of life, far more than any terrorist could ever hope to achieve. And my client, the People, are the true victims."

The lawyer stops, theatrically.

"Your Honor, we have seen the enemy. And it is our *own System!*" He points at the lawyer for the System accusingly.

The lawyer for the People sits down slowly, dramatically. Then he murmurs a somber, "Thank you, Your Honor. We rest our case."

Snapping out of your momentary mind-wander, you keep the proceedings moving. "The counsel for the System will now proceed with your case."

"Thank you, Your Honor," says the lawyer for the System as he takes a small sip of water. Then he begins.

"Your Honor, we stipulate that the System is not perfect. Yet we submit that it is still the best worst system in the entire world. And do you know why?"

The lawyer for the System pauses, letting the question linger in the warm air of the courtroom as he turns to the audience.

"It is…because…People…our *free* People…*you* People…have the power of *choice*. And this includes the freedom to make BAD CHOICES!"

The audience explodes in gasps as the counsel for the People jumps up and shouts his own "Obbbbbjecttttttttionnnnnnnnnn!"

You're banging your gavel hard now, as no one seems to be paying attention. BAM! BAM! BAM! "We will have order in this court or I will CLEAR this courtroom!" you shout. As the frenzy dies down, you continue banging your gavel for good measure.

"Over...ruled..." you say slowly and sternly. "Go on, counselor."

"Thank you, Your Honor. Ladies and gentlemen, we are living in an age when rampant consumerism and epidemic debt are colliding with, sadly, *the death of personal responsibility* in America. Yes, sometime over the past few decades we have lost our way, and devolved into a society where assigning blame for our own bad choices has become acceptable, even in vogue.

"What can we say about a People who sue fast food companies for their obesity, and *blame a lender* for actually giving them hundreds of thousands of dollars, often without requiring that the borrower put even one dollar down? If it pleases the Court, we also stipulate that indeed there were some cases of unscrupulous lenders who broke the law, intimidated consumers, faked paperwork, and inflated home values; we agree that those rogues of the system should be brought to justice and punished, and their victims should be compensated for their pain. But those cases are not what we are talking about here today. No, we are arguing against the vilification of the entire lending industry.

The counsel for the System pauses, and looks down at the wooden floor of the courtroom, in thought, then continues.

"Ladies and gentlemen, I submit to you that for every case of fore-closure or default, the industry that we are defending here today has responsibly, dutifully, and valiantly provided the American Dream for millions of other homeowners, who read the deals they signed, who thought through their limits and resources, and who prudently and responsibly shook the hand of these lenders and are *keeping* their promises!"

"Objection!" again shouts the counsel for the People.

"Overruled," you say simply.

"Your Honor, the same fast, easy, and reckless path that so many homeowners took in taking on debts they could not pay is the same fast, easy, and reckless process we are using to feverishly point blame at every lender in America, especially the one that happened to be guilty of only being the largest and most prolific, Countrywide. Like the witch hunts of Salem, isn't it possible—just possible—that we are unfairly demonizing a firm that has done so much good for so many, as well as made some mistakes? Almost all of the big lenders and banks created, offered, and granted 'exotic' loans; why are we zeroing in on just one company if we believe the whole system was at fault? Well, Your Honor, the System submits that there would have been *no offering* of such products *at all* if the People had not *chosen* to buy them!"

Again, there is a slight uproar from the audience.

"My esteemed colleague, the counsel for the People, contends that all corporations are only profit stalkers, pouncing on innocent people and unfairly persuading them to spend. Yet every consumer, at every moment of transaction, has total and complete control over the decision whether they spend, on what, and how much. In our free society, no one is *forced* to buy. Yes, companies tout their goods and services in the media, in the mail. That is how they communicate their offerings to those who may really need them, because these media *are where the customers have responded positively before.* Yes, they use legal and available data to try to target those consumers who have—through their past behavior—shown a propensity to respond to such offers. Is it truly wrong to offer people what they want or need? No, we say."

He shakes his head slowly.

"Long ago, companies such as Sears and Montgomery Ward were

sometimes the only source of goods and services to pioneers who headed out West, determined to build a better life for their families on a small homestead. With the growth of the railroads and mail service, these brave settlers needed pots, pans, soaps, stoves, and other essentials that their catalogs provided, when no general store existed as far as the eye could see. Were those companies evil? No. But then something started to happen. America drifted away from focusing on its *needs* to focusing on its *wants*. Economists, sociologists, and writers began observing behavior that came about through the industrial revolution, and the sudden trappings of wealth—idleness, leisure time, the explosion of obesity, and concerns about maniacal materialism. With new terms entering our lexicon such as 'affluenza' and 'conspicuous consumption,' we have somehow morphed into a society focused more on eating and buying than we are on principles, personal responsibility, and ownership of our own behavior, bodies, and decisions. In every aspect of our lives now, it seems we consume more than we need. Do people really *need* hundreds of handbags? Do they *need* four cars? Do they *need* to add onto the house or take that vacation simply because the neighbors did? Are we *nuts*? *Where* is the outrage at the death of personal responsibility?!!!"

The lawyer turns toward the audience and asks, "Show of hands, how many of you are homeowners?" Most of the gallery raises their hands. "Okay, how many of you are in good standing—how many of you pay your mortgage on time every month, with no problems?" Most of the homeowners keep their hands up.

"Congratulations, you all are in the *majority* who do the right thing and responsibly pay your mortgage commitments. So, I ask you, *why* should we bail out those other people? These are the choices *they* made—freely! Yes, these are the choices, the free, personal choices that many people made who cannot now pay the mortgage debts they owe. As I've said, there would be no corporations selling us anything if we did not buy it. Throw out that junk mail if you don't want it!

Turn off the television if you don't want to see it! If you don't want to be fat, don't eat it! If you don't want to be broke, don't overspend, be sure to know your resources, your true needs, and your limits! We submit, ladies and gentlemen, that to blame corporations for the things we buy is to say that we are perpetuating our own loss of personal responsibility.

"Regarding my colleague's assertion that government dropped the ball, well, we say, hindsight is twenty-twenty. We say that economists and the Federal Reserve did what they thought was best at the time, and, in fact, on the record, warned us against overspending, too much debt, and the dangers of what had been deemed 'irrational exuberance' of the housing and mortgage markets. Why did no one listen? Because they had the *choice* not to, that's why. Could they have raised rates sooner? Sure. But no one can know what effect that would have had at the time, and we will not waste the Court's time on speculation.

"Finally, it has been asserted here today that free markets are themselves inherently evil and nefarious. We strongly object to such an assertion, and challenge the People to come up with a better solution. Long ago our Founding Fathers based our new form of government on the basic principle that the *people* know best what is best for themselves, that they can and should be self-determinant in all things, including making stupid choices, and then being responsible for those choices. It is *that* faith, that the People will uphold that responsibility, on which the Founders based our America. Freedom itself is a serious responsibility of every citizen to handle carefully and thoughtfully, or the entire system can be put at grave risk, like we are experiencing now. The alternative is to say that a centralized, controlled system, devoid of freedom and choice, is the answer. We submit that this is the beginning of totalitarianism, and will not be debated further in this courtroom.

"If in a free society, people, some people, all people, make bad choices, commitments, promises, then we believe that they should be held accountable for those choices they made, even if that means the wholesale correction of a bubble that never should have been created. In fact, it could be said that the collapse, or overdue correction of housing values from their high, is and will be a natural cleansing, like a forest fire. It will allow a great many potential buyers who were priced out of the skyrocketing market to finally be able to afford a home of their own, too. And this is good. If we bail out those who made poor choices, and the government artificially keeps home prices high, we will be rewarding those choices, incentivizing the repetition of that behavior, and trying to put undue control on the natural correction of the system.

"And to those who say that coming to the aid of a massive financial firm and not individuals is just 'wrong,' we would argue that it is a question of scale. A giant financial firm on the brink, with tentacles of debt and commitments all throughout the world's financial system, adversely affected by market forces outside its control, could spell disaster for the entire economy and singularly affect *millions* of lives if not helped. I am sorry to state the cold, hard facts, but the awful truth is that a single home foreclosure by people who made their own choices in entering into those agreements is less painful to the entire system than the collapse of a corporate financial pillar of that system.

"Your Honor, our finest moments in our nation's history have come through overcoming adversities, and this one is of our own doing. While we agree that any illegal activities within the System should be brought to justice swiftly, we also contend—no, we *beg* the Court— that yes, we should now endure the pain of the choices the People have freely made; we urge the court to let this forest fire burn itself out. This is the only thing that will improve the People's condition moving forward and prevent this behavior from happening again. Please, Your Honor, although we are the System, we ask that the court let *the People* decide which offerings are made in the future through their own self-corrective behavior and the learning that we will all get from this suffering regarding our own debt and consumption habits. But it will pass and maybe it will finally wake us up. Thank you, Your Honor."

The lawyer for the System sits down, and you breathe out a hefty sigh, partly relieved that the speeches are over; partially overwhelmed with the decision you must now render. *Who is at fault?* The bailiff gets your attention from the side of the courtroom as you see him miming the banging of an imaginary gavel, mouthing silently the word *recess*. Realizing that he is reminding you of what you should do next (this is your first time on the bench as a "guest judge," remember), you blurt out "Okay, we'll take a five-minute recess while I determine the fate of our society." You tap the gavel as audience members file out of the courtroom.

You head to your private chambers, an office behind the wall behind the bench. You plop down into the rich leather of your large chair, exhausted, and stare at your silver-balled, clicking momentum trinket on your desk. You mindlessly pull the last of the six hanging metal balls and are left alone with your thoughts and the now incessant click-clacking of this hypnotic device. How will you decide? Who is at fault for this debacle of the housing and mortgage markets? The People who were overconsumptive, got greedy, or chose poorly? The entire System? Lenders, government, the Fed, free markets? You continue to focus on the infinitely complex yet playfully simple Newtonian device in front of you. It swings to one side, then the other, then back again in seemingly perpetual motion; polarized, balanced. Only the equal forces in partnership create the energy transfer before you.

You smile as the sudden light of your own epiphany shines upon you.

SOMETIMES, WHO IS a "victim" and who is a "perpetrator" depends greatly on one's point of view, particularly in the naturally occurring and free-flowing dynamics of the capitalist marketplace. Yet, who is *more* wrong? The fools who led, or the fools who followed them? Or perhaps no one was a fool. Maybe everyone was doing exactly what the marketplace expected them to do, and *that was the problem*.

Our economic system is as complex as it is chaotic, as structured as it is random, and prone to out-of-control momentum, and overcorrection, in directions both up and down. And much of this behavior is ingrained in the natural instincts of our own corporations, our government, and ourselves.

If the process of the legal agreement involved multiple parties all agreeing to enter into the terms of that deal (even if the ARM terms that were agreed to change midstream), then it could be argued that it is equally the responsibility of all of those same parties if something goes wrong. So in the final analysis, perhaps we were all simply acting as directed by our own self-interests, and as this all continued to feed on itself, we were all equally culpable.

Corporations' self-interest was to return value to shareholders as fast and as profitably as possible, by giving the marketplace what it wanted to buy. In Countrywide's case, they provided easy access to money and reaped the fees and revenue rewards of that service. But common sense says that to give anyone a loan with a "no documentation" review process is madness. To allow people to pay *less than* their mortgage demands every month is lunacy. To give anyone a loan who has a substantial history of poor repayment and bad credit, dumb—no matter how high the interest rate.

People's self-interest was to live the American Dream. Our egotism and our need to preen our plumage reached ridiculous heights as the explosive growth of overly built, overly gilded, so-called "McMansions" may have highlighted our loss of self-esteem and called into question our true motives for physical, visual statements of our own worth. To get into bigger, more expensive homes, buy more stuff, go more places, and consume more of everything. We became pigs. We got greedier. Our materialism took over our sense of purpose. Our industrial revolution, and now the information revolution, have made our leisure pursuits transcend our true, basic needs. It could be argued that the rebirth of personal spiritualism over the past generation is a direct reaction to our own feelings of consumptive guilt. The famous economist Thorstein Veblen coined the perfect phrase in his brilliant and breakthrough treatise on "conspicuous consumption." People gambled that it would only get better if they doubled down on "black." They bet that housing values would rise, that debts could always be refinanced. But they were wrong. "Red" came up instead for America, and now we are gasping in disbelief as the dealer takes our money—our homes—away.

The system's self-interest was to feed on itself. I am constantly amazed at how much of economics mirrors physics. Newton's First Law says that "Every object in a state of uniform motion tends to remain in that state of motion unless an external force is applied to it." Bubbles like this occurred because the motion of housing and mortgages was bubbling, and there was no external force to stop it—until, of course, it burst or collapsed under its own weight, from the "surface tension" of over-inflated prices. But why is America continually prone to such bubbles? What is it about even our world culture that pushes us to continue with financial frenzies—from gold, to railroads, to dot coms, to housing and mortgages, even going back to the Dutch tulip craze in the early-seventeenth century—every few decades, like clockwork? We never seem to learn. When will we learn to see the signs of irrationality and correct them before it is too late?

My own self-interest was to make as much money as possible as fast as I could. Aren't we all trying to do that? My way of doing this was to apply my expertise in marketing to help the largest mortgage firm in the United States achieve *its* self-interest. But I finally saw what was happening, and although it's easy in retrospect to say that I should have spoken up more vehemently, I did not. I did not have the power to change the entire system, to stop everyone from pursuing his own self-interests, to change human nature, and to yell "Fire!" in this overcrowded housing and mortgage movie house.

And besides, I, too, had a mortgage to pay.

Like our imaginary desk ornament, the metal balls of our mortgage mess would never have gained momentum without both sides feeding on each other. The bubble began feeding on itself when a too-easy supply of exotic loans collided with rabid consumerism gone hog wild, and when housing values skyrocketed because everyone demanded a house. By thinking we were doing *good*, by allowing much greater, and nutty, access to homeownership, we inadvertently deluged the marketplace with never-before-seen demand from many people who were not ready for the responsibility of ownership. Even today I can remember seeing news stories of potential homebuyers sleeping out on lawns in tents the night before an open house, shaking my head and thinking, *this is crazy*. And it was.

It is fair to say that corporations, in this context, may be guilty, but not responsible for their natural behavior. But what about people? Saying that homeowners share some personal responsibility and their part in creating this mess has become a touchy subject—a politically incorrect hot potato. Homeowners are usually viewed as victims, and some of them truly are if they were lied to, if they fell for the old "bait and switch," if forms were laced with misinformation. But people intentionally living beyond their means are not victims. Bankruptcy laws have created a safety net that enables and facilitates such spending in the wrong hands, and conspicuous consumption has become an epidemic. Yes, household financial management is an individual responsibility. But it affects all of us eventually.

Our culture of credit has gone mad, and it has undergone a transcendental evolution from where it began. Once upon a time, if I had told you that you would be able to make a phone call to order a product or a service, and that product or service would be delivered simply by providing a 16-digit, magical number verbally, you may have called me crazy. Who would trust enough to believe that a silly little number could buy you wonderful, magical things? The concept of credit was not new, as stores had been extending credit to good customers for years, but there had never been a device to cover multiple service establishments. The first was Diners Club, developed in the 1950s, where restaurant aficionados could use the same card at multiple restaurants that had been signed up to the program, followed quickly by my old client, American Express. Then, of course, the rest came along, to now, where *not* using cash has become the norm. In only two generations or so, credit, and the option *not* to have cash available to cover it, have taken over our system.

The emotional toll that this market correction, or implosion, if you will, has taken will continue to spread from individuals to the economy as a whole for a long time. As anyone who reads the *Wall Street Journal* can testify, our economy has just found itself locked in a debtor's prison of its own making, and that has widespread repercussions. When the government bails out—in other words, rewards those who, by their own doing, default on their financial commitments—there may be no future motivation for thoughtful owners who dutifully pay their debts to continue doing so.

If you run a red light truly by accident, your hefty traffic ticket is the punishment. But, should the government bail you out of this ticket? If you make the choice to put all your life savings on black at the roulette wheel, and you lose, should the government pay you back? You knew you had a 50/50 chance of doubling your money; it was your choice.

Our markets are flush with alluring paradoxes that can trap those who are not careful or experienced. In advertising, the moment something becomes cool, it is no longer cool. In housing—or any bubble, for that matter—the moment an investment gets hot, it begins no longer being hot. When everyone is buying, you should be selling, and when they are selling, buy it up, the investment saying goes. But this is a free country, and this also means that people have the freedom, dammit, the right to be *dumb*. Stupidity is not a crime, although maybe it should be.

Harry Truman is said to have once remarked that he wished he had a one-armed economic adviser, because he was sick of hearing wishy-washy advice from economists that "well, on the one hand, this might happen, but on the other hand, that might happen." Well, it is true that economics can appear to be counterintuitive, confusing, and notoriously difficult to predict. It is a system with as much chaos and variables as there are data. But one thing still usually holds true in Econ 101: *People respond to incentives, both positive and negative.*

This is one of the more commonsense aspects to economics, yet its effects can be misleading if not vetted thoughtfully. If you raise taxes and the overall costs of cigarettes, consumption, and sales go down, that's good, right? But this also lowers the revenue taken in for healthcare that some of the cigarette taxes pay for. When gas prices soar, consumption goes down. But this also means less revenue for infrastructure spending that gas taxes support.

But then there are some of the counterintuitive elements of the subject that have been written about recently. Somewhere I read the brilliant hypothesis that the legal requirement of seat belts may actually have *increased* the number of accidents (but still has saved lives) because people *feel* safer, and that if instead every car came equipped with a rusty spike sticking out of the steering wheel right at your chest, car accidents might go to zero. A silly, extreme example, perhaps, but the concept is sound.

The same is true of financial incentives. When the government rescues, bails out, helps—whatever you call it—those who acted financially *irresponsibly*, engaged in reckless speculation, or otherwise made their own mess, government potentially rewards that behavior, ensuring its perpetuation, enabling its proliferation into greater levels of nuttiness, and motivating even greater levels of risk-taking.

If someone is consuming ten thousand calories a day by choice, should we—our government—*really* pay for their stomach stapling procedure? Wouldn't then the government, in fact, become the *enabler* of such behavior? It can be solidly argued that lenders were the enablers in this metaphor, bringing us pound after pound of fatty loans and telling us not to worry about potential heart attacks; and yet we enjoyed eating it.

There is extreme danger for the future in rewarding bad decisions, yes, but a foreclosed home also does not pay property taxes, which is already beginning to cripple state and local government budgets. It is arguable, but it may actually be *less* expensive overall to bail people out than to let the system self-correct. Whether or not the math favors either action may come down to the final scale of the damage, which is, as yet, frighteningly undetermined. But the point is, the moral issue is very complex.

Some people see the government as a parental figure in our lives, an entity that should protect us from ourselves, which should control markets. As I and any parent know, rewarding bad behavior, even small things, can be disastrous in the long term and grow into unimaginable wrong turns in life. If we think of a fairly elected government as a parental overseer, is it not also their moral duty to punish us, and let us fail, when it will teach us something critically important about responsibility, doing the right thing, and being a productive adult? It hurts me deeply when I have to punish my children for some misdeed; hearing them cry when I take their toy away or when they get a "time-out" just rips me in half. But I also know it is my job to help them shape their character, to teach them truth, honor, responsibility, duty, and good choices; as John Adams used to say, "to do good, and to *be* good."

Yet it could also be argued that if the government, corporations, and society in general are to act as parental figures, they have failed miserably and are considerably inept in this regard. None of these entities can ever truly replace the proper guidance of a parent, nor should they, except in extreme cases of neglect. Parents should still lead by example, and may try, yet they don't always do it well. My own parents used to warn me about the dangers of smoking, even as a thick blue cloud of smoke hung over our dinner table from the cigarettes dangling from both their mouths.

Corporations can be awful at it: many dutiful drones at major corporations have their yearly bonuses tied directly to the success of the financial metrics within their responsibility (the same was true of my bonus at Countrywide), and yet many CEOs at those same firms still reap huge bonuses even if the value of their firms *tank* on their watch. (While I believe this sends the wrong message to front-line workers, I also understand that financial incentives for these critical leadership slots need to be powerful enough to attract the best candidates. The debate over CEO pay can fill an entire second book so I will not go deeper here.)

Our own government does not lead very well by example, either. It tells us to manage our own financial responsibilities well and to pay our bills, but that same government is itself deeply in very risky, crippling debt, for more than three times its yearly revenue.

A small provision in the new HOPE law quietly allowed the United States to raise its legal debt ceiling (the total amount that the law says the government can owe) to *$10.6 trillion*, up from the previous level of $9.8 trillion. (The more recent $1 trillion bailout put it even higher.) For historical context, the total debt held by the United States in 1993 was "only" about $4 trillion. Currently the national debt equals approximately $31,000 owed by every man, woman, and child in America (source: TreasuryDirect.gov). (More can be learned from the frightening and brilliant book about our national debt, called *I.O.U.S.A.,* by Addison Wiggin, Kate Incontrera, and David Walker.)

So we owe about a cool $11 trillion, (although some would argue our true debt should include unfunded *future* obligations as well, which could bring the number to more like $60 trillion) but the 2008 projected revenue for the United States is only about $2.7 trillion (source: U.S. Office of Management and Budget). And we deficit-spend, like crazy. So let's imagine your house is the United States.

Let's assume your household makes $100,000 per year. Equating the revenue vs. the debt of the United States ($2.7 trillion vs. $10 trillion) to your house, that would be like having a credit card balance—a revolving, increasing debt that continues to require greater interest payments as well—of $370,000 on your total household income of only $100,000, and you begin to get a sense of the hole we are all in. Imagine also that every year your credit card debt is growing and growing from your own overspending. Still want to go shopping?

ONE OF THE foreclosed people I interviewed for this book, if you recall, was a young twentysomething speculator who expected to get rich quick. She correctly noted that she was from the "microwave" generation—where she expected to simply push a button and she would always quickly and easily get just what she wanted. She accurately described the perceptions of her generation.

Recently I heard that former senator Phil Gramm of Texas was booted off John McCain's campaign team because he commented publicly that "America had become a nation of whiners." Maybe he was right. In this life we have to work hard, nothing comes simply by wishing for it, and any sense of entitlement is misguided. Most Americans understand this, but a segment of our population clearly does not; those who feel that the world owes them something for nothing need a serious attitude *reboot*.

Maybe the suffering brought about by this mortgage and housing crisis might in fact teach us some hard lessons in the long run; snap us into more financial intelligence and prudence, and, as some economists and apartment dwellers have said, do good by correcting inflated home values down to "normal" levels, so that not only rich people can afford them. If America's mortgage and housing markets were obese, it is possible that this intensive, year-plus-long "liquid diet" after our economic "heart attack" might be exactly what we need.

These mixed messages—from government, from society—are fast

becoming part of this "great moral hazard" for the future, and make focused, involved, consistent guidance from our teachers and parents more important in today's world than ever before. But as I recently heard Dr. Phil say, it is time for common sense to make a comeback in America. He's right.

But when a crisis reaches a level of critical mass that threatens the system, then shouldn't all bets be off? Shouldn't the self-elected government step in to save us from ourselves?

Not since the creation of the Securities and Exchange Commission and the Federal Deposit Insurance Corporation after the crash of 1929 have we entered into turmoil that has required a complete overhaul of the financial system. All of these players contributed to this reckoning—lenders like Countrywide and others who lent, perhaps recklessly; government regulators at state and federal levels who let this get out of control; central monetary policymakers at the Federal Reserve who perhaps too aggressively lowered interest rates, and perhaps kept them too low for too long; homebuilders who saturated the market by overbuilding; speculators who artificially added to the bubble of inflated home values; marketers like me who convinced consumers to borrow more and more against the value of their homes; and, yes, the consumers/homeowners who signed for these loans they cannot now pay—we all played a part in this tragic drama. Just like the tenor within the halls at Countrywide during the boom, all of America was foaming at the mouth, focused solely on the next quarter's spectacular results, never mind the potential long-term impact. Who cared if all the trees in the forest were being cut down or if the system itself was overheating; we were all getting paper-rich.

And yet, to dwell only on the question of who is at fault, and only the negative aspects of this drama, is in danger of missing out on the critically and equally important positive potential—the learning experience of the mess. In any system, any machine, the only way to make it pronounce its own weak spots is to push its limits to the maximum.

This crisis, as bad as it is, is here. Maybe it has done us a favor by identifying the areas of danger, of risk, that were inherently always there. The potential energy of the breakdowns has been turned into the kinetic "boing" of the springs flying out, where it was potentially broken all along. Good. Now we can fix it, and make those joints stronger. So, like previous generations, let's stop whining about it; let's just roll up our sleeves, come together, and get to work to fix it.

What We Should Do Now

1. Decide Who Deserves Help: Create the Foreclosure Fault Index (FFI)™

Although politicians eager to get elected have naturally made sweeping, populist statements saying "America needs to help families who are losing their homes by the millions," the truth is that not everyone deserves help. Remember, for every terrible story of foreclosure, as bad as they are, there are arguably a hundred other homes who are making their mortgage payments as promised, even if their loans have reset. Maybe they planned better for the new higher payments, or insisted on a fixed-rate loan product only, against the pushy recommendations of their broker. Maybe they are working more or spending less to cover the costs of the debt they signed on to and agreed to always pay. Maybe they intentionally made sure that their original payments were never more than 30 percent of their monthly take-home pay, making room for emergencies and the resets, too. If we help some, should we help all?

Yes, many have lost their homes. I, too, have included some of these heartbreaking and terrible stories in this book. And some are gut-wrenchingly real and awful. But what I believe the media has not expected, and the Internet world of blogs and opinion-shouting has facilitated on a massive scale never before seen, is the loud and angry voices of the new "Great (No Longer) Silent Majority"—and this book is partly for you: those homeowners who did *not* overspend, who did not overextend, who were prudent and smart and cautious when the housing and mortgage frenzy was under way. Those responsible, fiscally conservative homeowners who are keeping the pledge they made, who read their loan documents carefully, who spent less than they made, and who are now *outraged* at the thought of government—their tax dollars—bailing out other people who are losing their homes because they perhaps made bad decisions, overspent, or brought it on themselves.

It is critically important in this debate to articulate and segregate the different reasons for these foreclosures. As I have discovered in my research and interviews as well, every default, every foreclosure, although sometimes having common threads, is truly unique. Every case would need to be assessed by an independent, emotionless process that focuses on fairness, and doesn't engage in the dangerous game of rewarding, and thereby incentivizing, future overspeculation, overconsumption, and malfeasance.

Americans can be the most compassionate, most generous, most helpful people on Earth; but only to innocent people who really deserve it. We also have the death penalty, and show little compassion for those who made their own poor choices, or intentionally did wrong, and are now suffering from the results of those choices. America should indeed come to the aid of those who were legitimately swindled, or had events out of their control lead them to financial disaster. But for those in foreclosures that came from dumb decisions, poor planning, or out-of-control consumerism, they should reap what they sowed, and should not be given free money by the government, in my view.

But how do we make that decision on a case-by-case basis? My proposed framework would help determine which families in foreclosure should be aided by the government, and which should not. Potentially polarizing and incendiary, yet critically necessary, this proposed process is, I believe, a thoughtful, logical totaling of all of the poten-

CREATE A NEW FORECLOSURE FAULT INDEX (FFI)™

How should government determine who truly deserves assistance?
A basic, initial framework uses a 1–100 FFI score to determine eligibility:

	HISTORY OF GOOD CHOICES	HISTORY OF BAD CHOICES
Foreclosure Trigger Event *out* of Their Control	**FFI score > 75** Most worthy of government help: First served.	**FFI score 25–75** Gray area; focus of the debate.
Foreclosure Trigger Event *in* Their Control	**FFI score 25–75** Gray area; focus of the debate.	**FFI score < 25** Least worthy of government help: Not eligible.

Note: Assistance in no way should be decided by race, religion, or class, only evidence of financial data and past behavior

tial factors that may have caused a foreclosure, and the expected value of all its greater deleterious effects.

Calling upon a rating system relatable to the FICO grading system already known to many homeowners, credit-card holders, government, and financial entities, yet with a twist of irony for good measure, I propose the following:

Much like its evil twin, the FICO score, each foreclosure case would be judged on a set number of factors, each with a sliding scale of intensity, which would then create a numerical index from 1 to 100. Those with scores over 75 would clearly be eligible for some kind of assistance; those with scores under 25, none. The area that will require a sliding scale of tiered assistance would be those with scores of 25 to 75, not so clear at all.

The first step is separating the obvious "they definitely deserve help" group from the "are you kidding me?" group. Like everything in life, from our classrooms, to our society in general, everything eventually comes back to a *bell curve*. Even in college I can remember being truly stunned by the brilliance of a few select people, and also being equally blown away by the incompetence of some others, who surely must have been the dean's nephew or something. The same is true, probably, of those in financial trouble. Some will be clearly deserving; others not. The rest is that huge bell in the center of our curve, and we need to figure out who gets nudged to either end of the spectrum.

This structure is arguably oversimplified, but this is intentional on my part; the larger, more complicated the idea, the simpler the structure and the message should be. This crisis, and determining who the victims truly are and are not, will surely rank as one of the most complex, challenging issues of our time and be a top issue for the new president's administration's first one hundred days. (If it is not, then we chose the wrong candidate.)

This oversimplification of the structure is also so "We the People"—all relevant audiences, from the press, to homeowners, economists, legislators, and regular folks of all education levels—can grasp the fairness of its basic structure immediately and on the same level. The exact common-sense definitions of "good/bad choices," "trigger events," and other specifics would need to be debated publicly and hammered out in legislative committees. And there would be much to decide on in addition to definitions. A sliding scale of assistance would seem reasonable; not everyone would get the same amount. And who would actually provide that assistance—local, state, federal governments, or even corporations themselves through fines, etc.—also would need to be determined by lawmakers.

I believe that the two areas of immediate clarity and fairness appear at the two ends of the scale. Those who have a history of making smart, good, lawful, responsible choices, who had something happen to them legitimately out of their control (illness, death, job loss, proof that they were truly duped or ripped off or otherwise a "victim" of an unscrupulous lender, and divorce [although this one might be arguable, especially by the far right]) might achieve a score above 75. These people should be helped first, although we will need to have a realistic debate regarding the limits of that help. (Yes, the government should have helped victims of Hurricane Katrina faster and better, but, give them free housing for *years*?)

Those with a score under 25, we feed to the wolves.

These people have a history of very poor choices, or irresponsible and/or reckless behavior. They may be rampant speculators, lawbreakers, ridiculous overspenders, and shopaholics. They sign up for every credit card and max them out on crap. And the trigger event or events that precipitated their default or foreclosure were definitely within their control and of their own doing. Maybe they bought three cars when they could afford only one. Maybe they gamble. Who knows? But for them, it would be time to pay up. Maybe we should send Ray Liotta over to see them, as Henry Hill in *Goodfellas*.

Business bad? F*ck you, pay me.

Oh, you had a fire? F*ck you, pay me.

Place got hit by lightning huh? F*ck you, pay me.

I can only imagine how this dialogue might have been tweaked by the current "script doctors" at our nation's lenders:

Didn't "understand" or plan for the known impending reset to your 3-Year Adjustable Rate Mortgage that was due to go from $900 per month to more than $2,000 per month in the thirty-seventh month? F*ck you, pay me.

Didn't "expect" the value of your $300,000 home to drop to $200,000 even though you [wrongly] assumed that the value would magically go up to over a million bucks, and you could refinance over and over again forever? F*ck you, pay me.

At the same time, you went on a cruise, bought two Mercedes, bought a giant McMansion, stayed addicted to QVC, and saved nothing? F*ck you, pay me.

If you have a history of irresponsible financial behavior and are now in trouble because of events and decisions that were well within your control—and were due to your *own poor choices*—then the government should not bail you out.

The same is true of corporations—depending on the case. Those who were victims of market factors out of their control, who have a history of adding value to our economy in an ethical manner, should be considered for assistance, but *only* if their demise would do material harm to the internal machinery of the American system. Fannie Mae, Freddie Mac, Bear Stearns, AIG—even Chrysler way back when—to let these firms fail would do irreparable harm to the United States and create cascade failures of other industries. But, *The Sharper Image?*—yes, failures like these are sad, but, eh, not the end of the world. *Sorry, guys.*

Then, after the obvious "should definitely help" and "feed 'em to the wolves" groups are identified, there is the rest: the massive gray area. These are folks in the middle, with scores between 25 and 75, for which a thoughtful, rational, scaled, quantifiable assessment tool is really needed. People with a history of "good choices" but had a trigger effect *in* their control might be an upstanding citizen with a great credit score, clean record, but did not plan for their ARM to reset, and bought that Lexus anyway. Do we help them? Do we let them fold into ruin? One could argue that anyone is allowed to make one mistake and helping them now means they may be able to buy three new homes over the next 20 years, helping the economy in any number of ways.

The other gray area may be someone who has a history of bad choices but the event was out of his control. Did the owner show a history of irresponsible speculation, or ignorance of debts and obligations? Is there evidence proving that the owner was lied to by the lender about the reset terms of his Adjustable Rate Mortgage? For a hypothetical example, an ex-con might have put his life back together, gotten a job, started a family, volunteered at the local YMCA, and never looked back on his poor judgment and conviction that occurred when he was a teen 30 years ago. He now owns a home and pays his mortgage. Then he got hit by a car and couldn't work. Do we help him save his home? Maybe.

One critical recommendation is to avoid any possible accusation of unfairness or bias; nowhere on any of the applications or paperwork for this assessment should there be any mention of race or gender. Let's number the cases, perhaps even keep their names anonymous, allowing only the administrators of the assessment (with redundant objective reviews and audits to purge any undue bias) to know their true identity and access their history. I don't care if you are white or brown or a man or a woman or whatever; I believe that should not in any way determine the scoring and decide whether help is warranted. Only one's past *behavior* and the nature of the trigger effect should determine the outcome, in my opinion.

Either way, as the crisis continues to unfold and the lasting ripples are felt into the next decade, let's hope that America will still have the ability to help *anyone* when the time comes.

2. *Make Home Buying* Difficult *Again*

I personally helped sell the dream—Angelo's professed dream—of helping all Americans achieve homeownership. And this may have helped fuel the disaster; just because we *can* do a thing does not mean, perhaps, that we *should* do that thing.

Back when my parents bought their home in 1969, the same year when Countrywide was born, few people had so-called second mortgages. If they did, something was usually wrong with the household, and fueled neighborhood gossip. There were no "exotic" loans; at least not like during our most recent boom. Adjustable Rate Mortgages didn't really come into vogue until the out-of-control interest rates of the 1970s pushed the market to create them to allow people to get into homes and still be able to afford their monthly payment.

And buying a home used to be hard—*really hard*—by design. The responsibility and character that warranted a borrower being given a huge loan used to be forged in the furnace of struggle, savings, and past demonstration of credibility. Young people would work their fingers to the bone to save the 20 percent down payment, and not a penny less. They would be sure to pay their other bills so they would be considered a good risk, worthy of that ultimate of trusts granted when a bank would hand them all that money. They would act in a manner befitting an upstanding member of the community; showing themselves worthy of the *honor* of homeownership, and being a small yet important piece of the neighborhood fabric. Homeownership was granted only after the establishment of character, reputation, and trustworthiness. It was, through decades of economic Darwinism (but not counting any unfair racial or economic biases infecting its evolution), a system that was intentionally designed to filter out those who were not yet worthy of that trust or financial risk, to make it an uphill struggle, to make homeownership a *privilege to be earned, not a right to be granted* to every American.

We need to bring this thinking back again. To earn this privilege, I believe we should go back to insisting on 20 percent down payments; a track record of financial responsibility; and appropriate, stable income to show that they will be able to make their monthly payment with a level of certainty.

It is a sad truth that not everyone should have, or is ready for, the massive responsibility of owning a home. Although it could be a romantic notion that easily lends itself to the "American Dream," perhaps now from this crisis we should take another look at how we define the dream itself. Opportunity for self-improvement, progress and growth through hard work, justice, equality—perhaps these are the elements of the dream we should focus more on, moving forward. The language of our unique heritage speaks of "life, liberty, and the pursuit of happiness." It does *not* say anything like "life, liberty, and the pursuit of *stuff*," does it?

Freedom of choice—free will—is the great glue that binds together the fabric of our democratic republic. And yet we seem to have forgotten that with that power comes the great counterbalancing weight of responsibility; that we need to be smart about what we buy, how much we buy, what we eat, how we live, what medicines we take, what leaders we choose. Several of the cases I have interviewed for this book were astonishing. The speculator who took on more and more loans for properties she had never seen, and hoped she would be able to rent out; the woman who took a mortgage for $4,500 a month when her entire monthly income was tenuously only $6,500 per month. When I asked her incredulously how she expected to feed her children by taking on a mortgage that would essentially leave her nothing left, she replied, "I was told I would be able to Refi." *Huh?*

3. End the ARMs Race

If you put a gun to my head and forced me to find the single biggest trigger of this crisis, from my research and history from within Countrywide, I would have to say that the concept of the Adjustable Rate Mortgage (ARM) was the most powerful catalyst for disaster. America has shown clearly that it cannot handle ARMs. It is time for our government to take this dangerous financial toy away from us before we shoot our *other* eye out. Like weapons of financial destruction, lenders offered them and buyers grabbed them, with their fuses already prelit. One-year, three-year, five- and seven-year resets meant a cascading effect of implosions across America that continues. So many of the cases I have interviewed for this project said that they knew that the loans were adjustable and would reset. But what was unknown, and could not be known to the lender or the borrower, was just how high the monthly payment would reset to, when it did. This would depend on interest rates that no one can know for sure will be in the future. Many cases reported being told by their lender that if the new payments were too high, that "they would be able to Refi." This is, of course, ridiculous. The only way a lender can say that you *will* be able to Refi is if they *knew for sure* that the value of your home would still be greater than the amount you owed on the mortgage. And in an era of uberexotics like PayOptions, which could actually increase the amount you owed on your loan every month, combined with collapsing home values (I truly believe no one expected the speed and severity at which it has happened), it was a recipe for disaster.

If we reinstitute the stable, fixed-mortgage products that our parents had, this would remove a major trigger of future disasters, enable better planning, eliminate surprise resets, and allow better projections of risk and value of mortgage securities.

The average length of stay in any owned home is about seven years, so assuming that the mortgage lobby goes *apeshit* when they hear I am recommending that we go back to only 30-year-fixed products (and eliminate many of their array of product options that yielded huge fees), perhaps a reasonable compromise will be to set limits on ARMs; no loans to ever reset in less than ten years. By eliminating the one-, three-, five-, and seven-year adjustables, stability will still be improved. If borrowers cannot afford the monthly payments without something less than a 10-year ARM, and put 20 percent down, then sorry, they are not financially ready to own a home. Period.

Oh, and while we're at it, do away with all those *ginormously* idiotic "optional payment" loans. There should be no *option* to pay back one's debts in a steady fashion, ever.

4. Completely Separate the Appraisal Process from Lenders

Countrywide owned a title company called LandSafe, which, by handling the closing process allowed Countrywide to own much of the homebuying process from end-to-end. Now before you jump to conspiratorial conclusions, note that at the time I, too, saw this as a way to make the homebuying process faster, smoother, and easier for every Countrywide customer. It seemed to represent the future of the process at the time, ensuring fewer errors, more revenue for the firm, and happier customers. But, in hindsight, I can now see how this setup might have allowed the potential for the *perception* of a conflict of interest. During any homebuying or Refi process, the critical step is the appraisal of the value of the home. Licensed by the state, these hardworking, mostly honest people measure the home, inspect it, and assess the value using comparable properties recently sold in the same neighborhood. Then they apply their professional recommendation regarding the home's true value on paperwork that then enters the loan process with their trusted, good-faith signature. Now, I never saw or heard of any conflicts of interest at Countrywide regarding the appraisal process, and all lenders required them for loan paperwork. But if the appraiser is hired by title companies that are somehow affiliated with the lender processing the loan, this could mean trouble. In this setup there is the natural possibility that the appraiser could somehow be unfairly pressured, however subtly, to set the appraisal at a certain amount to ensure that the loan be granted if they are in any way compensated by the lender's organization. For this reason, I believe that in the future all appraisers should remain completely independent of any lender affiliate, including title or escrow companies that may be owned by a lender. Or, we prevent any lenders from owning any title or escrow companies at all. But this will be up to our policymakers and regulators to decide.

5. End Sales Commissions Based on the Generation of Loan Applications

In the past, mortgage salespeople were sometimes paid their commissions on the number of loan applications they managed to finagle from their prospects. This motivated the salespeople to grab as many people to process applications as possible, regardless of whether they could or even should be getting that loan. It also sometimes relinquished them from any follow-up or obligation related to their prospect getting approved for the loan or the borrower's potential default down the road. Once the salesperson completed the "app," they would churn through other prospects to get another application done to get more commission. Don't blame these salespeople; this is what salespeople do. And people do what financial incentives (in this case, their commissions) motivate them to do. Sometimes they are paid based on the leads they get, or apps, or end sales. Sometimes they get higher commissions for the particular products that the lender is pushing. But to spiff them based on the application "tonnage" alone yields a recipe for potential disaster.

We should revert to flat-salaried people, using a similarly refined model from the stock brokerage industry. When consumers know that the salesperson is not compensated on a commission from this sale, they are more likely to trust that salesperson's advice, and the salesperson is more likely to tell the consumer the truth. This is just human nature.

6. End All No-Documentation, and All No-Income, No-Job Loans

These were madness. Total, stupid madness. To give someone hundreds of thousands of dollars simply based on their filling out a form is to know nothing about human nature. And any lender who approved a loan simply based on a borrower's *word* regarding his income and assets, without verification, deserves to lose that money. Period.

7. Formalize and Mandate Pre-Loan Closing Counseling Sessions

Many of the cases I have studied said that if the borrower had been properly counseled on the basics of what they were signing, they may not have signed after all. During the loan process, each borrower should be assigned an objective counselor not in any way connected to the lender or title company. Their job would be to walk the borrower through all of the obligations of the loan, in clear, plain language, and, most importantly, explain to the borrower the potential risks, including how high the payment could get if it is due to reset, when it would reset, and any potential penalties or fees. Borrowers would need to formally acknowledge their understanding of the risks they are taking, and the debts they are assuming, by signing the document.

And this presigning "breather"—perhaps including a 24-hour waiting period—would assess borrowers' true understanding of what they are signing; a consistent element missing from many of the foreclosure stories I have seen.

8. Create Both a Lenders' and a Borrowers' "Bill of Rights and Responsibilities"

In travel, healthcare, and many other contentious customer service models that are prone to conflict, confusion, and misunderstanding about who owes who what, there exist customer Bills of Rights and Responsibilities. We should mimic that model in mortgage lending so it will obligate the lender, the borrower, and both together to certain promises, rights, and responsibilities. Topics enlightened may include a borrower's obligation, and the meaning of the promise, as well as their right to contest the agreement through some sort of arbitration, etc. On the lender side, perhaps clarity over their fees, penalties, and the process by which they would have a right to act in case of default. Also it must include a provision that the lender can never *guarantee* that a borrower will *definitely* be able to Refi in the future (this is dependent on the home's value, and the equity in the home, if any), and language that clearly states that any adjustable product may reset by as much as X percent. Much of this is already embedded within the existing mountain of loan paperwork that borrowers need to sign, but we need to simplify it and bring it to the surface for clear review by the layman or, frankly, uneducated borrower. Either way, the handshake that the lender and borrower are making would be formalized in writing—in a simplified, plain-English manner, versus the mind-numbing legalese of standard mortgage paperwork.

9. Create a Mandatory "TurboCharged" Version of Mortgage Insurance

When I got my first house, I was able to put down only 10 percent. By my own recommendations for the new rules making it again difficult to buy a home, I would not have been eligible yet to secure the privilege (not the right) to own a home. But when I got the loan, I had attached to it a $150 payment each month for "mortgage insurance." This, I was told, was assigned to anyone who did not put down 20 percent.

We need to institute a policy that every loan in America should have with it cataclysmic mortgage insurance, in case of unforeseen disaster. Like car, life, and earthquake policies, a complete mortgage default is no less a disaster for both the lender and the borrower. The concept needs to be refurbished with sweeping changes mandating it on every loan, ensuring that the mortgage will be paid off in case of emergency as stipulated in the policy, regardless of the financial standing of the borrower. Armies of actuary accountants would need to determine the premiums, limits, and coverage amounts, just as in life insurance and all other insurance models; if you are a smoker, your life insurance rates might be 30 percent higher than for nonsmokers. The same would be true if you defaulted before, or had very poor credit, etc.

The current system does indeed charge higher interest rates on a sliding scale (FICO score) for so-called riskier loans, but if the current crisis has taught us anything, it is that some guru finance jock got that math, and those quantitative definitions of "risk" *way wrong.* It will be critical to protect the system better against loss based upon your conditions and past financial behavior. Given the failure of the old system, a more formal, "total loss" insurance model should be added to hedge against risk in the future, in addition to sliding scales of interest rates.

10. Institute a Mandatory "Financial Responsibility" Curriculum in Grade Schools

In the quaint old days of yesteryear, public schools taught something called "Home Economics." Back then the curriculum focused more on the 1950s archetype of American homemaking, teaching the finer points of cooking, cleaning, sewing, and the like. I can recall in my own high school days in the early 1980s, God help any boy who was caught dead taking "Home Ec." Perhaps it was in its last days in the curriculum, as budget cuts went deeper and deeper every year since then, but I believe we need to bring it back, updated, refurbished, and reformulated for the true needs of today's society: We need to bring it back as a *personal finance* course.

Clearly, America needs a refresher course in the responsible handling of money, and especially the smart handling of debt. Yes, adults need this, too, but the way to do this is to focus on the future needs of our society, by formally providing some kind of financial education for our kids. I would liken it to the arguably successful education programs regarding nutrition that came about in the 1970s, educating people about what is healthy and what is not (yet still allowing them the freedom to make their own decisions and order the "number three," supersized, with the ubiquitous Diet Coke as if to justify it calorically). I can recall in school, and on Saturday morning cartoons, information about portions, the "food groups" pyramid, and recommendations on servings per day. I believe this template could be a powerful best practice to develop a consistent, effective, concerted effort toward teaching American families, and kids, the benefits, dangers and optional paths of personal finance. Yes, "Mr. Mortgage" or the evil "Mr. Debt" could be characters that teach children. *Don't laugh; this stuff works.*

My little ones are in elementary school, and besides a brief chapter on what money is, and a kindergarten unit related to identifying each of the denominations, I have yet to see any material focused on teaching them financial responsibility with money. That is why I teach them at home.

Every week they have a list of chores they need to do. They get a set amount of money each week for the chores they complete. Then I work with them to teach them what I hope will be good habits for a lifetime. They are told that they need to save 30 percent of it, they can spend 30 percent of it, they need to eventually invest 30 percent of it, and 10 percent is set aside to donate to charity. It's a utopian process, perhaps, but it feels like the right thing to do at their ages.

They are not quite old enough yet to understand the investment concept, so they are saving 60 percent of their income for a rainy day. One of my youngest son's favorite hobbies is counting all of his one-dollar bills; he glows with pride at "how rich he is," no matter how small the pile is. And when they spend it, they learn the punch to the gut that can sometimes come from handing over cash for a thing that suddenly doesn't look so cool at that moment at the register. I think this is a critical lesson; spending should be thoughtful, considered, and sometimes painful. Indeed, I believe that when we in America charge things on a credit card, it is too easy to forget the cash it represents; when I spend cash only, I know that I tend to spend much less. There is something inherently more difficult in handing a cashier a wad of twenties for some jacket I might wear twice; I wonder how much household debt could be lessened in America if somehow everyone were forced to use cash only.

And let's also teach kids early the danger of value bubbles, at least how to recognize them. Adults create bubbles because we are taught as kids to fuel them. Sometimes they are called fads, but from Hula-Hoops, to pet rocks, to Smurfs and Cabbage Patch dolls and now from Beanie Babies to Webkinz, materialistic bubbles based on only perceived value abound in kidland. Although I don't pretend that this element of the new curriculum will prevent such bubbles, perhaps it will at least make them more aware of their dangers in adulthood and teach caution.

Now, I am not saying that I am some kind of perfect parent or anything; God knows I am not. But I believe that this manner of teaching needs to come from the partnership between parents at home and teachers at school. When I was at Countrywide, the educational aspects of homeownership, and teaching about the finances required for it, were deeply rooted and pounded into all of the web pages and paper literature, especially to minority borrowers. We wanted all borrowers to be smart about their decisions, and we took this educational role very seriously, even as we were pushing whatever exotic loans would be necessary to get them in the house. In retrospect, like a fast-food company that displays its nutritional warnings and offers "apple fries" while pushing the new Angioplasty Burger, it is truly schizophrenic behavior.

I actually recommended a "kids' program" when I was at Countrywide Bank. Then, as I do now, I believed that there was a vacuum—a marketing opportunity—for a financial services brand to "own" educating kids about money. Roundly rejected by the management of Countrywide because apparently there was no profit in it, perhaps Bank of America could plant this flag. I think some banks have kids' programs, but no one has stepped forward with a large investment in the message to *own it* and do it well from a branding or marketing perspective. I believe that emerging as the altruistic bank that cares enough to try to teach children about money is an enormous opportunity (feel free to take this as free marketing advice, Mr. Lewis [CEO of Bank of America]). But while they would be doing "good," it is not completely without hidden motives. Kids loyal to your bank brand because they see you as teacher, advocate, and sage about money are more apt to choose you as their checkbook bank when they go to college. I don't need data to prove this, I just know it to be true.

Through the development of a newly revised "Home Economics" curriculum in late elementary school, I would bet that future generations of Americans could be made at least more aware of the dangers of debt, the power and responsibility of money, and, like those cartoons of the past regarding food and nutrition, educated on what will make them financially or physically unhealthy, long term. Then, they can make their own free, considered choice to be obese or enter financial ruin if they wish.

———————

THIS IS A repeating story in our America: irrational, overly enthusiastic bubbles, followed by cataclysmic overcorrections. And we always wait until it reaches crisis levels—like global warming—to even recognize it and actually do anything about it. Gold, railroads, dot coms, housing—we have seen it a hundred times, and we never learn. The pattern is easily recognizable: a feverish run for profits and get-rich-quick wealth that is ultimately unsustainable, followed by an equally feverish witch hunt to find fault, and to point blame at anyone but ourselves, especially those corporate leaders who fed us exactly what we asked for. And I gorged myself on it as well; if the mortgage business had been a dessert, I spent more than three years with chocolate all over my face.

Maybe we simply don't want to learn, or are incapable of learning. Maybe our greed prevents us from doing what we know is good for us. Maybe we have some sort of sadistic need to experience ecstasy, then severe pain every now and then. I can only hope that this tale describing life from inside the corporate bubble, providing the answers to the question that all of America seems to be asking—"What *were* they thinking?"—will serve as an education and a warning for future generations of companies, consumers, and government.

The arguments under way over the merit and nature of debt, and the role of government as parent or people as the better deciders of their own choices and fates, are as old as the republic and may never be resolved. Hamilton and Jefferson argued about these very themes within George Washington's cabinet as our modern day two-party system was in the larval stage. Jefferson, forever fearful of a strong and potentially corruptible central authority; Hamilton, a firm believer that the people needed to be watched over like sheep. And yet it is the yin and yang balance of this argument that motivates markets to seek out new opportunities and then potentially suffer those corrections. Is this capitalist tug-of-war a good or a bad thing for America? It doesn't matter; it is America. I would give anything to hear Jefferson's and Hamilton's thoughts on our current state of affairs. *Sigh.*

But as seen from deep inside the bubble, as a senior executive at what was then the largest mortgage lender in the United States, and the first giant to fall—Countrywide—it was initially difficult to see, let alone question, if what we were doing was truly good for America after all. There was a moment when I felt like it was my fault, but I don't feel that anymore. At the time everyone was doing exactly what their own self-interests and assigned roles told them to do; borrowers borrowed more and more to spend more and more on inflated housing values, because they could; lenders created exotic new products to feed that need, and reaped the rewards of fulfilling that mandate that society designed them to do, because they could; government tried to stay out of the way of the momentum, because a rich, fat electorate is a happy electorate. In the final analysis, everyone was at fault, and no one was at fault.

And looking back now, my story was America's story.

When I giddily saw the golden opportunity for growth, wealth, and prestige as I joined Countrywide in 2003, like the new crop of potential homeowners and those who wished to gain wealth from the growing equity in their homes, I *was* America.

When Angelo put his hand on my shoulder and passed on the gospel that we were doing *good* in bringing the American dream of homeownership to all citizens, just like all those people who responded to tons of television advertising and direct mail seeking to be part of this dream, I *was* America.

When I personally believed that the idea that homeownership was the *right*, and no longer just the *privilege* of every citizen, I *was* America.

When the turning point came around the conference table in the Vault, when I realized that something terrible might happen (yet still with unsettling uncertainty), I was like those hundreds of thousands of homeowners who opened newly reset mortgage payment envelopes around their kitchen tables, seeing their new higher mortgage payments, and saw the end staring them in the face, yet were helpless in the cruel knowledge that I, and they, could do nothing about it, I *was* America.

When I partially blamed myself for the mess I had helped create within a system designed to foster that same mess, I *was* America.

And then, with belief and dreams and faith in institutions and leaders in ruins, I was left numb, seeking ways to make sense of it all, and to recover.

I was—I *am*—America.

THIS MORNING, LIKE most summer mornings, I took my sons to day camp. In the car, as we had done so many times before, we passed the rows and rows of white picket fences and newly built homes amid an ocean of realty signs in our Southern California neighborhood. Except this time I heard their small voices from the backseat, blurting out one of their trademark non sequiturs that can sometimes come from elementary schoolers.

"Dad, can we get a new house?" my youngest said, seemingly out of nowhere.

"Why do you ask that?" I said.

"Well, I like *that* one. And *that* one. Can we get a swimming pool? Oh, and air hockey, we play that at camp. Can we get a dog, and a big backyard for him?"

Then my other son piped in. "Noah has a backyard bigger than ours. And my new friend Benjamin has a swimming pool. And a game room. Can we, Dad?"

The laundry list of their preferences for our newly imagined estate just kept coming. As they quickly entered their now louder, unison chorus of "Can weeeeee, Daaaaaaaaaad ppppppppppplllllllllllleeeeeeeeeee-eeaaaaaaaaaaassssssssseeeeee?" I smiled, shook my head, and loved them more than ever before.

Yes, indeed, they were American kids, I thought.

"We'll see, boys, we'll see. Let's see what next year brings."

Afterword

SOME OF THE LANGUAGE I used in telling this story was considered by some who saw the original outline to be histrionic hyperbole. Phrases like "Second Great Depression," "financial weapons of mass destruction," and even the book title, *The Foreclosure of America,* seemed over the top by some. And truth be told, at the time I felt they could be right. After all, I am a creature of marketing, and have been trained my whole career to sell stories. But in this unique case, I also felt that the words were authentic reflections of how I viewed the potential future, based upon my knowledge of the loans outstanding throughout the United States, many of which I helped sell during the boom. My awareness of the very real potential danger, and my passion to get the warning out as quickly and as broadly as possible to the current population as well as to future generations, was what pushed my pen to paper in the first place.

Then in late September and early October 2008, as this book was reaching its final stages of editing and production, it seemed that this financial crisis might actually take on nightmarish proportions, and my words would become horribly prophetic. In other words, all hell broke loose.

It seemed that the world began turning upside down for many Americans. We all were so incredulous at the acceleration of unthinkable financial events, that suddenly, nothing seemed unthinkable anymore. It seemed that even our leaders in Washington and the Treasury Department, behind closed doors, began to panic, and struggled to maintain their composure for the television cameras.

Was it possible? Could the Second Great Depression actually *happen*? That kind of world only appeared in scratchy old film footage: breadlines; families, dirty and hungry, crossing the Plains in dust storms searching for food; children playing in squalor; people fighting over medicine and baby food; society almost breaking down. Then again, I never thought I would actually see two jet planes slam into the Twin Towers in a conflagration that would look like a movie about the end of the world. Yes, unimaginable things happen.

Within only a few short weeks, it seemed like America had gone haywire; as if I had fallen asleep in reality and awakened in a nightmare. From the financial world to the political world, everything felt wrong, like this "couldn't really be happening." In quick succession, shortly after the collapse of the unsinkable Freddie Mac and Fannie Mae, other titans of Wall Street and Main Street fell into the abyss of greed, loss, and hubris. If this were fiction my editors would have deleted this with the comment "not believable."

Like Bear Stearns before it, Lehman Brothers went under, wiping out the retirement savings of many of their employees, and the fortunes of shareholders. Merrill Lynch, like Countrywide, was one of the lucky ones, and found a savior in the nick of time, being bought by Bank of America. The American insurance colossus, AIG, whose tentacles reached into and affected almost every facet of American financial life, as well as many of the world's economies, was literally bought by the United States. Huge banks like Washington Mutual and Wachovia buckled. Washington Mutual was bought by JPMorgan Chase, and Citigroup made overtures to what was left of Wachovia, with the U.S. government brokering the deals. But within a week after Citi offered to help Wachovia, Wells Fargo swooped in with a better offer, and a dramatic buyout showdown began. The story twisted and turned every few hours until Wells Fargo's offer prevailed.

Like in 1929, both banks finally collapsed under the weight of depositors withdrawing their accounts *because they thought the banks would go under*; "financial collapse" is one of the most dangerous self-fulfilling prophesies in our modern world. Both WAMU and Wachovia probably came within a micron of closing their doors to depositors.

In these failures there were also two side stories that just added to the increasing absurdity. The closely watched vice presidential debates a week later were said to have been proudly sponsored by (*yikes*) Wachovia (maybe they served soup to the hungry crowds). And, the seizure of WAMU occurred while the CEO was literally in the air— on a flight from New York to Seattle—and he was told of the shutdown when he landed. The press reported that, after being on the job for less than three weeks, he may still walk away with millions.

Also during this same time a former beauty queen was possibly in line for the *presidency*, touting her foreign relations experience as being solid *because she can see Russia from her house*, and in an unprecedented, Communist-style restriction of our free press, reporters who were with her during her visit to the United Nations were only allowed to photograph her meeting foreign leaders, but were not allowed access to her to ask questions and vet her ideas. Instead the press was ordered by her campaign handlers to "treat her with deference." Shame on what *was* our free press for agreeing to this shameless replication of how the North Koreans do it.

Did I doze off and wake up in another reality? The United States was now *in* the insurance business, *in* the mortgage business, and dangerously liable for all of the serious risks that entailed. Just because America comes to the rescue and buys up terribly bad debt, it does not magically make the debt any less bad. It is conceivable that although we have saved some firms from having to write down a trillion dollars in bad debt, America itself may eventually be forced to write down this same trillion dollars. The inevitable losses *have* to go on a ledger book *somewhere*. But, who then will bail *us* out? A foreign nation? Who would then hold the deed to the United States? The potential ramifications of this serious turn of events is so large, few people I have spoken to can even get their heads around it.

Capitalism cannot exist without capital. And yet in late September, the credit markets, which lubricate the entire system with that capital—cash—for all levels of business functions throughout the country, seized up like a racing car that had lost all its oil. Banks were afraid to lend to anyone or any institution. With shocking speed and an even more shockingly breezy, almost matter-of-fact process, we morphed from the once great beacon of free-market capitalism in the world to a quasi-socialist America.

Then it just kept getting worse and weirder, and quickly.

Fed Chairman Bernanke and Treasury Secretary Paulson called congressional leaders to an emergency meeting in Speaker Pelosi's office on Thursday evening, September 25. Reports stated that the tone of the meeting was so dire, so cataclysmic, that one congressman said that it felt like the air had left the room as the weight of the true emergency hung in the air. A proposal was hurriedly cobbled together by the administration, which had seemingly lost all credibility with America, and the House vetoed.

The Secretary of the Treasury *got down on one knee and begged* the House Speaker to get the package passed, in front of a stunned press corp. The president aired a nationally televised address expressing the urgency and danger. The presidential candidates both theatrically rushed back to Washington. The House, inundated with angry citizen calls to not "bail out" Wall Street and the "fat cats," vetoed the bill on Monday September 29, 2008, and the market precipitously fell 777 points in one day. It was eerily similar to the date of Black Tuesday, October 29, when the Great Depression is considered to have officially begun in 1929. With ominous foreshadowing, for the first time in recent memory, on that same Monday, September 29, an electrical glitch caused the opening bell of the NYSE not to ring.

As a marketing professional, I knew the original package would fail as presented the minute it was presented to Congress; I could clearly see that none of those finance jocks were marketers. Product names can make or break their success, and calling it a "bailout" at any time would make it dead on arrival. Calling it "The Recipe for Change," the "Financial Rescue Plan," or even "The New Tomorrow Law" would have been more palatable to an already bewildered public. And I find it hard to believe that the obviously smart Treasury Secretary Hank Paulson would ever actually think that America would anoint sole power over almost a *trillion* dollars (borrowed partially from not-all-friendly foreign governments) to just one person's control—him. (Oh, and by the way, he'd probably be gone from the job on January 21, 2009.) Economists could not even agree that the package would work at all, some saying that the downward momentum was already too late.

At the time of this writing, the Senate just approved a revised version of the bill, and quickly thereafter nonchalantly went on recess until mid-November. Luckily the House approved it by the end of that week. Of course, now, ironically, the bill is reportedly wrought with pork barrel spending earmarks we clearly can't afford, such as rich tax breaks for wool research, auto racing tracks, and other miscellaneous items to simply put us even further in the hole. Consider: the bill to save our union from bad debt has been laden with even more unessential debt. Have we learned *nothing*? And yet the news stations showed the press conference where legislators tripped over themselves to shower each other with praise; shame on government for letting this crisis get this far in the first place.

The single greatest risk the market—indeed now, our entire economy faces—is not risk itself, but the *uncertainty* surrounding any potential risk or reward. And now we are faced with the *mother* of all uncertainties—will our economy recover from this crushing debt? We have arguably entered an uncharted time, where the uncertainty is so enormous, it threatens the system itself. The terrorists must be laughing their asses off as they watch us do this *to ourselves*.

The markets and the population as a whole are, in my view, so nervous that we are now only one unforeseen shock away from the final tipping point of economic depression. We are at the very edge of panic, that psychologically ethereal and unknowable moment when it becomes too much and the psyche of the markets "snap." Regular people—and now, many finance experts, too—feel helpless and lost, as the crisis is simply too large and too complicated for many to digest.

Fear used to be the single, greatest natural regulator of our markets and our behavior. Fear is useful. Fear has power. Fear of consequences, of loss, of pain, of failure. It motivates kids to do their homework, drivers to stop at red lights, and in the old days, banks to not lend to risky borrowers. That fear for centuries kept risk-based firms from going under. The Great Depression, as well as many other lesser-known, nineteenth-century, smaller market crashes, eventually proved that government does need to regulate Wall Street; the fox can never guard the henhouse, as they say. We need a third-party validating that indeed they are not taking any frightening risks. Ironically, that very same fear instinct is now greatly intensified, because we did not heed it earlier. Likewise, there is sad irony in the fact that years of no regulation may now create a greater level of regulation than ever before.

The government's economic socialism that is now being enacted is, in my opinion, terrible. Yet in the words of many of our leaders, it has become, unbelievably, "less worse" than the unthinkable alternative. I can only hope that a decade from now, as the crisis hopefully has faded into the history books, the wise government of 2020 figures out how to ease the government *out* of the insurance and mortgage business, and morph back into a capitalist model of sensibly regulated, yet free markets.

As this manuscript was originally being written, the collapses of Bear Stearns and IndyMac Bank, as well as the monumental falls of giants Freddie Mac and Fannie Mae had, I thought, provided more than enough drama to prove what I felt might happen eventually. But now, even as I need to finish this Afterword for the book's production deadline, it is still unclear if America will survive this crisis. And no one, including me, could have known that Countrywide would simply be the first giant to unthinkably fall.

The story will continue to evolve throughout 2010 and beyond, but it all may have started at that meeting in 2003, in an underground, nuclear-proof bunker at Countrywide, at the time the largest mortgage company in the world, and at all the other similar "exotic loan" launch meetings that were held at financial services companies all throughout the United States during the boom.

In the final analysis, all we can do now is hope, and fervently wish, may heaven help the United States.

Acknowledgments

JUST AS WHEN I was at Countrywide, the execution of this project and its success were not accomplished by me alone, but were done with the help of a much larger team of talented professionals supporting me, and I want to thank them all. To the wonderful team at Berkley Publishing Group (a division of Penguin Group), I want to thank publisher Leslie Gelbman for her great support and faith; Denise Silvestro for her brilliant, insightful editing and guidance; Adrienne "Andie" Avila for helping the book through its final stages; Meredith Giordan for helping to keep all the plates spinning; and to the intrepid publicity team of Rick Pascocello, Craig Burke, and Julia Fleischaker for their excitement and tenacity.

Eternal thanks to my agent, Jeremy Katz (and to Richard Laermer for connecting us), who never stopped believing in my ability to tell this story well; his friendship, talent, and nurturing have been rare gifts; and to his fearless assistant Iris Hsieh for keeping all the paperwork straight.

To Meredith Pahel for her fast and accurate interview transcriptions; to Jason Sikes for his amazing web design; to my wise and supportive legal counsel from Alan Kaufman and my publisher's lawyer Ellis Levine; to Charles Jackson and Jolie Dugas at ACORN.org, and to Martyn Brown for sending me interview candidates.

Thanks to Professor Ed Leamer, director of the UCLA Anderson Forecast, for his wise counsel and feedback; to Dean Judy Olian of UCLA Anderson School of Management for her kind words of support; and to Rita Costello of the UCLA Anderson Library for her generous access to UCLA's vast resources.

A special unexpected thank you to a hero of mine, American historian and author David McCullough; through his example he unknowingly inspired me to dedicate myself to telling meaningful stories well, and to never stop trying to *excel*. And to all of my wonderful family and friends, especially my parents, for their unwavering belief in me and this project, I will forever be grateful.

I also extend my deep thanks and admiration for all of those brave souls who came forward to tell me the difficult and painfully private details of their own financial hardships and the reasons for them. Hopefully their stories will provide others who are suffering a sense of hope; help them know that they are not alone; and provide a dramatic, visceral telling of a story that has too often been told simply through cold numbers.

Finally, I want to thank all of the dedicated professionals who ever worked at Countrywide, who without their passion for what we were doing, many Americans would never have been able to get into their own home at all.

And finally, to Angelo Mozilo, for creating Countrywide in the first place, and for pushing us all, at one time, to believe.

Index